MW00675559

Romantic Michigan

a guidebook for couples
seeking unique romantic experiences

Carol Bruyere

Eagle Feather
Press

Front Cover Photo: Provided by Diane O'Shea
Northern Light Inn,
Ontonagon
Copyright © 1998 by
Richard Tandlund

Cover Design
and
Back Cover Photos: by Carol Bruyere
Copyright © 1998

Inquiries and orders:
Eagle Feather Press
526 West 14th Street, Suite 179
Traverse City, Michigan 49684

Romantic Michigan is a trademark of
Eagle Feather Press

Copyright © 1998 by Carol Bruyere

ISBN 0-9661313-0-4

All rights reserved. No part of this work covered by the copyrights hereon may be reproduced or copied in any form or by any means, either stenographic, graphic, electronic, or mechanical, including photocopying, voice recording, eletronic scanning, videotaping, or facsimile or internet transmission, without the express written permission of the publisher, except in the case of brief excerpts in course of fair comment or critical review.

PRINTED IN THE UNITED STATES of AMERICA

#3-

*To my husband, Dennis –
the ultimate romantic!*

CONTENTS

For a romantic rendezvous in ...   *See page ...*

The Sunrise Side &
Top-O-The-Mitt.. 1

The Thumb &
Surrounding Areas.. 18

Those Irish Hills &
The Southeast Corner 40

River Country
(South Central) 54

Harbor Country
(Southwest)... 70

The Lakeshore -
South Haven 89

The Art Coast -
Saugatuck, Douglas, etc. 98

The Shoreline -
Grand Haven... 122

CONTENTS

For a romantic rendezvous in ...   *See page ...*

The Cities by the "Sea"
Ludington & Pentwater 135

The Port Cities - Manistee, Onekama, Frankfort,
& Elberta, with Beulah & Benzonia 157

The Leelanau Peninsula - Glen Arbor,
Leland, Northport, Suttons Bay 172

Grand Traverse Bay
Traverse City & Old Mission Peninsula 203

Bay Country South - Chain-o-Lakes Area
Elk Rapids, Alden, Ellsworth, etc. 218

Bay Country North - Charlevoix, Petoskey,
Harbor Springs & Points North 227

The Upper Peninsula 256

Mackinac Island 308

Thank you to all the Innkeepers,
Restaurateurs, Chamber and Tourist
Bureau Directors, and everyone else
who graciously gave their time for
interviews and tours, and generously
provided photos or artwork.

You are appreciated.

•

Thanks, also, to all the wonderful
friends who encouraged me.

A very special Thank You to my friend
Adelle, who spent hours proofreading
this text.

You are treasured.

Introduction

*S*eeking *romance?* Look around you. Michigan is not only one of the most beautiful of the 50 states, it also boasts some of the most romantic destinations in the Midwest. Surrounded by four of the Great Lakes, and surrounding thousands of inland lakes and rivers, Michigan is truly a "water wonderland" - and a treaure chest of romantic opportunities.

What is romance?
ro•mance (rö mans´; *also for n.* rö´ mans)
[ult. <L. Romanicus] **n.** excitement, love, etc.

It's a combination of timing, setting, and ambiance, plus who you are, and what you do . . . to make it special . . .

Sometimes you need a break - a getaway - a weekend, an evening or a moment alone . . . together . . . to put you "in the mood". Most people think of the perfect "atmosphere" for romance, as quiet, secluded (more private), comfortable, scenic, and beautiful. Settings on or near the water are perceived as especially perfect - that's Michigan, of course!

The addition of those "little touches" like soft lighting, candles, a fireplace, a gurgling fountain, flowers, a pleasant fragrance (pot pourri, scented candles, etc.), and soft, sensuous music will enhance any romantic "scene". And how about those "sense-ual" personal details? A bit of velvet, lace, or slinky silk, a touch of perfumeor cologne, a dashing sweater or tux, and you, looking your most attractive and alluring. Ah, yes, perfection!

Certain activities enhance and encourage romance - perhaps a few stolen moments in a hot tub, or by the fireside; a dining, concert, or theater outing; strolling hand-in-hand on a beach or quiet lane; sailing; dancing; canoeing; a massage; a sleigh ride; something really fun (or funny); or that secluded picnic.

In "matters of the heart", nothing is more endearing than showering loads of attention on the object of your affections! Combine thoughtfulness, caring, selflessness, giving, sharing, and pleasant surprises - like planning a weekend getaway, like a dinner invitation, a love poem, or a single rose!

Yes, romance is . . . the right place, the right time, those extra little touches, and . . . the two of you!

What is romantic?

ro•man•tic (rö man´tik) *adj. 1.* of, like or characterized by romance **2.** fanciful, not practical; visionary **3.** suited for romance **4.** Michigan

Michigan is home to hundreds of Bed & Breakfasts, Inns, and unique resort lodging destinations. Though it would have been impossible to include even a brief listing of every lodging choice, Romantic Michigan™ has tried to feature the most intriquing and romantic of these. Occasionally it was not possible to coordinate with, or enlist the cooperation of, Innkeepers or management. We regret the ommission of any otherwise attractive lodging possibilities, but offer a sizeable collection for you to sample!

Thousands of dining and activity choices also sparkle throughout our magnificent state. Again, with the cooperation of their management, local Chambers of Commerce and Visitors Bureaus, and written and personal recommendations, we have tried to mention or feature the "stars" among them.

Though everyone's idea of romantic things to do may be different, we've tried to suggest activities designed to encourage relaxing, virtually stress-free, non-competitive togetherness! Names, phone numbers, and details of service providers are offered to our readers as an information starting point for your romantic journeys. A listing herein does not imply a recommendation by Romantic Michigan™, nor do we guarantee your satisfaction with their fees or services.

Every little corner of Michigan offers a variety of seasonal and annual festivals and events for your enjoyment. Our task is not to list those events, but simply to make available to you Chamber of Commerce or Visitors' Bureau contacts so you may investigate further.

It is our sincere wish that all of your romantic experiences, especially those inspired by this guidebook, are perfect and wonderful. We cannot, however, assume any responsibility if they are not. We believe all information tucked lovingly into these pages will prove to be as accurate a representation of available services as was possible at the time of printing. Please forgive any errors or omissions - none were intentional.

The State of Michigan tourist information bureau offers comprehensive listings and brochures of area Chamber and Tourist Bureaus, cider mills, art galleries, wineries, herb farms, cross-country ski trails, bike paths, trails, state parks, color tours, etc. You may wish to contact them before your trip at . . .

Travel Michigan
1-888-78-GREAT
www.michigan. org

or contact:
Upper PeninsulaTravel & Recreation Assn.
1-800-562-7134
West Michigan Tourist Assn.
1-800-442-2084
www.wmta.org
Michigan Sunrise Side Travel Assn.
1-800-424-3022
www.misunriseside.com

Additional valuable assistance may be gained by visiting the following web sites:
www.mlive.com/travel
www.travelassist.com
www.bbonline.com
www.laketolake.com

"There are so many ways to love,
and each one has its own delights".

- Sara Teasdale

Painting by Donna Critchfield

Sunrise Side & Top-O-The-Mitt

*T*hose peaceful wide open spaces, and abundant natural beauty, make this corner of Michigan an especially relaxing destination.

Several of the state's most beautiful rivers are this area's crowning glory. Winding lazily through Huron National Forest, the Au Sable offers many a spot for picnics and quiet interludes. Paddlewheel boat tours, canoeing, tubing and kayaking are popular, as well as stops at the mystical Iargo Springs Viewpoint, or famous Lumberman's Monument. River Road - a designated National Scenic Byway - keeps the river company, and provides a superb chance for leaf-peeping and leisurely drives. The Black, Pigeon, Rifle, and Sturgeon Rivers, and thousands of acres of state forests, wildlife preserves, and wilderness areas, promise plenty of

additional opportunities for outdoor adventure. Trails abound for hiking, cross-country skiing, , snowmobiling, horseback riding, or nature and wildlife viewing.

Lake Huron invites lovers to it's pristine beaches for swimming, sunning, strolling, or even scuba diving at Thunder Bay Underwater Preserve. And don't forget the *sunrise!* Magnificent sky-color displays are a very romantic way to start your day!

Michigan's unique "Inland Waterway" beckons boaters for a *one-of-a-kind* cross-country excursion, and can be entered from **Cheboygan** or the Alanson/Indian River area.

Huron's port cities, with their historic streets, quaint shops, and fun activities, also call to boaters (and landlubbers, too!).

Bike or stroll the ten mile paved Shoreline Lighted Path on *Tawas* Bay; watch the freighters pass by Rogers City; ride the River Queen in *Oscoda*; in *Mackinaw City*, tour the Fort, the Butterfly House, Historical Pathways, and Courtyards' shops, listen to strolling musicians, attend Voyageur's Jubilé Dinner Show, take a Vesper Cruise, or tour nearby Old Mill Creek State Historic Park; attend summer bandshell concerts, or the year-round professional Thunder Bay Theatre in *Alpena*; or try one of the fascinating performances at Cheboygan Opera House. (Not to mention the delights of all the inland communities!)

From Cheboygan to Standish, this Great Lake's shoreline is guarded by numerous lighthouses. Visit one! Be inspired! Send out your beacon of love!

Any season, any reason, Michigan's Sunrise Side and Top-O-The-Mitt invite you to "unwind in Nature's backyard!"

Sunrise Side Travel Association
517-469-4544
www.oweb.com/upnorth/sunriseside and
www.misunriseside.com
Elk Country Tourism Bureau
517-742-4732
Mackinaw Area Tourist Bureau
1-800-666-0160
www.mackinawcity.com
Cheboygan Area Tourist Bureau
1-800-968-3302
www.cheboygan.com
Alpena Area CVB
1-800-4-ALPENA
www.xmission.com/~gastown/balaam/alpena.htm
Oscoda Area CVB
1-800-235-GOAL
www.oscoda.com
Tawas Bay Tourist & CB
1-800-55-TAWAS
www.tawas.com

Thunder Bay Resort - HILLMAN

"romance with a different dimension"

*N*othing seems more romantic than an old fashioned horsedrawn sleigh ride! And Thunder Bay Resort promises a superb experience, with the added attraction of possible elk, deer, and wildlife sightings, as well as a gourmet dinner at Elkhorn Cabin. Snuggle with your darlin' on a 40 minute ride through the Pigeon River State Forest, and arrive at the rustic gas-lit cabin to watch Resort chefs prepare your meal on wood-fired stoves (what a special flavor!) Tuxedoed servers bring palate teasing appetizers including pear and apple crepes and shrimp cocktail. Homemade soup, Caesar salad, and pan-roasted red skin potatoes complement the ever-popular Crown Roast of Pork. Your repast is accompanied by choice of wines, and dessert Pizzeles with raspberry sauce and white chocolate mousse. Mmmmm! Not quite how it was on the frontier! Sated guests enjoy coffee in front of the stone fireplace prior to their ride back to the resort for a 1-3 night stay in cedar and fieldstone lodges, a soak in the year-round enclosed hot tub, and complimentary breakfast. 36-66 people enjoy scheduled winter weekend rides or private parties (book 6 weeks to 2 months in advance). Thunder Bay also offers Fall color tour hayrides/dinner packages, which include Big Buck beer tasting and guitar sing-a-long entertainment back at the resort (call for dates 3-4 weeks in advance).

Spacious luxury suites, and whirlpool suites with split bath, bedroom, living room, deck and full kitchen, provide comfortable contemporary lodging options for your retreat. Package rates vary from $250-562 per couple, depending on dates and length of stay (1-3 nights), and include winter activity passes for cross-country skiing, snow-shoeing, ice skating on the Resort's lighted rink, or snowmobiling. Call Thunder Bay for lodging only, or summer golf and tennis package rates.

Resort dining options include: casual light meals in the Clubhouse Bar & Grill featuring traditional breakfast fare plus specialties ($1.95-4.95), sandwiches, soups, luncheon salads and Mexican favorites ($1.95-5.95), and pizza; The Loft Restaurant - where casual attire is *Dining* appropriate, even with the fine linens and fine *Delights* dining choices like "Eggplant Parmigiana", "Chicken Stir Fry", "BBQ Ribs", "Lake Huron Whitefish", and "Seafood Linguine" (priced from $6.50). Special menus, catering, separate porch dining , and entertainment available for private parties. Take out service is also available (sorry no room service!); or cook-your-own in your private kitchen or on available gas grills.

Enter a new and different world of romance! Call . . .

Thunder Bay Resort
1-800-729-9375 or 517-742-4502
27800 M-32 East, Hillman, MI 49746
www.thunderbaygolf.com
email:tbg@thunderbaygolf.com
Sorry, No Smoking inside Elkhorn Cabin

Inn-spired Activities

Hike the High Country pathway; try viewing elk, birds, and the glorious Fall colors!

Fireside Inn - PRESQUE ISLE

"a relaxing, rustic retreat"

*F*rom the moment you turn onto the "Fireside Highway" for the 1/4 mile drive to this old-fashioned lake resort, you'll feel as if you've entered "serenity".

Tucked along the quiet shores of "shimmering" Grand Lake, Fireside Inn offers a comfortable choice of accommodations, from seventeen private sleeping or housekeeping cabins, to five sleeping rooms with private bath in

a wing of the rambling main building. If you long for a quiet, peaceful escape at a reasonable price, this is it! Rustic, and informal, but comfy getaways are yours for $40-80 a night Spring and Fall or: rooms with meals $60-80 June, July and August; cabins $500 per couple weekly in summer including "American plan" meals.

Cabins are cozy and appealing with historic original furniture, private bath, and a fireplace and refrigerator in most. How about a secluded log hideaway for your romantic tryst? Or perhaps the very special Cabin 16 - right on the lake and enhanced by the mellow "music" of gently lapping waves!

Relax! Unwind! Walk along the lakefront, "sit a spell" on the wide porch of the main Inn building, or curl up in the "Fireside Room" for a taste of the old days, a roaring fire, or a game of checkers. Two firepits on the beach are oh-so-inviting for the twilight to midnight hours! Swimming, diving, canoeing, row boats and kayaks, tennis, volleyball, ping pong, horseshoes, swings, shuffleboard, and forest hiking trails await the more adventurous guest.

Guests gather throughout the summer in the bright dining room, for plentiful samplings of good old American cooking. Simple breakfast fare of French toast, pancakes, and eggs is individually  served ($5 charge to drop in visitors). Dinner reservations are required, so hosts can plan ahead for the plentiful home-cooked feasts like roast beef, ham, chicken, or pasta (complimentary to Inn guests, $6-7.50 for dinner guests). No meals are served during Spring and Fall, though your hosts will happily direct you to local eateries.

 Dining Delights

Fireside Inn is "another place guests return to again and again", so schedule your visit up to one year in advance. Your hosts will start a waiting list in January for popular summer dates or Fall color tour weekends. Plan ahead to "make the connection" at . . .

Fireside Inn Resort, Inc.
517-595-6369
18730 Fireside Highway, Presque Isle, MI 49777
No Smoking in Dining Room

Inn-spired Activities ───────────────

Go hiking; pick wildflowers; step into a different era at the Hideaway Bar; or go boating on beautiful Grand Lake!

Huron House - OSCODA

"a luxury retreat for couples"

*N*o indoor common areas here! This beachfront Inn is designed for *private* "Key West type" laid back getaways. The perfect place for couples!

Each of 12 ultra-private rooms/suites provides a pair of binoculars for watching the intrepid sailors, or soaring eagles pass on Lake Huron. Spacious or cozy, all are gorgeous, with beautifully appointed traditional decor. Each has its own unique character - perhaps a beach flavor, or Victorian flair, with large TV, private bath, and private whirlpool tub or outdoor deck spa.

Several rooms offer a mini-fridge, wet bar with microwave, private deck or balcony, and a fabulous Lake Huron view. Five fireplace rooms provide cozy winter  "cocoons", while all upper guestrooms offer private outdoor hot tubs. Rates vary from $65-145, depending on room and day. Your welcome? A personal greeting on a tray, accompanied by homemade cookies!

Four choices stand out as most popular for that guaranteed extraordinary romantic experience: Iasco Suite for summer retreats, Iargo Suite for winter; while Moonshadow and Sunrise have it all, anytime. Mid-June to Mid-September these rooms book very early, so call a minimum of 3 mos. in advance to assure your reservation.

Ample outdoor decks seem to hang over the "Big Lake", and are separated from its rolling waters only by an enticing strip of white sand beach. Firewood is supplied for use in the beach fire pit; charcoal is supplied for cookouts on the deck grill. A complimentary bubbly beverage is supplied for your special occasion. Quiet is supplied for listening to the waves - from the deck, from the beautiful gardens, from the beach, or from your lakeview room!

Though innkeepers at Huron House respect guests' privacy and generally "let clients alone", they do serve a Continental Plus breakfast to your room (or on the deck if requested). Homemade goodies, fresh fruits in season, and a choice of breakfast specialties brightens your breakfast tray - along with another personal card.

Your perfect romantic memory is assured with the Innkeeper's arrangements (by special order) for flowers, champagne, cake, dinner reservations, or suggested activities.

Your perfect romantic getaway is enhanced by a glorious sunrise on the ice, or a spectacular "moonrise" reflected on glassy water.

"Refresh your spirit", renew your love, at . . .

Huron House
517-739-9255
3124 N. U.S. 23, Oscoda 48750
www.oscoda.com/huronhouse/
Smoking permitted on deck only

Inn-spired Activities ————————————

Take your bottle of wine to the quiet of Lumberman's Monument, sit 2-300 feet up on the dunes and watch the sunset over the river; enjoy our 'uncrowded paradise' in summer; ski the riverbanks and 130 miles of scenic groomed trails in winter; check out local art galleries, Fall colors, and some of the most breathtaking scenery in Michigan!

Garland - LEWISTON

"It's beautiful! It's Relaxing!
It's witchcraft!"

G arland will cast it's magic spell over all who enter the gate! Perfectly melded into 3500 acres of unspoiled beauty, this magnificent, expansive lodge-style resort is known as "the ultimate four-season...retreat."

Visitors are enchanted with thousands of twinkling white lights reflected on the sparkling winter snows; with acre after acre of perfectly manicured grounds and "out of this world" landscaping; with the rustic warmth of mammoth lodge-pole pine construction and numerous stone fireplaces; with glimpses

of deer, turkey, fox, and rare nesting bald eagles; with the "delicate balance between luxury and the environment" that only Garland achieves so well!

This is not a typical large resort. Though massive and including plentiful accommodations, Garland still offers abundant opportunities for intimacy and romance! Couples stroll the sun-dappled or softly lit grounds and nature trails (there are "lots of PRIVATE SPOTS!"), skate arm-in-arm around the lighted ice rink, schedule a moonlit wagon or sleigh ride, or treat themselves to a romantic dining experience...

And dining at Garland *is* an experience! Whether you choose the casual atmosphere of Herman's Grill, summer outdoor dining on Herman's Terrace, or more formal ambiance (dress code applies, and reservations recommended) of Herman's Main Dining Room, you'll enjoy gourmet cuisine stressing freshness, quality, and creativity. *Dining Delights*   Chefs here are always "trying new ideas and refining old" ones. To perfectly complement Garland's hunting lodge theme, signature dishes are wild game specialties like "Venison Sauerbraten", or "Raspberry Glazed Pheasant". "Broiled Naubinway Whitefish with hazelnut and dried cherry crust", "Veal and Forest Mushroom Meatloaf", and "Adobo Seasoned Free Range Chicken with chili cornbread stuffing". These are but a taste of tempting dinner entrees for $14.50 to $28.00. Ask your server to suggest the perfect wine. In addition to the dinner menu, Herman's Grill offers munchies and sandwiches ($2-$8.95) for lighter meals, and nightly summer entertainment (weekends in winter) . Garland's capable Conference Services staff will coordinate receptions and special occasion arrangements.

Still getting the hang of relaxing and renewing your relationship? Ease into it, together, with one or more of these fun

activities: golf one of 4 fabulous courses; try out mountain biking, snowmobiling, or cross-country ski trails; energize with tennis, volleyball, or basketball; encourage each other in the fitness center or lap pool; swim in the outdoor pool (summers only - pool house stocks extra towels); schedule a therapeutic massage; or relax in the glass-enclosed outdoor, or the cozy indoor, Jacuzzi® or sauna.

First class overnight accommodations are guaranteed at Garland, whether in the richly colored pine-furnished Lodge Rooms, the more elegant English manor hunt-club style South Wing, the Jacuzzi® rooms, or the beautifully appointed Suites - with fireplace sitting area, refrigerator, 2 person Jacuzzi®, all the amenities (even coffee), and a bathroom "to be lost in". Your privacy is even better assured in one of the resort's popular single or double villas, complete with separate sitting room, cozy dining table, high European-style bed, gas fireplace, wet bar and Jacuzzi® tub.

Garland is open all year, except for a short respite in November and March. You'll want to call for rates, since seasonal offers and discounts apply, and many exciting packages, special events, and theme weekends are hosted year-round.

Two of the finest "au deux" escapes? The "Penthouse Package" - dinner served "en suite" by your personal server, champagne, chocolates, dinner wine, roses, breakfast in Herman's, and accommodations in the elegant Penthouse suite; and "Zhivago Night" - a horsedrawn sleigh ride to the resort's Buckhorn Lodge for a gourmet 5-course feast "worthy of the czars" (*Detroit Monthly*), a roaring fire, refreshing beverages, luxurious villa lodging, breakfast, and cross-country skiing.

Discover the rest of Garland's uniqueness. It's peaceful! It's unforgettable! Experience it! Call . . .

Garland
1-800-968-0042
County Road 489, HCR-1 Box 364M, Lewiston, MI 49756
www.garlandusa.com
Smoking and non-smoking accommodations available

Inn-spired Activities ———————————

Try golf, hiking , xc skiing, or take a romantic sleigh ride!

Lakeview Hills Country Inn -

LEWISTON

"a paradise for lovers"

*T*his inviting four-story lodge sits atop
the highest point in Michigan's lower peninsula. Its winding
wooded drive is lighted by century old street lamps from Belle
Isle. Its broad wraparound porches overlook the panoramic
beauty of East Twin Lake, and commanding views of rolling
country hills and forests up to 35 miles distant.

Guests frequently "disappear" to the lodge's rooftop
Observatory - a quiet spot filled with rockers and comfortable
seating; or to the downstairs Common area - furnished with
hand-crafted log furniture, TV, VCR, stereo, and board games -
and adjacent to the cedar-lined exercise room, complete with
various workout equipment, dry sauna, and Jacuzzi® tub.

The really unique feature of this country Inn? A
professional croquet court, where guests don the required
traditional "whites", and spend some time enraptured by the
slow-paced nostalgic sport of 1800s Europe. Play amid ghostly
images of ladies with parasols and white-clad gents!

Guest enjoyment also includes use of a cross-country ski
trail, and putting green, or hiking the 365 acre property.

Summer sun, glorious fall color, or pristine snowy landscapes provide a peaceful backdrop for the 14 guest rooms, each with private bath, unique furnishings and antiques, and historical information about the area and the rooms' namesake. Select a respite with railroad theme and log furniture (Au Sable Room); Victorian flair with claw-foot tub (Goldie Wheeler Room); more primitive appeal (Mitchelson-Hanson Bunkhouse); 50s theme and birdseye maple furnishings (Otsego Room); or Native American decor with "John Wayne bathtub" (Chippewa Room. Many rooms offer lake views, and access to balconies for outdoor cuddling! Most popular? The Lakeview Room with upper balcony and view of the entire valley and lake. Honeymooners often book the Lewiston Room - an airy floral retreat with balcony. Rates range from $98-125.

By all means, let your hosts know if you're having a "sweetheart celebration"! They'll arrange a special treat including flowers and champagne. Weddings happen here on the lawn or porch, with catered great-room or downstairs receptions (20-30 guests) a possibility.

Valentines Day is extra special at Lakeview Hills! Ask about packages for that lovers' holiday, and other theme weekends such as skiing, tubing, canoeing, or croquet luncheons and dinners.

While guests may drop in the kitchen anytime to enjoy tea and snacks, they'll dine together by the Great Room fireplace each morning. A favorite feature of the Deluxe Continental Breakfast is sausages and "Banana Pancakes", though you may enjoy a quiche, or hot oatmeal, with your bagels, muffins, cereal, fruit, and beverages.

You'll find "beauty, warmth, and hospitality ... like at home, but better!" at . . .

Lakeview Hills Country Inn
Resort and Croquet Club
517-786-2000
Fleming Road, P.O. Box 365, Lewiston 49756
Smoking outdoors only, please

ℋack-ℳa-𝒯ack 𝒥nn - Cheboygan

A century-old log lodge on the Inland Waterway's Cheboygan River, featuring rustic decor accented with decoys, lures, canoes and rowing sculls. Arrive by boat or by car, and enjoy a leisurely meal with a panoramic "theater" view of the river. Try specialties like "Baby Spinach Salad with almonds, oranges and raspberry vinaigrette", Prime Rib, Lake Perch, Salmon, Walleye, "Whitefish Almandine", or "Baked Whitefish with dill sauce". Save room for Hack-Ma-Tack Pie - vanille ice cream, crème de cocoa, crème de menthe, pecans, and chocolate sauce". Tasty!

Open May-October / Full Bar / Smoking in designated areas /
8131 Beebe Road • 616-625-2919

𝒯he ℬoathouse - Cheboygan

Anchor's away! Dock your boat (or your car) at this nautically-themed eatery for some great Boathouse Specialties like "Chicken ala Hondro - stuffed with ham & mild peppers, with tequila lime sauce and jack cheese", "The Boathouse Pasta - shrimp, crab, seafood, mixed fettucini, and sundried tomatoes", Prime Rib, "Salmon-Artichoke Fettucine", "Mediterranean-style Lamb Rack", "BBQ Baby Back Ribs, Northern Michigan Whitefish, "Sesame Grilled Tuna", "Spicy Shrimp with peanut sauce", Steaks, or "Seafood Stuffed Ravioli" ($12-20). Lighter meals, sandwiches, and salads are available for luncheon or dinner ($4.95-8.95). Tantalizing!

Open all year / Reservations accepted for parties of five or more / Smoking in designated areas / Full bar & wine list / Outside deck dining / Private parties up to 75 / Call for entertainment schedule

106 Pine Street • 616-627-4316

Dining Delights

The Courtyard Restaurant & Lounge - *Alpena*

Combining an "Old-world" flair with a nautical flavor, popular private booths, and an up-beat, casual lounge. Serving Italian Pastas, Steak, Seafood, and "finger food" like Pizza and Nachos. Try "Norwegian Salmon Florentine on sauteed mushrooms and spinach with asiago cheese," "Veal Marsala with mushrooms and side of pasta Alfredo", or Shrimp - steamed, hand-breaded, or combination, all with homemade garlic bread. Mama Mia!
Open all year / Smoking in designated areas / Reservations accepted, and a good idea weekends / Full bar & extensive wine list / Private parties possible for 30-35 guests
2024 U.S. 23 South • 517-356-9511

Dining Delights

Fieldstones - *Harrisville*

Warm and casual European-style dining featuring a varied menu of Soups, Salads, Fresh Whitefish, Pastas, Seafood, Prime Rib and German specialties like "Beef Rouladen", and "Jaeger Schnitzel" ($6.99-14.99). The menu changes yearly, so expect some surprises. Relax in a comfy chair at the sunken bar, or sample homemade cheesecake, pie, torte, or specialty foods from the "Craving Corner". Sunday Breakfast Buffet ($6.99) features fresh baked goods and fruit, eggs, breakfast meats, biscuits and gravy, hash, cheddar potatoes, Belgian waffles, etc. Wunderbar!
Open May 1 - October 1 / Separate smoking room / Full bar and wine list / Reservations accepted / Banquet room seats 30-50
676 N. Huron Road • 517-724-6338

15

Lakewood Shores Resort - Oscoda

This golf club is "known for their flowers!" Glass walls surround the dining room and overlook fields of over 60,000 annuals and 3500 day lilies. Candlelight, fresh flowers, and linen-bedecked tables bring the beauty indoors to enhance luncheon options like Open Face Sandwiches, Salads, and "Shrimp or Ham Hawaiian" ($4.95-7.95); or dinners such as "Stuffed NY Steak with mushrooms and onions", Perch, Walleye, "Stuffed Orange Roughy", "Chicken Oscar with crab, broccoli and hollandaise", or "Chicken Dijonnaise on a bed of spinach with dijonnaise sauce" ($9.95-18). Call for dates of summer Dinner Theaters. Always a feast of beauty and good taste!

Open April - October / Smoking in designated areas / Reservations recommended / Outdoor dining on patio / Full bar and wine list / Cocktails and Sandwiches available in "19th Hole" / Banquet room seats 65, main dining room -135, 19th Hole -50

7751 Cedar Lake Road • 1-800-882-2493

The Pack House - Oscoda

A registered 1878 Michigan historic site, with period decor, original woodwork, and small intimate dining rooms graced with marble and oak tables, Victorian chairs, candlelight, flowers, linens and four fireplaces. Serving fine dining selections like "Planked Whitefish encased in Duchess potatoes", top of the line Sterling Silver Beef, "Garlic Roasted Prime Rib", and a popular "Pasta Specialty with lobster and shrimp morsels in crab sauce over fettucini" ($9.95-16.95). Add special zest to your meal with a bottle of private label wine. Or, enjoy a burger or appetizer in the cellar bar. Legendary!

Open April - October / Smoking in designated areas / Reservations recommended / Full bar & wine list / Two upstairs banquet rooms seat 8 or 60

5014 N. U.S. 23 • 517-739-0454

À Deux Adventures

- Sunrise Side and Top- o-the-Mitt

Mackinaw City
Voyageur's Jubilee Dinner Show 1-800-230-SHOW
Therapeutic Massage 616-627-4345
Wings of Mackinaw Butterfly House 906-847-3742
Old Mill Creek State Historic Park 616-436-7301

Indian River
Cross In the Woods 1-800-EXIT310
Sturgeon & Pigeon River Outfitters 616-238-8181

Oden - inland waterway
Windjammer Marina - Boat Rentals 616-347-6103

Grayling - Vanderbilt - Hillman - Johannesburg
Grayling Area CVB 1-800-937-8837
   or .... www.grayling-mi.com
Hartwick Pines State Park &
   Lumbering Museum 517-348-7068
Green Timbers Recreation Area
Fletcher Pond Floodwaters
The Depot Restaurant (casual dining) 517-732-3115

Cheboygan
Cheboygan Opera House 616-627-5841
Therapeutic Massage 616-627-4345

Alpena
Thunder Bay Theatre 517-354-2267
Alpena Civic Theatre 517-354-3624
Middle Island Lighthouse Keepers Assoc., Inc.
   Aerial lighthouse tours 517-356-6361
Alpena Soaring Club - introductory
   Rides ($48) 517-354-4496
   or 517-354-4496
Besser Natural Area - Presque Isle County

Oscoda
Au Sable River Queen 517-739-7351
Reid Lake & Hoist Lakes Foot Travel Areas
Three Mile & Oscoda Beach Parks

The Thumb & Surrounding Areas

*O*ur Michigan mitten's "Thumb" area offers a treasure trove of peaceful rural and shoreline retreats close to Detroit, Lansing, and other metropolitan centers.

Take a scenic shoreline auto tour on M-25 with stops perhaps at charming Victorian communities like *Lexington*, Croswell, and Harbor Beach; *Port Austin*'s Lighthouse Park and underwater shipwreck preserve; restored "ghost town" museum buildings of Huron City; Gagetown's unique Octagon Barn; or the Thumb's only sand dunes at Port Crescent State Park. Visit lighthouses, berry farms, cider mills, harbors, gardens, museums

and parks. Peruse the shops of historic *Holly's* Battle Alley, *Linden, Chesaning,* or Lake Orion's Canterbury Village. Have some fun, or some "holiday magic" at Crossroads Village and Huckleberry Railroad - not too far away. Don't miss the "Tridge" - Midland's 3-way foot bridge, the Holz Brucke wooden covered bridge in Frankenmuth, or the couples ritual "Be Good to Your Mother-in-Law Bridge" in Croswell - a swinging suspension footbridge offering that sage advice!

Top attraction here is Michigan's "Little Bavaria" - *Frankenmuth!* German-style onion towers, flowerboxes, and glockenspiels lend that old-world European atmosphere to a marketplace of more than 100 shops. Watch woodcarvers, sausage makers, doll makers, and leather crafters. Stop in candy shops, wine cellars, breweries, and

bakeries. Get in the spirit at Bronner's fascinating CHRISTmas Wonderland. Experience the satisfaction of a family-style chicken dinner as only Frankenmuth can do it. Take a romantic carriage ride through town, or take a peaceful riverboat tour. *Willkommen!*

One star of the area's entertainment offerings? The *Chesaning* Showboat of course! Pride of Shiawassee River's historic Chesaning, the showboat features summer performances of well-known entertainers. Or, you could schedule a music break at nearby Pine Knob or Meadowbrook outdoor concert theaters.

Another very special nearby attraction is the singularly beautiful Dow Gardens in *Midland*. Waterfalls, streams, ponds, and manicured lawns highlight acres of ever-changing seasonal floral displays, ornamental trees, and shrubbery. You'll find that, together, "it's paradise - that was only a garden a moment ago".

From shore, to shops, to gardens, to Inns - "where the countryside meets the lakeshore" they give "Thumb's Up!" to romance!

Huron County Visitors Bureau
1-800-35-THUMB
www.huroncounty.com
St. Clair County CVB
1-800-852-4242
Lexington-Croswell CVB
810-359-2262
Frankenmuth CVB
1-800-FUNTOWN
www.frankenmuth.org
Chesaning C of C
1-800-255-3055
Midland County CVB
1-888-4-MIDLAND
www.macc.org

𝒯he ℛaymond ℋouse 𝒥nn -

" affordable luxury"

*I*t's an easy drive from the city to serenity. Escape! Experience the quiet elegance of this classic Victorian landmark. A warm, friendly haven from May to November, Raymond House is also a showcase for the "Lady of the Manor's" unique 32" tall Artistic Doll Creations.

Seven individually decorated, and spacious "bedchambers" (each with private "en suite" bath) await your romantic pleasure: perhaps a dramatic Art-Deco style; Victorian with hand crocheted lace accents; or the very popular "Lincoln Room" with its namesake headboard, fainting couch, and painted pine floor. (Rates from $65-85). You'll want to plan 4-6 weeks in advance for a stay on busy weekends.

Unwind and get to know each other again in the large main parlor. Enjoy the warmth of the historic decor, the fireplace, your choice of hot teas from the tea wagon, sherry, or homemade cookies.

Be sure to check out this Inn's "pamper room" - a fully equipped workout sanctuary with massage room and on-call therapist.

Guests are encouraged to relax on the quiet deck, overlooking the terraced garden and fountain, or to stroll leisurely to the beautiful nearby harbor and watch the moon rise over Lake Huron. This port's lighthouse still winks a warning to passing freighters and pleasure craft.

Expect a filling Breakfast Buffet including muffins, breads, coffee cakes, hot and cold cereal, beverages, and on weekends a hot entrée such as "Baked Cinnamon-Raisin French Toast", or "Perogies a la Hispanic with salsa or sour cream".

Satisfy your appetite, and satisfy your soul . . .at . . .

Raymond House Inn
810-622-8800 or 1-800-622-7229
111 Ridge Street, Box 438, Port Sanilac 48469
www.bbonline.com/mi/raymond
Smoking on deck or front porch only, please

Inn-spired Activities ————————————

Take a moonlight stroll over to Lake Huron and the adjacent lighthouse, watch freighters pass; stop by the Harborview Cafe in the marina and sip coffee on the top deck overlooking the harbor.

Governor's Inn - LEXINGTON

"more than just a place to rest . . .
a place for love!"

A summer retreat for a former Governor, this Inn could be *your* retreat from life's hustle-bustle!

Nestled in the quaint resort village of Lexington, Governor's Inn offers a peaceful Victorian ambiance featuring wicker-filled parlor, large formal dining room with sitting room, and a wraparound porch for spoonin'!

Three delightful floral themed guest rooms, each with private bath, welcome you to the charm of yesteryear and the romantic possibilities of today! Climb the hand-carved staircase to your private quarters, and enter a world of antiques, flowers, and cozy quilts. Year-around rates are $55-75 (book 2-3 weeks in advance). A favorite is the Cottage Rose room - bathed in morning sunlight - but you'll enjoy the Lilac Room, or cozy Morning Glory Room as well. *Do Not Disturb!*

Until breakfast, that is! You'll want to join the other guests in the dining room for an ample Continental Plus buffet, highlighted with the Innkeeper's fresh-baked muffins or coffee-cakes, and fresh fruit. Feel a chill in the air? Huddle around the pot-bellied stove and hug your honey!

Nearby Lake Huron beach will beckon you for some quiet moments. Watch the sailboat races, picnic at the pier, take in a local festival, or enjoy a color tour. Let the gentle lake breezes carry you back to . . .

Governor's Inn
810-359-5770
7277 Simons Street, P.O. Box 471, Lexington 48450
Smoking on outside porches only please

Inn-spired Activities _____

Go to the beach and pier; watch the sailboat races; check out the nearby Petroglyphs, annual art fair, Ciderfest, Fall colors, annual Christmas event; try cross-country skiing and tennis. Just be together!

"Love is most nearly itself
When here and now cease to matter."
                    - T.S. Eliot

Powell House - LEXINGTON

"one of life's simple pleasures . . .
overlooking Lake Huron"

*O*n the shore just North of the quaint village Lexington, this warm gracious Inn welcomes guests in Victorian style. Call at least 3-4 weeks in advance for George's Room, one of three with private bath. All the rooms here are

adorned in comfortable period decor, with a hint of lace at the windows. (Rates $65-75).

Settle in to your bright, airy room and wander to water's edge for a swim, a picnic, or a tennis match. You'll greet with pleasure the woods and gardens at this charming destination, and may wish to continue your stroll on the harbor promenade. Or, the nearby bike path may beckon you for a four-mile trip to historic Croswell.

The Powell House parlor offers the "simple pleasures" of a fireplace, piano, and many books. But don't forget a few moments alone in the adults-only Tree House!

Guests can pile their plates high next morning as they're served an elegant full breakfast in the formal dining room. Look for such special dishes as "Amish Egg and Sausage Bake", "Calflute - French fruit custard bake", "Herb Baked Eggs", or "Cinnamon Twists". Early birds will be happy to note - coffee and juice are out at 7:30 a.m.

What a "great place to relax, eat well, and become uncomplicated!"

The Powell House Bed & Breakfast
810-359-5533
5076 S. Lakeshore Road, Lexington 48450
Smoking outside only - garden and porches

Inn-spired Activities _____

Check out the beautiful marina and harbor, quaint shops, indoor Harbor Bazaar (all year on weekends), and the Lexington Players; swim, play tennis (on grounds), go diving to 16 sunken vessels in the underwater preserve; take the bike path to Croswell; go to the beach!

"If you would be loved, love."
- Hecato

Bonnymill Inn - CHESANING

"a wonderland of love"

I t's Country Victorian splendor in all eighteen rooms and eleven suites of this spacious, inviting Inn. You're welcomed in the atrium, which also serves as a perfect gathering spot for warming by the fireplace, enjoying the games and books, or the complimentary Afternoon Tea with home-made goodies and seasonal beverages. You could even enjoy your favorite cocktail, since Bonnymill has its own liquor

license! Fair weather visitors especially enjoy a mellow moment on the huge wrap around front porch. You will too, if you like rocking chairs - there's 50 of 'em!

Guests gather in the atrium too, for the Full Buffet Breakfast, featuring such delicacies as "Bonnymill Inn Baked Eggs", and daily homemade, warm "Cobbler" and "Cinnamon Rolls".

Complimentary coffee is ready for the guests at all times, and a complimentary bottle of champagne greets wedding-night couples. Your host can also arrange for flowers, fruit baskets, or goodie baskets with homemade chocolates!

All twenty nine of this Inn's charming rooms and suites have private bath, and comfortable period decor combining lace and antiques with bright, pretty colors. Each one is unique, delightful, and very appealing, but couples may prefer to reserve a suite, since each one has its own sitting area and 2-person Jacuzzi® tub. Thirteen of the rooms have the added attraction of a cozy fireplace to put you "in the mood"!

This busy Inn is full year-round, so be sure to call at least two months in advance for a weekend suite reservation. Off-peak rates are $32.50-72.50, while high season rates range from $65-145. Ask about special packages available Sunday - Thursday, eleven months of the year.

Though available dates are limited, Bonnymill Inn does plan on-site weddings for those who rent the entire Inn (50 guests indoors, 100 in the garden). Receptions are planned in conjunction with family-owned Heritage House restaurant across the street.

Plan a "relaxing, quiet time, just to be spent with each other". Plan to visit . . .

Bonnymill Inn
517-845-7780
710 W. Broad Street, P.O. Box 36, Chesaning 48616
Smoking in atrium and hallways only, please

Inn-Spired Activities ———————

Visit our area's two delightful parks, and stroll down "the Boulevard" in town - Chesaning is "Old-fashioned America"!

Stone House - CHESANING

*"a perfect stop on your
journey to romance"*

*L*eaded glass windows, hardwood floors, and magnificent oak woodwork are merely a hint of the warm welcoming atmosphere found here.

Lured to the parlor by the tinkling of the ivories on the 1930 player piano, you might just stay for a fireside tete-a-tete, or to share a good book. Parlor weddings (50 guests max) are always beautiful here.

Stone House' traditional hospitality includes afternoon snacks, coffee, tea, and complimentary soft drinks, as well as a non-alcoholic sparkling beverage for those special occasions.

Non-traditional, however, is the unique Full hot Breakfast with many house specialties like "Breakfast Pizza", "Baked French Bread", or "Grandma's Coffee Cake".

Check into the Murphy Suite (Bridal Suite), an elegant two-room suite perfectly suited for a two-hearted union! Queen

Anne cherry-wood furnishings include a king-size bed. Fireplace, Jacuzzi®, and wet bar are the special amenities enhancing its cream and rose decor.

The Emily Anne Room could also provide that perfect memory. It, too, has a fireplace and Jacuzzi®, though its ambiance is distinctly Victorian, enhanced by a rich wine backdrop.

Three additional rooms, each uniquely designed to enchant, offer private bath and Jacuzzi®. Phones and TV grace each of the five guest rooms with modern amenities. Special rates are in effect in winter mid-week, but standard rates are $100-160. Innkeepers suggest weekend reservations be made 1-3 months in advance.

With all that this "most romantic" Inn has to offer, perhaps you should re-route your romance to . . .

Stone House Bed & Breakfast
517-845-4440
405 W. Broad Street, Chesaning 48616
email:stonehousebb@juno.com
Sorry, no smoking indoors

Inn-Spired Activities

Go to some of the antique shows and sidewalk sales Memorial Day through Labor Day; experience the weekend-long Candle Walk (Friday -Sunday after Thanksgiving) when homes are decorated and on tour; stop in Market Street Square shops and famous Dottie's Deli; be here for Show Boat week in summer; go to the movie theater or dancing - only 20 minutes away!

Pine Ridge - FENTON

"a paradise for lovers"

This is the ultimate metro-getaway! Privacy rules at Pine Ridge, with each room luxuriously appointed and including a hot tub spa, fireplace, stereo,TV, sitting area, and private bath. These sixteen very romantic, inviting hideaways are designed for couples to "cocoon", relax, and enjoy each other for midweek rates of $145, and $195

Friday, Saturday, Sunday and holidays. Be sure to book 4-6 weeks ahead, and remember the Inn is closed Christmas Eve and Day.

Though this retreat has 40 acres of wooded trails marked with red hearts, and a lovely pond guests will enjoy, there are no common areas - that's the idea, remember? *Privacy!* (Though you may wish to share the moment of your matrimony with 10-15 invited guests on the lawn or at woods' edge.)

A Continental Breakfast of warm, gooey cinnamon rolls, Havarti cheese and orange slices, coffee and juice arrives at your door at a time you request. The same heart-handled trays deliver to your room an evening "snack" of four cheese varieties, crackers, four kinds of hot puff pastries, hot stuffed clams, marinated artichokes and mushrooms, gourmet raspberry cookies, chocolate mints, and a carafe of wine!

If your romantic fantasy is to have your mate all to yourself, Pine Ridge is the perfect experience! With no children, pets, or phones, "its heaven for so many couples" at . . .

Pine Ridge
810-629-8911 or 1-800-353-8911
N-10345 Old U.S. 23, Fenton 48430
Smoking and non-smoking rooms available

Inn-Spired Activities _____

Though most of our guests choose to stay right here, there are movie theaters and dancing twenty minutes away. Enjoy!

"love is like a precious plant. You can't just accept it and leave it . . . or just think it's going to get on by itself. You've got to keep watering it. You've got to really look after it and nurture it."

- John Lennon

Michigan Star Clipper DINNER TRAIN
AND BED & BREAKFAST CARS   - WALLED LAKE
"a shining star - recapturing a grand era"

*A*h! What ambiance! The aura of fine rail dining and travel! Not only will this award-winning old-fashioned train take you on a journey to a slower, gentler day, but their fabulous staff will return you to a time when service was superb!

Begin your journey with an elegant five course gourmet meal prepared on board by 5 chefs with the freshest of daily ingredients. Choices, changing monthly, may include seasoned and slow-roasted Prime Rib, "Morrishes Island Poulet - filet of chicken with red pep-

pers, mushrooms, zucchini, and gruyere cheese sauce", or "Salmon Creme Dijon with radish Dijon creme, wild rice, and garden vegetables". A full service cash bar is available on board in dining cars or lounges. All dinners are

Dining Delights complemented by a dessert from the Chef's repertoire.

Spacious cars are richly appointed in mahogany, burgundy, spruce green, and tan furnishings and Victorian carpets, accented with tilted mirrors and soft lighting. China, crystal, and large picture windows at each table, as well as exterior viewing lights, enhance the beauty of your dining experience.

Dinner excursions, departing Tuesday through Sunday all year, include a Murder Mystery, or a more romantic Musical Revue, performed table-side for your personal enjoyment ($68.50 per person - Gents! Coat and tie required. Ladies! Dress appropriately!).

Tickets for the two hour Luncheon excursions (no entertainment) are $38 per person, with menu selections of "Beef Bordelaise", "Baked Cod", or "Italian Chicken". For celebrations of any kind, ask about The Star Clipper's especially designed gift packages with gorgeous bouquets, balloons, and "scrumptious tortes". Private parties? Absolutely! Charter an entire car for smaller, intimate groups, or for up to 243 guests.

For a truly unique, first class romantic adventure, reserve one of seven private sleeping compartments. Dine with the other B&B guests in the Cleveland drawing-room car, or dine privately in your cozy, romantic compartment. Silk moiré wall coverings and gilt-framed paintings set the mood in the French-style rooms, or you can have a bit of 50s-style nostalgia complete with half bath, if that's more to your liking.

Dancing, dining, entertainment, accommodations, stellar service, and an Enhanced Continental Breakfast, are all included in the Bed & Breakfast package for $248 per couple weekdays, $279 per couple weekends. You'll have nothing but compliments for the staff of this warm, welcoming *amazing* train!

Be transported to a place for love. . . a world of romance. . . on . . .

The Michigan Star Clipper
Dinner Train &
Bed & Breakfast Cars
248-960-9440
840 N. Pontiac Trail, Walled Lake 48390
(6-7 Minutes North of Novi Twelve Oaks Mall)
Small smoking section available in each car (filtered)

Dining Delights

Chesaning Heritage House -
Chesaning

This imposing 1908 Southern-style mansion has an open stairway off the front entry atrium, and two floors of first-class dining pleasure with three glassed-in porches. The glow of four fireplaces is reflected on linen and flower bedecked tables with pewter charger and goblet settings. Over 30 entrées on lunch and dinner menus may include "Chicken & Fruit Combo - homemade chicken salad with fresh fruit and fruit dip", "Swiss Family Wellington - burger with swiss cheese, mushrooms, and spicy tomato sauce in puff pastry" (lunches $6-12); "Stuffed Pork Tenderloin - rolled with bread stuffing", "Hickory Charred Salmon Filet - coated with hickory-char crust rub", "Pork & Mincemeat en crouté with apple schnapps & pecans in puff pastry", the very best Lobster tails available, famous blueberry muffins, and an extensive monthly list of Seafood specials (dinners $12-22 + market). Wonderful!

Open 363 days - closed December 24 and 25 / 90% Smoke Free / Full bar & wine list / Reservatioins Recommended / Several banquet rooms seat 10-80 / Entertainment weekends in "Rathskeller" lounge / Carriage Shop Gifts open in rear bldg.

605 W. Broad Street (M-57) • 517-845-7700

Dining Delights

The Farm - Port Austin

Overlook the three acre "farm" from the bay window, and enjoy the harvest - presented in such "cuisine of the heartland" specialties as "Grandma Lizzie's Chicken with lemon-thyme dumplings", "Swiss Steak in red wine sauce", "Herbed Farm Bread", "Roasted Eggplant Soup", "Bread & Butter Pudding", and "Rhubarb Cobbler with homemade ice cream". ($8.95-20) It's "country-style comfort food", and it's superb!

Open Tues.-Sat. in Summer - Weekends only in May and Fall / Smoke free / Full bar & wine / Reservations appreciated

699 Port Cresent Road • 517-874-5700

Dining Delights

The Bank 1884 - Port Austin

A "casual atmosphere" in a restored historic building alight with candles, fresh flowers, and linen service. Serving appetizers such as "California Style Pizza" and "Smoked Norwegian Salmon", and gourmet dinners like legendary "Chicken Wellington", certified Angus Steaks, a variety of fresh Fish, "Shrimp Scampi", and at least two daily specials like "Seafood Enchilada", or "Salmon Profiterole wrapped in thinly sliced potatoes" to complement a wide variety of regular menu items (menu $15.95-19.95, specials $14.95-21.95). Memorable!

Open mid-April to mid-December, call for seasonal hours / Full bar, beer & wine list / Screened porch seats 40 for Summer parties / Christmas parties possible / Reservations advised especially in Summer / Designated smoking areas

8646 Lake Street • 517-738-5353

Dining Delights

The Garfield Inn - Port Austin

Imposing 1830's architecture, linen, candlelight, and pewter chargers set the mood. Fresh market ingredients create gourmet specialites like "Florida Rock Shrimp Crespelle with grilled vegetables, pecorino romano, and tomato basil crème", "Jamaican Jerk Chicken with peas, rice, and mango relish", "Roasted Yelloweye Rockfish tomato provencal with quinoa pilaf", or "Roasted Pork Loin Adobo with chimichurri sauce and cheddar cheese grits" (luncheon $5.95-7.95, dinner $13.95-18.95). "Where expectations are not just met, but exceeded . . . and service is not just a word - it's a promise!"

Open all year - call for seasonal hours / Smoking only at the bar / Garden weddings for 200, indoor parties for 80 / Full bar and private label wine / European-style shared bath Victorian bed & breakfast rooms available ($80-110)

8544 Lake Street • 517-738-5254 or 738-5255
1-800-373-5254 or email: garinn@aol.com

Dining Delights

Fogcutter - Port Huron

Overlook the St. Clair River, Lake Huron, and the stunning panorama of Blue Water Bridge from the 6th floor vantage point of this traditionally-styled restaurant. Linen service and candlelight set the stage for a repast of perhaps "Mignonettes of Beef en Brochette", "Prime Rib", "Almond-Fried Jumbo Gulf Shrimp", "Broiled Breast of Chicken with Mandarin orange sauce", ($10.95-19.95 + market price), or a lighter lunchtime "Spinach Salad with mesquite chicken and warm bacon dressing", "King Rueben", or "Jr. Fogcutter Hot Brown" ($6.25-9.95). All that, and the view, too! What more could you ask?

Open All Year / Full Bar and Wine List / Private Banquet room seating 150 / Reservations Appreciated / Smoking in designated areas / Keyboard organ dance music Fri. & Sat. eves + Sun. aft.

511 Fort St. • 810-987-3300

Dining Delights

Thomas Edison Inn - Port Huron

Three magnificent Victorian dining rooms set in candlelight, fresh flowers, and fireplace glow, look out on the St. Clair River and the reflected lights of beautiful Blue Water Bridge. Sample "Honey Mustard Chicken Croissants", "Mushroom Encrusted Pork Medallions", "Seafood Orechietti Pasta", or other lunch specialties ($6-13). How about evening fine dining choices like "Char Broiled Provini Veal Chops", "Salmon with sundried tomato crust", "Sauteed Southern-style Paella (14-21), "Surf & Turf" or "Twin Lobster Tails"? (market price) Delish!

Open all year / Full bar, lg. cocktail lounge / Private banquet room seating 600-700 / Outside dining in courtyard / Smoking in designated areas / Reservations recommended / Variety of live bands Wed.-Sat. in lounge

500 Thomas Edison Parkway • 810-984-8000

Dining Delights   *Huron Shores* Golf Club -Pt.Sanilac

Admire tournament plaques, historic photos of the club, award winning paintings of a talented local artist, or the greens and fairways visible from those window tables. Enjoy a frequently changing menu with lunches like "Terrific Black Bean Soup", "Seafood Chowder", or the "Bunker Burger" and "Bogie Burger" (avg. $4.95 incl. soft drink); or dinner choices including Prime Rib, fresh Whitefish, Pickerel, and Perch with herb and butter sauces ($11.95 avg.) and weekend dinner specials that "You're not apt to make at home"!

Open March - New Year's Eve / Designated smoking area / Reservations recommended on Summer weekends / Full bar / Parties in back room with view - seats 40; Spring and Fall - 90

1441 N. Lake Shore Road • 810-622-9961

Dining Delights   *Broad Street* - Linden

You're invited! - to the casual comfort of Broadstreet - with lunches of generous-cut Prime Rib, Sandwiches, Pasta, and specialties like "Spinach-Wild Mushroom Turnovers", and "Sweet Potato Shoe String Fries ($5.50-9.50); over 20 appetizers (under $10); dinners like "Pan Roasted Cajun Duck with portabellos & ginger", "Planked Porterhouse Steak with Saratoga fries & sauteed pepper, onion, & mushroom ramoulade", "Grilled or Blackened Filet with Hawaiian Shrimp and Oriental bean sauce", Duck, Seafood, or Vegetarian & Asian specialties ($12.50-22.95); Sunday "Wine Thieves" with tasting & special menus; and "Wednesday After 6" cigar-friendly live jazz evenings. It's "food off the beaten path"!

Open all year except 2 weeks following New Year's / Smoking section in bar / Full bar and very extensive wine list / Parties for 50-70 in upper dining area

103 E. Broad Street • 810-735-5844

37

Find a romantic candlelit corner in this historic Queen Anne Victorian's five dining rooms, set in Holly's Battle Alley "antique" shopping district. Enjoy classic and "creative American" cuisine like "Stuffed Portabello Mushroom with parmesan vegetables", "Pheasant Sausage Stuffed Artichokes", and signature "Escargot en Phyllo" appetizers ($4.95-6.95); luncheons like "Spinach Salad with mandarin oranges, almonds & poppyseed dressing", "House-made Linguini with vegetables & cream", signature "Chicken Strudel Hollandaise" and "Victorian Onion Soup with puff pastry top", or "Fresh Vegetable Pita with avocado cream" with Hotel-made fresh potato chips! ($4-8); and daily changing dinner selections

such as signature "Filet of Beef Wellington", "Fresh Norwegian Salmon Filet in white wine with champagne & feta cheese sauce", "Fresh Roast Lingonberry Duckling", "Fresh Lobster Wellington with citrus hollandaise", and Chops, Steak, Seafood, and Chicken specialties ($15-25). A historic dining adventure!

Open all year / Limited smoking seats available / Reservations recommended / Full bar and wine list / Banquet room seats 175 / Piano music in main bar / Weekend comedy club - lower level Ask about dining club / Agoura Antiques open in lower level

110 Battle Alley • 248-634-5208

À Deux Adventures

- Thumb and Surrounding Areas

Midland - Saginaw - Flint Area
The Dow Gardens...1-800-362-4872
Shiawassee National Wildlife Refuge............................517-777-5930
Crossroads Village 1-800-648-PARK
Frankenmuth
Riverboat Tours...517-652-8844
Zehnder's of Frankenmuth (chicken dinners)..............1-800-863-7999
Bavarian Inn Restaurant 1-800-BAVARIA
Bronner's CHRISTmas Wonderland......................... 1-800-ALL YEAR
  and ....www.bronners.com
Fantasy Carriage Company, Inc. 517-777-4757
Chesaning
Chesaning Showboat (c/o CofC)..................................1-800-255-3055
Dottie's Deli 517-845-7101
Caseville - Gagetown - Port Austin - Bad Axe
Lipprandt Orchards & Dried Flowers 517-453-2851
Friends of the Thumb Octagon Barn............................1-800-369-8882
Huron County Nature Center Wilderness Arboretum
Tip-A-Thumb Canoe Rental..517-738-7656
Tip of Thumb Air Tours...517-738-5546
  or...517-269-7299
Port Austin Community Playhouse 517-738-5217
Sanilac Petroglyphs 517-373-3559
Lexington
David X. Regan Memorial Harbor
Patrick Tierney Memorial Park
Holly - Fenton
Michigan Balloon Corp. (hot air balloon rides)............1-800-968-8368
Capt. Phogg Balloon Rides (Balloon Quest, Inc.)...........810-634-3094
Pine Knob Concerts...248-377-0100
Lapeer - Lake Orion
Past Tense Country Store
Olde World Canterbury Village 1-800-442-XMAS
Meadowbrook Concerts...248-377-3300

Those "Irish Hills" and the Southeast Corner

O.K. all you "city folk", discover the many surprises that await in this beautiful close-by getaway corner - fine dining, quaint lodging, entertainment, and history galore!

The natural beauty of **Irish Hills** is punctuated with lakes, parks, and seasonal amusements like a dinosaur tour, a buffalo  ranch, an exciting motor-car racetrack, a space center, and numerous fascinating museums. History buffs will love the frontier charm of Stagecoach Stop USA - a mixture of old style architecture, shops, demonstrations, displays, street shows, live dinner theater, and FUN!

Another intriguing stop is Walker Tavern at Cambridge State Historical Park. See a renovated roadhouse and reconstructed wheelright shop, then toddle off to the "Antique Alley" chops of fourteen area communities.

Treat your sweetie to a soda in Tecumseh's "The Chocolate Vault Old-Fashioned Ice Cream Parlour & Candy Company", or "The Parlour (Jackson Dairy, Inc.)" in Jackson.

A summertime tradition for over 60 years is a visit to **Jackson**'s Cascades illuminated waterfalls. Evening performances of this unusual man made fountain display are accompanied by constantly changing music and colorful lights.

Highly recommended for that romantic interlude is a peaceful stroll through MSU's Hidden Lake Gardens - a 755 acre landscape arboretum with year-round exhibits, one-way driving and hiking trails, and a sheltered place for the perfect picnic! Plan an evening at historic Croswell Opera House - Michigan's oldest theater; an excursion on Adrian & Blissfield Rail Road's Old Road Dinner Train, or Murder Mystery Dinner Train; or an

autumn drive to Irish Hills Towers' spectacular overlook.

Tours and attractions, hayrides, lakeside picnics, lazy paddleboat trips, horseback riding, campfire dinner, hikin', swimmin' cross-country skiin', or plain ol' relaxin', you'll appreciate the Irish Hills area "where good times and good people come together"!

Lenawee County Conference & Visitor's Bureau
1-800-536-2933
www.tc3net.com/travelenawee

Jackson Convention & Tourist Bureau
1-800-245-5282
www.jackson-mich.org

Brooklyn/Irish Hills C of C
517-592-8907

H. D. Ellis Inn - *BLISSFIELD*

"return to an era when the pace was slower,
and life was easier"

*R*eturn to 1883, with true-to-the-period antique furnishings, artworks, quilts, and lace.

Ask anytime (until 9 p.m.) for coffee or tea to be served in the Inn's formal parlor. Get a look at what life was like in Victorian times through the lenses of a stereo-optican. Or, peruse special books of the era, including signed first editions by Michigan author Edgar Guest.

Upstairs, the sitting room is a bit more casual with games and books for relaxing pleasures.

Four guest rooms, each with a different color scheme and private bath, rent for $75-95 including midweek Continental Plus Breakfast. Jams made from locally grown fruit top homemade breads and muffins (like the popular "Walnut Raisin Bread"), and go along with beverages and a fruit tray at the serve-yourself buffet. Weekends will find the addition of a hot dish such as "Sausage Egg & Cheese Strata", "Baked French

Bread with walnuts and brown sugar", or perhaps "Ellis Inn peach or apple Cobblers".

Innkeepers here will arrange weddings and parties for up to 100 guests, and special packages to include the Dinner Train, or dining at Historic Hathaway House. Romantic packages encourage couples to "spend time with each other" with one of those options, or at a picnic lunch, concert, play, garden or museum tour, or shops. Sample some relaxing spa services - a massage or body treatment, steam or whirlpool bath, or other pampered experience. Then take a sunset walk by a lake, or simply try some world-class porch sitting!

Busy times at this comfortable, relaxing Inn will fill up 4-6 weeks in advance so book early. And, oh yes, please let the Innkeeper in on your honeymoon or anniversary plans - you'll receive a bottle of champagne (or non-alcoholic beverage), and a flower in your room to help you celebrate in Victorian style!

You'll have your heart set on returning to . . .

H.D. Ellis Inn
517-486-3155
415 W. Adrian, Blissfield 49228
web info with Hathaway House at www.hathawayhouse.com or
with Michigan Travel Bureau at www.michigan.org
Smoking on the front porch only, please

Inn-spired Activities ————————————

Do a pampered spa package; see Hidden Lakes Gardens; visit antique malls, craft malls, the Lenawee County Historical Museum, Irish Hills attractions, and Stagecoach Stop USA; take in a performance at Adrian's Croswell Opera House; and treat yourself to a train excursion!

Chicago Street Inn - BROOKLYN

"step back in time...to a time of dreams...a time of romance!"

*I*f your romantic dreams include a nostalgic trip back in time, this is the perfect place to make them come true! Surround yourself with the rich elegance of hand wrought oak and cherry moldings and trim, European stained glass, and a wonderful collection of antiques and portraits. The entry, sitting rooms, and dining room are highlighted year-around by the glow of original electric chandeliers, and warmed seasonally by the cherry fireplace that's framed with Romeo & Juliet tiles.

Add to your old-tyme adventure with tours of local antique shops, museums, and historic sites. Then return to Chicago Street Inn for your private "journey" to old-fashioned peace and relaxation on the porch or in your room.

Stay in your choice of four delightful rooms or suites in *The Victorian Swallows Inn,* or *The 1920s Bungalow.* The Inn *rooms* and Jacuzzi® suites recall the simple, rich beauty of the 1920s. Three of the suites feature gas fireplaces for your enjoyment on cooler days, and three also include TV, VCR, and refrigerator for a very private hideaway. You'll want to book at least 1 month in advance, though specific room choices cannot be guaranteed. Rates range from $80-165.

Top off your "trip" with a full buffet breakfast including one of Bill's special "Herb & Cheese Omelets", "Baked French Toast", or another specialty hot dish, cereal, fruit, and homemade baked goods.

Ah, Chimera! Oh, Romance! For occasions, surprises, or fulfilling your dreams - try a visit to the past at . . .

Chicago Street Inn
517-592-3888
219 Chicago Street, Brooklyn 49230
www.getaway2smi.com/csi
email: chiinn@aol.com
Smoking outside only, please

Inn-spired Activities —————————

Enjoy canoeing, bowling, or walking the quiet village streets; seek out the parks and lakes; sample fresh treats from Flavor Fruit Farm orchards; share a bicycle tour "in our quiet area"!

Dewey Lake Manor - BROOKLYN

*"return to...a time of lamplight and lace,
love songs and flowers, picnics and sunsets!"*

*F*or your anniversary - a rose. For your honeymoon - champagne and breakfast in bed! For your anytime getaway - the peaceful quiet of this century-old home.

From the comfort of the large sitting room, enjoy the yard and lake vistas, or sit by the fire in the parlor with your sweetie and read a book together. Snack on cider and donuts, coffee or lemonade. This is a place to relax and refresh!

For your private hideaway, you may most enjoy the Lake-view Room (its name implies its best feature!), or perhaps the Mapleview or Floral Rooms, each with its own fireplace. All five comfortable country Victorian rooms offer feather beds or quilts, private bath, TV, radio and a homemade cookie treat! (Rates from $69-75).

A hearty breakfast buffet is served in the glass enclosed porch or formal dining room. You'll enjoy fruit, cereal, raisin bread, muffins and bagels, along with varied hot dishes like

"Waffles by Joe", or "C h e e s e - B r o c c o l i Quiche", and your favorite breakfast beverage.

Wander 18 acres, play piano in the parlor, or ponder the reflection of the moon on Dewey Lake. Or, feel free to use paddleboats, canoes, grills, picnic tables, horseshoes, croquet court, or bonfire area.

Wedding or reception? Reserve the entire Inn and make it memorable with a ceremony in the parlor (35 guests max), or on the hill overlooking the lake (max 200 guests). And *do* inquire about the Valentine Package!

You'll come back again and again to the "quiet country atmosphere" of . . .

Dewey Lake Manor
517-467-712
11811 Laird Road, Brooklyn 49230
www.getawaytosmi.com/dewey
Smoking outside only, please

Inn-spired Activities —————————

Sample the area's ice cream parlors; have fun at the festivals and home tours; lunch at the Beach Bar in Clark Lake; see the Twin Towers, and the Country Jamboree; canoe the River Raisin at Sharon Hollow Acres; toast and taste at St. Julian Winery Outlet in Jackson!

The Munro House - JONESVILLE

"say 'I love you' with style and grace...
say it at Munro House!"

*T*his imposing 1834 American Greek Revival-style mansion was once a station on the underground railroad. Today Munro House offers it's guests an atmosphere of stately elegance with all those "little extras" that make your stay one of comfort and pleasure.

You'll be welcomed in the double parlor, where a baby grand piano and victrola are available for your enjoyment. Or, while away some time in the library, selecting a 19th century or

current volume, or a video for viewing in your room later. Don't forget to peak into the Bottomless Cookie Jar in the dining room, or wait for coffee and dessert to be served every evening.

Imagine treating your significant other to a relaxing stay in one of this Inn's seven rooms, five of which offer fireplaces, all of which include TV, desk, phone, and full sit-down breakfast.

Select one of four classic colonial-style rooms, or one of simple Shaker decor. For a special memory, why not reserve Clara's room - a garden getaway? Or, perhaps check into the lodge-style comfort of George's Room. Guests in these popular Jacuzzi® suites may order breakfast served in their suite. You may want to call at least two months in advance to be sure your room choice is available. Rates range from $75-150.

In the morning, join the other guests in front of the open-hearth fireplace for a hearty serving of the house specialty - "Orange-vanilla French Toast with orange-apricot syrup", or perhaps "Eggs Florentine Crepes", with all the accompaniments.

Notify your host in advance if it's your birthday, honeymoon, or anniversary, so you may receive their very special gift.

Munro House is available to host your garden or parlour wedding, reception, or anniversary party for up to 75 guests.

You'll never forget your "I love you" at . . .

Munro House
517-849-9292
202 Maumee Street, Jonesville 49250
www.getaway2smi.com/munro
A non-smoking Inn

Inn-Spired Activities ────────────────

Experience the Amish country; skip off to a picnic or buy fresh fruit; visit Grosvenor House Museum; go cross-country skiing; enjoy our local summer theatre!

49

Dine among the Victorian splendor of beautiful chandeliers, fine period furnishings and antiques, oil paintings, and charcoal sketches. This his-
toric mansion offers truly fine dining in six intimate dining rooms accented with five glowing fire-places, fine china, linens, candlelight and fresh flowers. Certified Chef Miguel Cueto spe-cializes in "Rack of

Lamb" "Seared Salmon with roasted peppers, olives, pine nuts, and raisins", "Charleston Chicken with cream, Canadian bacon, and mushrooms over farafelle pasta", and "Potato Crusted Wall-eye", to go along with Prime Rib, Seafood, Pasta, Poultry, and meat entrées ($15-23). Featured luncheon items ($6.95-9.95) include "Chicken Frangelico with cream liqueur sauce, pecans, and dried Michigan cherries", "Fresh Broiled Lake Superior Whitefish", and "Shrimp & Crabcake Sandwich with zesty dill mayonnaise". More casual dining, and a tempting Sunday Brunch, are featured in the more rustic atmosphere of the carriage house (the Main Street Stable & Tavern).

Open all year - call for seasonal hours / Reservations recom-mended / Smoking in backroom parlor only / Full bar and wine list / Cocktails and hors d'oeuvres on the porch or in the gardens / Private parties in Hathaway House for up to 90 guests - in the Loft of the Stable, 60 - Meeting & Harness Rooms,10-25

424 W. Adrian Street • 517-486-2141

Michele's at the Brooklyn Hotel
and *Brooklyn Bistro*
at the Brooklyn Hotel - Brooklyn

"Formal dining with a pleasant small village attitude" - in a restored Victorian hotel. It's "elegant but casual!" Enjoy the paintings of a local artist, a hand-painted tin ceiling, linens, silver, candlelight, and a rose on every table! Plus "unstuffy gourmet" French continental cuisine like "Deep Fried Pickles", Fresh Oysters, "Bacon-wrapped BBQ Shrimp", "Raspberry Rum Baked Brie and 'almost famous' pita chips" for starters; and "Monterey Tuna Steak Sandwich", "Vegetarian Boursin Flatbread", "Brooklyn Blue Chicken with ham, blue cheese, pecans, and Alfredo sauce", "Honey macadamia Shrimp Salad", "Raspberry BBQ Duckling", and "Vegetarian Combo (ravioli veggie bake)", Veal, Prime Rib, and "Rack of Lamb Dijonnaise" (lunch $5.50-11.95, dinner $10.95-19.95).

Weekend breakfasts feature specialties like "Brooklyn Omelette with ham, jack cheese, and roasted pepper salsa", "Eggs Benedict", and "Vegetarian Tortilla" ($2.75-5). The menus change seasonally, the historic magic and the quality cuisine - never! Ce magnifique!

Closed Mondays and January / Smoking in designated areas / Reservations recommended for weekends / Full bar, wine list featuring Michigan wines, and micro-brew beers / Private parties for 25 - Semi-private parties for 60 / Inquire about four spacious, non-smoking, restored suites available on upper level

131 N. Main Street • 517-592-0700

À Deux Adventures

Adrian - Blissfield

Old Road Dinner Train / Adrian-Blissfield Railroad
  Dinner or Murder Mystery reservations please call
  Hathaway House...517-486-2141
  Private Charters, Special Event, and Excursion
  train schedule 1-888-GO-RAIL-1
Three Bridges

Irish Hills

Walker Tavern...517-373-3559
Stagecoach Stop USA 517-467-2300
Waterloo Riding Stable & Dude Ranch 517-522-8920
Waterloo Area Farm Museum.................................313-596-2254
Croswell Opera House.. 517-264-SHOW

Jackson

Jackson Dairy, Inc. (The Parlour)..........................517-782-7141
Cascades Park...517-788-4320
Ella Sharp Museum 517-787-2320
Michigan Space Center 517-787-4425

Jonesville

Grosvenor House Museum.....................................517-849-9596

Manchester

April Victoria (Victorian Faerie Tea)....................517-428-0040
Healing Hands (massage therapy) 517-428-9660

Clark Lake - Concord - Hanover - Tipton - Tecumseh

Beach Bar 517-529-4211
Mann House Museum 517-524-8943
Child's Buffalo Ranch...517-563-8249
Hidden Lake Gardens 517-431-2060
The Chocolate Vault (ice cream & candy) 517-423-7602

*Note: For an additional dining choice, please see Victorian
    Mansion Inn, Coldwater, page 68, River Country*

"How do I love thee?
Let me count the ways.
I love thee to the depth
and breadth and height
My soul can reach."

- Elizabeth Barrett
  Browning

River Country and other *Historic Rural Havens*

*E*xperience the peaceful pleasures and warm hospitality of Michigan's "unpretentious" rural heartland.

Surrender yourself to the restorative powers of Southern Michigan's clear, cool liquid pathways! Surprise yourself with the calico charms of a country fair! Indulge yourself in lazy, relaxing natural beauty!

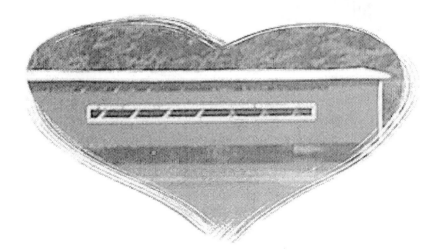

If your honey has been hounding you to *relax*, this is the place. What a great "homebase" for tours of slow-paced Amish country, for quiet walk-and-talks, for Fall color tours, Sunday drives, and swingin' on a swing. Appreciate nature from the seat of a bicycle, the back of a horse, on cross-country skis, or your own two feet. Float away your cares - in a rented canoe, pontoon, or boat. Snuggle in a sleigh ride or lift your spirits in a hot air balloon. Treat yourselves to an ice cream, an apple, some cider, or wine. Watch a parade. Tour a garden. Sit on the lawn and let the melodies of a summer band concert flow over you. Meditate. And make yourself at home!

You can surround yourself with hometown heritage: *Coldwater* shows off its historic treasures - 1886 Skeels House, 1875 Wing House Museum, 1800 train station mall, and the 1882 Tibbits Opera House - where audiences still applaud; *Marshall* invites you to its annual Historic Home Tour featuring close-up looks at selected 1800s homes and buildings, as well as museum tours of popular Honolulu House, Governor's Mansion, and others, a Civil War Encampment, and special shows and entertainment; and Centreville celebrates with a picture of the past (its covered bridges!), and a chance to buy a memory in its antique market.

Sample a winery, visit a farm, toboggan down the hillsides, have some fun at Cornwell's Dinner Theater, stop for coffee, lunch or supper in Marshall's Espresso Yourself coffee house, or make a little magic in Colon!

This could be the start of a grand love affair with River Country!

River Country Tourism Council
1-800-447-2821
www.rivercountry.com/

Branch County Tourism Bureau *(Coldwater)*
1-800-968-9333

Marshall Area C of C
1-800-877-5163
www.marshallmi.org

Sturgis C of C
616-651-5758

Three Rivers Area C of C
616-278-8193

Christmere House Inn - STURGIS

"history . . . romantic destiny"

*D*isappear into the gracious living of bygone days. The antique charm of this Queen Anne mansion sets a grand and elegant tone for your visit to the heart of rural Michigan.

Restoration of this imposing "executive" Inn accented fascinating examples of original craftsmanship including carved oak woodwork and fireplace mantels, magnificent stained glass windows, and a marvelous "grand oak staircase".

Two first-floor sitting rooms, and a lower-level English style smoking area, beckon guests to comfort and hospitality

highlighted with books, three fireplaces, player piano and victrola. Summer visitors take afternoon tea on the porch.

Victorian ambiance extends into each of the ten guest rooms unique period decor - soft florals, dramatic backdrops, simple stripes, or delicate lace, and of course antique furnishings galore! All rooms have private bath, phone, TV, and desk (for writing love letters and poetry dedicated to your own amour!) The four suites are marvelous escapes, with those added amenities designed especially for romance - hot tub, stocked bar, cappuccino service, and fireplace or unusual stove. Couples may want to request the Queen's Tower or Country Squire - spacious third floor suites with cathedral ceilings and leaded glass. Rates vary from $80-125.

Food "treats" and gifts honor that special event. Honeymooning? You'll receive a commemorative mug and gift certificate towards your first anniversary stay! And, oh yes, front parlor "fireside" wedding ceremonies (65 guests max), or garden events (225 max) are capably hosted at the Christmere. Cocktail and hors d'oeuvre receptions (165 max), and sit-down parties can be easily accommodated as well, since Christmere House is a full service Inn with fine dining. Plan your intimate "at-home" romantic dinner in one of the candle-lit formal dining rooms (Mon-Sat. 6-9 pm, reservations strongly recommended). Cocktails and wine complement a selection of fine cuisine entrées such as "Crab Stuffed Shrimp", "Lambchops with mint jelly", and "Chicken Royal".

Dining Delights

Guests also gather in the stately dining room for their individually served Full Gourmet Breakfast featuring such delicacies as "French Toast with fruit filling", "Ham and Cheese Egg Bake", or "Fruit filled crepes with ice cream topping".

For a very special occasion, the Innkeepers offer "Romance Christmere Style" - a delightful package with a wine-cheese-fruit-and-crackers welcome, and a complete champagne candle-light dinner in one of Christmere's own dining rooms (p.s. check your pillow "for a take-home surprise!)

Relive those days of splendor, at . . .

Christmere House Inn
616-651-8303 or 1-888-651-8303
110 Pleasant Street, Sturgis 49091
www.rivercountry.com/christmere/
email:christmere@rivercountry.com

Inn-Spired Activities ———————

For the out-of-doors couple we suggest a nearby state park for superb hiking & picnics;take an Amish country tour!

Mendon Country Inn - *a Wildwood Inn in*
MENDON

"the right place, and the right time for romance!"

$\mathcal{P}$ eddle away on this Inn's bicycle-built-for-two or paddle your way down the stream in one of their canoes! Either way, you'll be glad to return for your overnight stay at this history-filled former stage coach stop.

Filled with country antique furnishings, each of nine spacious rooms in Historic Wakeman House display a different theme. Perhaps the "Nautical Room", the rustic "Barn", or Southwest "Sundance" will be your favorite. Six with fireplace, two with Jacuzzi®, (all have private bath), the rooms range from

$69-129. The Adams Wakeman Room, with creekside porch, is a favored jewel. Why not plan to read, relax, or sunbathe in the "Rooftop Garden" overlooking the creek? Barbecue, picnic area, and country swing await as well.

Will a comfy suite be more to your liking? Two uniquely stenciled Jacuzzi®/fireplace suites sit across the drive in the Innkeeper's Cottage (rate $139). Or, for an even more private and quiet getaway, reserve one of five Native American motif suites in the Creekside Cottage ($159 per night). While each

suite in this round contemporary Lodge has its own Jacuzzi®
and fireplace, you may wish to socialize in the common-area
Kasha or Kiva Rooms, enjoy the full cedar sauna, or sit on the
creekside deck and watch the wildlife.

Propose to your darlin' in the "Country Canoe" (ask about
this package), then plan your wedding on the "island" (150
guests max, or 50 indoors).

Special packages here include "Candlelight Tavern Dinner",
"Old Tyme Amish Thanksgiving", and "Country Christmas", as
well as Canoeing, Massage, Winter, and of course Romance
offerings.

All guests at Mendon Country Inn are treated to a Deluxe
Continental Breakfast in the Puddleburg Room. It may feature
"Baked French Toast", or "Sour Cream Coffee Cake". Stay over
on a Friday evening, and you'll also experience a special dessert
buffet.

Stay over *any* evening, and you'll experience small town
friendliness, a warm "family" welcome, and a romantic mood
at . . .

The Mendon Country Inn
616-496-8132 or 1-800-304-3366
440 W. Main Street, Mendon 49072
www.rivercountry.com/mci
email: wildwoodinns@voyager.net
Smoking in designated areas only, please

Inn-spired Activities ————————————

Play some tennis; visit a local winery or Amish settlement; go
canoeing with us; kiss under a covered bridge!

The Sanctuary at Wildwood -

a Wildwood Inn in JONES
"for (nature) lovers only!"

*D*oes Mother Nature speak to your heart? If so, you'll feel right at home here, since this Inn's decor is designed to reflect the splendor of its 90 acre wildlife sanctuary. Great Room, Dining Room, and the themed Guest Rooms' private balconies/decks look out on seasonal outdoor panoramas of woods, meadow, and pond.

Inside, you'll still delight in such samples of Nature's splendor as Tree Beds, scenic Landscape murals, hand-hewn tables, and wildlife sculptures. Each Lodge Room and Cottage

Collection Suite is especially romantic with fireplace, Jacuzzi®, service bar, refrigerator, and private bath (rates $129-159). Couples will be particularly pleased with "Keeper of the Wild", and its unique birch grove headboard, or with any of the six new Cottage Suites.

After a Deluxe Candlelight Buffet Breakfast, featuring perhaps a "Finnish Pancake", "Bacon and Egg Bake", or "Baked French Toast", your outdoor odyssey begins. Hike the four miles of Inn trails, take a dip in the pool, or join the geese for a leisurely afternoon beside the pond. Your hosts can arrange horseback riding, bicycling, sleigh rides or tobogganing, skating, or cross-country skiing. For a one-of-a-kind treat, your hosts can reserve a specially designed "courting canoe" at a local livery. Settle amongst the pillows, and under the parasol, for an old-fashioned float down the St. Joseph River, including a champagne country picnic!

Shopping, exploring, and touring may all enrich your visit, but be sure to save some time for pure relaxation at the Sanctuary. Challenge each other to checkers in the Great Room, or curl up in the den/TV Room with your favorite magazine, while you snack on cookies-n-cocoa, coffee or tea. Then steal away to your private quarters for a fireside toast, or some Jacuzzi® time. Perhaps you'll want to order the "Romance Package", with flowers, champagne, confections and dinner for two at a local restaurant, or gift your love a massage and aromatherapy bath kit. Ask about Country Christmas and Golden Getaway packages, too. Weddings, honeymoons, anniversaries, or just a quiet escape, you'll want to make several trips to this fabulous retreat.

Escape! Enjoy these tranquil surroundings . . . enjoy each other! at . . .

The Sanctuary at Wildwood
616-244-5910 or 1-800-249-5910 (Res. Only)
58138 M-40 North, Jones 49061
www. rivercountry.com/saw
email: wildwoodinns@voyager,net
Smoking on balcony or patio only, please

Inn-spired Activities ——————————————

Take a walk through Russ Forest; explore our wine country; shop our antique and specialty shops; discover nature!

The National House Inn -MARSHALL

*"steeped in historic significance with
a wealth of contemporary hospitality"*

S imple Treasures:

A rustic entryway warmed by a massive open-hearth fireplace; a dining room lined with country green woodwork,
furnished in oak; two large parlors with an upstairs sitting
lounge featuring unique fireplace and hand-crafted cabinets. Ah,
authentic 19th century ambiance!

Sixteen guestrooms (each with private bath) display unique
styles from elegant Victorian to country primitive. Sizes range
from small and intimate to two-room suites, and rates from

$66-130. Most romantic havens? The Ketchum Suite, with
adjoining sitting room and overlooking Brooks Memorial Fountain, or H.C. Brooks Room bedecked in Country French.

Simple pleasures:

Ah, 20th century comforts! Breakfast "like you've never
seen"! A plentiful selection of homebaked goods and English
muffins, beverages, and fresh fruits, plus gourmet treats such as
"Morning Apple Tart", "Egg Strata", or "Sam Hill Cake"
(named for one of the rooms). Guests enjoy a light afternoon

tea, freshly popped corn, "the best coffee in Calhoun County", and family-style warmth.

A fun diversion? The Inn's Tin Whistle Gift Shoppe featuring country gifts and antiques. And, of course, the private Victorian Sitting Garden, a place of peace and beauty.

"Candlelight Tour Weekends", "Fall Tea", "Christmas Tea", Cooking Classes and all of historic Marshall's favorite festivals and events, offer you even more simply-special pleasure possibilities!

"The serenity is contagious, the sense of history infectious . . . the fast lane ends at" . . .

The National House Inn
616-781-7374
102 S. Parkview, Marshall 49068
www.innbook.com
Sorry, No Smoking

Inn-Spired Activities ——————————

Don't miss our local festivals, events, and home & garden tours; share the Calhoun County Fair (oldest in the state); hold hands at one of our summer band concerts!

"A man falls in love through his eyes, a woman through her ears."
- Woodrow Wyatt

The Victorian Villa - UNION CITY

"truly the past . . . unsurpassed!"

This elegantly restored 19th century getaway beckons. Which of ten distinctive Victorian-style "bed chambers" will you choose? The Victorian Renaissance or Master Suite, with separate parlors and gas fireplaces? The secluded Victorian Tower Suites? Or perhaps the "Victorian Country" with private garden-view balcony and antique clawfoot tub-shower? Any of the ten guest chambers (each with private bath), will delight you. Rates vary from $85-145 depending on day and room selection.

The Breakfast Buffet Saturday and Sunday is full gourmet, with fresh baked pastries, fresh fruit, homemade granola, and perhaps the "Villa's 3-Onion Egg Scramble". Monday through Friday, expect satisfying expanded continental fare. After your hearty complimentary breakfast, be as active as you like - enjoying local attractions, adventures, or events, then returning for afternoon English tea, or wine tasting.

Be sure to reserve a candlelit table for one of the Villa's champagne and wine dinners (not included with your stay). Served Tuesday through Saturday at 6, 7, or 8 pm seatings, this unique romantic 7 course Victorian dining experience may feature wild game, fish, pasta, or steak - all accented with especially selected beverages.

Ask for a calendar of special theme events. Victorian Villa is famous for its Victorian Christmas weekends, Victorian Summer Daze dinner theatre productions, and Murder Mystery weekends. Holidays are very special here (including Valentine's Day, of course!)

The staff will do whatever they can to help make your stay "as sparkling and romantic" as you wish by arranging tea-for-two, cheese and cracker plates, fruit baskets, a wicker-picnic-basket lunch, or Sweetheart Packages (with roses, chocolates, and champagne). Simple or lavish, indoors or out, Victorian weddings in parlor, Gingerbread Gazebo, at fountain or gardens, can be coordinated down to the smallest detail (150 guests max).

Dining Delights

Experience the old-fashioned ambiance and unhurried reflection of the 19th century. Experience . . .

The Victorian Villa
1-800-34-VILLA or 517-741-7383
601 N. Broadway Street, Union City 49094
www.innbook.com
A Completely non-smoking Inn

Inn-spired Activities ————————————

Visit a cider mill or apple orchard; taste our local wines; don't miss our colorful festivals; treat yourselves to summer stock theater and ice cream emporiums!

Dining Delights   *La Cantina*™ *since 1936, in Paw Paw*

Step into an Italian garden! Pass through the wide entry draped with grape vines, grapes, and decorated with dozens of Chianti bottles. Enjoy a view of beautiful Maple Lake from the spacious, candlelit, newly re-decorated dining room, or the overstuffed comfort of the "vineyard" bar. Order simple American Steak, Seafood and Chicken; gourmet or regular Pizza Napolitano; traditional Pastas; or one of the popular pasta specialties like "Seafood Pasta with clam sauce, clams, crab legs, scallops, shrimp, and mussels" or "Emilio Vegetarian Pasta with veggies, roasted red peppers, herbs and romano cheese" (lunch $4-6, dinner $10.95-15.95). Magnifico!

Closed Christmas Day / Full bar / Reservations accepted / Private banquet room seating 100 inside-200 with patios / Outside dining on upper deck or patio / Entertainment on special occasions / Smoking in designated areas

139 W. Michigan Avenue • 616-657-7033

Dining Delights   *The Seasons of Three Rivers*

For dining in a light and airy, soft atmosphere, ask for a candlelit, linen-draped table, or a very private high-back booth. Sit and watch the Rocky River flow lazily by, while enjoying a dazzling Sunday Brunch Buffet ($10.95); luncheon soups like "Carrot Caraway", Salads like "BLT", or "Salad Nicoisse", Sandwiches like "Open Face Prime Rib" or Portablello Mushroom" ($5.25-8.95); and dinners like "Duck Breast Salad", "Wild Rice Pancakes with Chicken Tenders", "Marinated Pork Tenderloins", or "Ahi Tuna in mustard crust with basmati rice" ($9.95-18.95). "Excellent food - relaxed atmosphere!"

Open all year/ Smoking in bar area only / Reservations welcome / Full bar & wine list / Banquet room seats 25 - weekday private parties in main dining room - seats 95

601 W. Hoffman • 616-279-5144

*Dining
Delights*

Malia - *Marshall*

If you appreciate the finer things, you'll appreciate Malia! Serving homemade-to-order fresh Italian specialties in a tiny, fun and intimate 100 year old building. It's oh, so romantic! Watch the chefs prepare homemade pasta in the open kitchen. Dine amongst antiques, ancient brick walls, and hardwood floors, or morning glories, ivy, black-eyed susans and pansies on the garden patio! "Wild Mushroom Fettucine with sundried tomato pesto", "Pork Tenderloin Linguine with cranberries and portabello mushrooms", "Crawfish Linguine with roasted corn", and their famous Cream of Mushroom Soup, are but a few menu items complementing eight to nine daily chalkboard specials (lunch $6.95-10.95, dinner $9.95-21.95). Delicioso!

Closed Christmas, New Years & Sundays / No alcoholic beverage service / Parties possible - max 40 indoors, 16 patio / Reservations highly recommended / Patio dining / No smoking
130 W. Michigan Avenue • 616-781-2171

*Dining
Delights*

Schuler's - *Marshall*

Run away to merry Old England - right here in Marshall! This warm, welcoming restaurant feels so cozy with its wood paneling, strong beams (engraved with English quotations), a fireplace in every room, and lots of stained glass and fresh flowers in the lobby. Open all year, except Christmas day, and serving in the dining room, or on the patio, a variety of fresh, enticing foods such as Prime Rib, Whitefish, and German specialites like "Sauerbraten ($6-10 lunch, $12-20 dinner). A perennial favorite? The Bar Scheeze appetizer spread!

Reservations recommended / Smoking in designated areas / Private banquet room seating 120 / Entertainment occasionally in the Pub / Outside dining on the patio
115 S. Eagle Street • 616-781-0600

Dining Delights *Victorian Mansion Inn* -Coldwater

This 125 year old brick Victorian home-turned-restaurant is "large, beautiful, and phenominal"! Set in candlelight, fresh flowers, and crisp linens agains a backdrop of rich, dark colors, the Mansion serves authentic Italian food, made fresh from scratch to order, and "worth the wait". Try Anitpasto, and Roasted Garlic appetizers, Gourmet Pizza, Lamb, Veal, Chicken, and Grilled Swordfish in addition to specialties like "Lasagna di Polo - with chicken, vegetables, ricotta, provolone & romano cheeses", "Fruitti di Mare Alfredo with shrimp, scallops, and snow crab", or "Bistecca 'ala Prime Rib' - grilled over an open flame" ($12.95-18.95). "It's awesome!" Their motto? To provide the greatest dining experience possible."

Open all year / A non-smoking establishment / Reservations recommended / Full bar, extensive wine list, large variety of margaritas, cappucinos & espressos / Parties possible - max 48
90 Division Street • 517-279-8852

Dining Delights *River Lake Inn* - Colon

Enjoy "Casual Elegant Dining", in one of three themed dining rooms: The Winery - with a vineyard/wine bottle decor; the Captains Quarters - filled with ships & lighthouses; and The Rookery - a favorite with its wildlife theme, bird-feeding stations, and "hoards of hummingbirds" to watch in Summer. Sample a varied menu of Seafood, Steaks, Pork Chops, Ribs, and Sandwiches ($8.95-19.95), or visit Friday & Saturday evening for The Buffet with Chicken, Fish, Crab Legs, Shrimp & Seafoods ($15.95). The Sunday Brunch Buffet is very inviting, and only $9.95. Be sure to check out the brand new "Blue Bird Trail" - a one mile nature walk with benches. Marvelous!

Open all year / Smoking in designated area / Full bar & wine list / Inquire about parties
767 Ralston Road • 616-432-2626

À Deux Adventures

-River Country and Historic Rural Communities

Centreville
Caravan Antiques Market....................................312-227-4464
Covered Bridge Park (shelter reservations)............616-467-5519
Colon
Abbott's Magic Company 616-432-3235
Jones
Swiss Valley (skiing)...616-244-8016
Marshall
Cornwell's Turkeyville USA (dinner theater).....1-800-228-4315
Espresso Yourself (coffee house & light meals)....616-789-1136
Sturgis
Klinger Lake Marina (boat rentals)
Sturgis-Young Auditorium & Council for the Arts
   (exhibits, concerts, plays)..................................616-651-8541
Three Rivers
Barb's Garden Gate (garden tour) 616-278-2108
Carnegie Center of the Arts (exhibits) 616-273-8882
Corey Lake Marina (boat rentals)..........................616-244-5878
White Pigeon
Tasty Nut Shop (soda bar).....................................616-483-7566

"Love is everything it's cracked up to be . . . It really is worth fighting for, being brave for, risking everything for . . ."
                                                    - Erica Jong

Harbor Country - *"Gateway to Michigan" & the Southwest Corner*

*W*hether you find it awakening with fragrant Spring blossoms, ablaze with Autumn's fire, awash in Summer sunshine, or adrift in Winter's whiteness - you'll absolutely *love* Harbor Country!

The area's picturesque harbors, dunes, and beaches have caused it to be dubbed "the Riviera of Lake Michigan". Aside

from the expected swimming, windsurfing, boating, beach walking, and sunbathing, visitors flock to Warren Dunes State Park (and other area Lake Michigan beaches) for dune climbing, hang gliding, picnicking, kite flying, and even cross-country skiing, sledding, and snow tubing.

Glowing water-color sunsets are best viewed from the popular Tower Hill, atop a 240 foot high sand dune. Inland parks and nature centers also provide a peaceful getaway or picnic spot. Some feature formal gardens, some wildflowers and nature trails or exercise trails. Some offer biking, day and night cross-country skiing, putt-putt golf, or volleyball. Dewey Cannon Park even lays out a unique "disk" (Frisbee®) golf practice area. And where else could you trek through "A Maze in the Maize" in a farmer's cornfield?

Marked motor tours, mapped Back Roads Bikeways, unique museums, and miles of beaches decked with majestic dunes, await. Delightful shops and galleries interspersed with roadside fruit stands and u-pick orchards, dot the Harbor Country map. The "Red Arrow Ride", from *Union Pier to Sawyer,* features over 40 such discoveries - marked with a Red-Arrow flag.

One of the pleasures of this corner of the mitten is its abundance of local wineries. Tour their gardens, vineyards, and wine production areas - gather tips on "judging" wines, taste the wine, or dine "en cellar", and select the perfect bottle to enhance your own romantic experience.

Do some grape stomping! Select your Jack-o-lantern from a local pumpkin patch! Climb an ice mountain! Watch a lighted boat parade! Ride a carousel! Join a hay or sleigh ride party! Enjoy December's Festival of Lights - all 50,000 of 'em! Discover Harbor Country!

The Harbor Country C of C
1-800-362-7251
www. harborcountryguide.com

Southwest Michigan Tourist Council
616-925-6301
www.swmichigan.org

"Love is an act of endless forgiveness, a tender look which becomes a habit."
- Peter Ustinov

Sans Souci Euro Inn -NEW BUFFALO

"your dream escape . . . through the gates
to 50 acres of pure serenity"

A private lake. A sunrise. The whispering pines, and "life without a care".

Welcome to the contemporary comfort of Sans Souci. Your choice of a full furnished guest house, a cottage, or a romantic suite awaits at a nightly rate of $98-185.

Each accommodation features a private living room and

light, airy European decor, with large picture window overlooking lake, meadow, or woods. Six of the 9 private retreats offer fireplaces, and 5 have whirlpool baths. All are soundproof, with private tiled bath, hardwood floors, king beds, TV, VCR, stereo, and telephone. Reserve 6 months to 1 year in advance to assure your selection during peak times.

Cottage guests prepare their own breakfast in their luxuriously outfitted kitchen, while guest house "tenants" (as well as those in suites) are given the option of using their own modern kitchen for meal preparation, or being served breakfast in their private accommodation. At a time of your choosing, your hosts will deliver a Full Breakfast including a variety of homebaked goods, beverages, yogurt, fresh fruit, granola, and an egg dish with meat and cheese. Special requests or individual dietary requirements are cheerfully accommodated.

Celebrating? Request flowers and champagne and toast your love in a rowboat or in the gazebo! Or, better yet, renew your vows on the shores of Lake Sans Souci with 20-120 guests to share your joy.

Do you need some R, R, and R? (Rest, Relaxation, and Romance!) This is definitely the place. Why not plan some volleyball or basketball, skate, swim, or enjoy a bonfire, "discover that intimate path", or fall asleep in a maple-shaded hammock? Yes, why not?

For "a lovely combination of European and American hospitality", try . . .

Sans Souci Euro Inn
616-756—3141
19265 S. Lakeside Road, New Buffalo 49117
www.sanssouci.com
email: sans-souci@worldnet.att.net
Smoking permitted in fireplace areas only

Inn-spired Activities ———————————

Get out on "the Sans Souci Trail"!; snowmobile, xc ski, take a hike or horseback tour; do some fashion shopping or gallery hopping!

Tall Oaks Inn - NEW BUFFALO

"an irresistible departure"

"Let the charm of this vintage 1914 Inn wrap its nostalgic glow around you." A magnificent ten foot fireplace adorns the living room - warm yourself. Three walls of glass enclose the garden room - lose yourself. Available for guests are games, books, a 52" TV with VCR, and a small library of tapes - amuse yourself. All guests are welcome to gourmet cookies, popcorn, snacks, coffee machine, soda, juice,

or milk, while couples celebrating a special occasion receive a split of champagne, chocolate chip cookies, strawberries, and a candle by the whirlpool - indulge yourself.

Yes, treat yourself - to a stay in one of 12 rooms (10 with private bath) at this lovely Inn. Decors vary, with some Country, some Southwest, or Victorian. For an extra special stay, select a room with private fireplace (4 available), or a whirlpool tub (8 available). Perhaps the Tiger Lily or Dutchman Breeches would be most to your liking for a night of romance. Let your tastes, (and your budget!) be your guide, rates range from $50-200, and selections should be made 4 weeks (off season) to 2 months (May 1-Nov. 1) in advance.

Part of the treat at Tall Oaks is being served a Full Breakfast, with choice of 2 entrées, in the dining room, or on the porch (weather permitting), or in your room. Menus may include such specialties as "Malted Waffles with sautéed apples", "Hazelnut French Toast", or "Three-cheese Egg Pie." Mmmm!

Get warmed, lost, amused, and indulged at . . .

Tall Oaks Inn
616-469-0097 or 1-800-936-0034
19400 Ravine Drive, New Buffalo 49117
www.harborcountry.talloak.com
email: talloaks@hc.cms.net
Smoking outdoors only, please

Inn-spired Activities _____

Don't miss Warren Dunes!

"Falling in love consists merely in uncorking the imagination and bottling the common sense."
- Helen Rowland

Ꮐarden Ᏽrove - UNION PIER

"a flower-filled reminder of a time . . .
when the world moved slower"

*O*h, so dramatic in yellow and peach - "The Sunflower" becomes your intimate hideaway in this Inn of year-round botanical pleasures. It features private bath and balcony, whirlpool tub, fireplace and TV/VCR/cassette radio - all for your personal pleasure.

Perhaps, instead, "the Rose" - a pink and green creation (with added mini-fridge) for romance and relaxation. Or, "The Violet", or "The Arbor", with their clawfoot tub/shower, and their more old-fashioned flair.

Whatever your choice of room, Garden Grove will surround you with the beauty, charm, and comfort of a 1925 summer cottage. Rates vary from $80-150 - be sure to book at least 6 weeks in advance.

Your honeymoon? or Anniversary? Expect fresh flowers, and a bubbly beverage. But all the guests will feel like royalty with day-long munchie treats available, robes, and special bath amenities.

Be alone, or feel free to gather, in parlor, den, library, or dining room. Be lazy or active, enjoy fireplace, outdoor hot tub, games, books, and an evening social hour. Or borrow a bicycle and pedal (or walk) to shops, beach, lighthouse, or dining. At day's end, gaze at a glorious sunset over Lake Michigan, then gaze at each other and fall more in love.

Wake up to a Full "Scrumptious" Breakfast - maybe "Luscious Lemon Pancakes", "Breakfast Pizza", or Quiche, complemented by fruits, muffins and breads, juice, and gourmet coffee and tea.

With wooded gardens pretty enough for weddings (15 guests max please), and common areas so cozy and entertaining, you'll never want to leave. This may become your favorite stopover in Southwestern Michigan. Remember, a garden is for lovers. Find your garden - inside, outside, all year long, at . . .

Garden Grove Bed & Breakfast
616-469-6346 or 1-800-613-2872
9549 Union Pier Road, Union Pier 49129
www.laketolake.com/gardengrove
email: gardenbnb@aol.com
Smoking outdoors only, please

Inn-Spired Activities ————————

Walk out to the lighthouse at Silver Beach; watch the sunset over Lake Michigan; shop the boutiques and look for antiques; visit our galleries, orchards, vineyards, and excellent beaches; experience some exciting water sports; take a slow, leisurely backroads ride!

The Inn at Union Pier - UNION PIER

*"it'll warm your heart . . .
and set your romance on fire!"*

*W*hat's so special about this Inn? The
unique collection of antique Swedish *Kakelugns* - wood burning
ceramic fireplaces - that warm twelve of the sixteen rooms, and
the Great Room, from mid-fall through Spring.

The decor, a mix of Scandinavian Country and Lakeside
Cottage, is casually elegant and highlighted by furnishings from
the early 1900s. Spacious, individually themed rooms feature
private baths, sitting areas, and telephones. Most have porches or
balconies overlooking English gardens. Select one of six rooms
in The Great House, five rooms in The Pier House, or four in
The Cottage of
the Four Seasons
- all will delight
you at standard
rates of $125-
195. Honey-
mooners toast
with complimen-
tary champagne,
and nibble choco-
late chip cookies
in The Captain's
Quarters or The
Garden View

Suite, two favorite choices for intimate entertaining. Curl up in
classic officer's style in the king sized cherrywood sleigh bed
near the warmth of your Kakelugn after enjoying a relaxing
whirlpool bath. Or soak in the skylit Jacuzzi® of the private
third floor suite, which includes a fireplace, TV, kitchen and
covered balcony.

Be sure to ask about package rates, discounts, and available custom services to help make any occasion special. Weddings can be arranged for up to 100 guests who reserve the entire Inn.

Complimentary afternoon refreshments (lemonade/hot chocolate and freshly baked cookies), as well as Michigan wines and popcorn each evening, are served in the spacious Great Room. Settle back in one of the numerous seating areas, and enjoy some games or the grand piano. The Pier House features a library for guest enjoyment, or you may do some star gazing from the year-round outdoor 8-person hot tub and adjacent sauna. Feeling adventurous? Borrow two of the Inn's bicycles for a local tour of this area's fabulous countryside.

Wind up your stay with a leisurely Gourmet Breakfast served in the Dining Room at your private table. Savor hot entrées like "Vegetarian Eggs Benedict", "Lemon Pancakes with blueberry sauce", or "Tomato, Fresh Basil & Mozzarella Frittata", along with fruit, muffins, and breakfast meat on the side!

Any season (book 3-4 months in advance for peak times) you'll appreciate this Inn's "genteel charm", privacy and comfort. You'll have a burning desire to return to . . .

The Inn at Union Pier
616-469-4700
9708 Berrien, P.O. Box 222, Union Pier 49129
Smoking on outdoor grounds only, please

Inn-spired Activities _____

Play croquet; go for a Fall color bicycle ride; hike the dunes and walk the beach; take a quaint hayride; visit a u-pick orchard; taste some of our area wines; picnic at Warren Dunes; go night cross-country skiing by *torchlight* at Madeline Bertrand State Park!

$\mathcal{C}ine$ $\mathcal{G}arth$ $\mathcal{I}nn$ and COTTAGES -UNION PIER

"just what you've been yearning for"

$\mathcal{U}$ nion Pier's only lakefront Inn, this former summer estate perches on a dune bluff over a private sugar-sand beach.

The look - "country eclectic", a mix of antiques and twig pieces, with Laura Ashley and Ralph Lauren prints. Each of the seven rooms has its own charming personality, TV/VCR, and private bath. Melissa's Room, with private deck, Lake Michigan view, and whirlpool tub; or Jennifer's Room with deck view, whirlpool tub, and unusual twig canopy bed, are the most

romantic choices. Emma's Room boasts the addition of a private fireplace. Rates are from $115-170 depending on room choice and season. For that very special occasion, at peak times, plan to reserve 1 year in advance.

The feel - is pure hospitality, with many personal touches and attention to detail. Like the Full Breakfast, served at individual tables, in dining room or outside deck - or even in your room or private deck by special request. Feast on "Buttermilk Pancakes with nutmeg and pecans", "Welsh Rarebit with tomatoes and bacon strips", "Belgian Waffles with fruit", or a strata, quiche, or frittata, along with fresh fruit, homemade breads, muffins, and coffee cakes.

Available throughout the day are homebaked cookies, candy jars, hot chocolate, tea and coffee. Wine and hors d'oeuvres are served daily from 4-7 pm, to be enjoyed fireside in the Great Room, lakeside in the screened porch, or on six common or five private decks. Nothing is more romantic than sharing a bottle of wine on the decks at sunset!

Or, how about the gift baskets, champagne, and restaurant gift certificates for those twosome celebrations? Holiday surprises include Easter baskets, Valentine candies and flowers, champagne toasts for New Year's, and silly Halloween treats. Complimentary use of bicycles is a delightful surprise, too. And, no surprise, each room and common area are flower bedecked, always. No one is more pampered, or special, or important than guests at Pine Garth. ... "Celebrate the uninhibited satisfaction of appetite, companionship, and rest ..." Celebrate romance at...

Pine Garth Inn & Cottages
616-469-1642
15790 Lakeshore Road, P.O. Box 347, Union Pier 49129
www.pinegarth.com

Note : Pine Garth also offers 5 charming housekeeping cottages with daily maid service. Each offers stone fireplace, private hot tub, gas grill, TV and phone, beach and screened porch access, for a different kind of intimate interlude.

Inn-Spired Activities ————————

Take a bicycle ride in the country with a blanket and a picnic basket!; enjoy drinks at the Harbor Grand Hotel, and overlook the harbor!

The White Rabbit Inn - LAKESIDE

"a romantic couples retreat"

I n the heart of Harbor Country, and specializing in "the romantic getaway" lies a small Inn which guests deem "an oasis in the desert", "a truly memorable experience", and a great place to "kick back and unwind", "put your feet up and just do nothing", find "peace and quiet", "rejuvenating tranquility", and "find each other all over again"!

Relax in the airy Lodge building, overlooking the woods. Take advantage of the inviting comfort to sit back and read, listen to CDs, select a movie, or have a complimentary late night snack. A hearty Continental Buffet Breakfast is served here, in

the company of "visitors" like deer, birds, chipmunks, and Bill the "extremely friendly" orange cat.

Settle into your choice of eight rooms or cabins, each with private bath, radio, TV/VCR, antiques, and unique "rustic" woodland decor. Several rooms have private patios, sitting areas, or fireplaces, while each offers a relaxing whirlpool tub, or outdoor hot tub/spa and private entrance. Ah, the magic of a twosome-soak in the tub!

The Inn's most popular rooms, and the two cabins, feature hand-crafted birch beds, with bent twig and willow accents. Room rates vary from $90-150 (with minimum stay requirements), while cabins with fully-furnished kitchens, and warm knotty pine interiors, rent for $175-200 a night. Special romance and honeymoon packages are available. Be sure to call ahead at least 30 days to assure your choice will be waiting for your arrival. White Rabbit is  closed Thanksgiving Day, Christmas Eve, and Christmas Day.

Spend a night or a weekend, and perhaps you, too, will "leave feeling rested, your senses alive . . ."! Call . . .

The White Rabbit Inn
Bed & Breakfast
1-800-96-RABBIT (967-2224) OR 616-469-4620
14634 Red Arrow Highway, Lakeside 49116
www.whiterabbitinn.com
email: basicnewf@msn.com
Smoking allowed only on your patio or outdoors

Inn-Spired Activities ——————————

Visit area antiqe stores, art galleries, and gourmet restaurants; see our wooded trails, Lake Michigan beaches, and majestic dunes!

Dining
Delights

Kent's - New Buffalo

A casually elegant atmosphere cloaked in warm blues and yellows, candlelit tables, and fresh flowers. A place to indulge in contemporary American food highlighting local products, like dry aged organic steaks, fresh fish and seafood, homemade pasta, and specialties like "Horseradish Crusted Salmon", "Pot Roast with herb dumplings", "Clay Pot Baked Chicken", or "Baked Tomatoes & Goat Cheese with fresh basil" ($11-22). The menu changes daily, but expect it to include pastry specialties like "Banana Chocolate Strudel". Innovative!
Open all year - closed Mondays / Reservations highly recommended / Smoking in the bar only / Full bar & wine list
203 W. Buffalo • 616-469-6255

Dining
Delights

Millers Country House - Union Pier

A California-style 1927 roadhouse with two large, airy dining rooms overlooking the garden, the woods, and a lily pond with fountain. Dinner selections include outstanding "New Zealand Rack of Lamb", "Hawaiian Fish - grilled mahi mahi with tropical pineapple/banana salsa", Steaks, "Shrimp Scampi", "Southwestern Grilled Vegetable Pasta", "Chevré Chicken - goat cheese, chicken, wild mushrooms, and spinach on pasta with madiera sauce", Gourmet Pizza, Ribs, and award-winning "drop-dead great" "Flourless Chocolate Cake" ($13.50-22.50). Or, have a relaxing lunch in the cozy, intimate barnwood Grill Room with its 100 year old bar, antler chandeliers, and casual Burger & Fajita type menu ($4.95-8.50). Millers offers Sunday Brunch, too (around $10). Millers - "People Crave it!"
Closed Tuesdays Sept. - June only / Seasonal outdoor dining & cocktails on deck / Full bar / Tented garden weddings for up to 400 / Summer Mellow Jazz Nights
16409 Red Arrow Highway • 616-469-5950

Dining Delights   *Red Arrow Roadhouse* - Lakeside

An actual roadhouse with a casual knotty pine lodge theme, area antiques, and memorabilia. Luncheon features may include Burgers, Pastas, "Roasted Portabello Sandwich with roasted red peppers, carmelized onions, and herb aole mayo", "Spinach Salad with sweet potatoes and dried cherry vinaigrette, or with strawberries & sprouts", or "Michigan Cobb Salad with roast sweet corn, blueberries & smoked whitefish" (Sat. & Sun. only, $6-8). Dinner choices like Pasta, "Char-grilled Top Sirloin over wild mushrooms & garlic risotto", "Fresh Salmon with parmesan crust over white bean ragout", or "Achiote Citrus Marinated Chicken over pinto beans & rice with blood orange salsa" average $11-17. Superb!

Open all year / Smoking in designated areas / Sorry, reservations not accepted / Appetizers, cocktails & small parties on screen porch / Ask about quiet lake cottage avail. for rent
15710 Red Arrow Highway • 616-469-3939

Dining Delights   *Jenny's Restaurant* - Lakeside

Jenny's new home is eclectic modern with a "more swanky" club-type atmosphere. Four dining rooms with romantic booths and candlelit tables, and a parlor-style lounge for cognac and after dinner drinks. Featuring an eclectic dinner menu of signature "Thai-style Chilean Sea Bass", "Pecan Encrusted Pork Chops", "Chicken Panisse with curry-coconut marinade, rice & Thai BBQ sauce", Lamb, Old-world Steaks, "Mushroom Lasagne", Brick-Oven Pizza, and much, much more ($11.95-25.95 + market). Sublime!

Open all year - 7 days Memorial-Labor Day / Smoking at 5 tables around bar (sorry, no cigars) / Reservations recommended / Small private parties possible / Full bar & wine list
15460 Red Arrow Highway • 616-469-6545

Tabor Hill Winery & Restaurant - Buchanan

Welcome! To a country vineyard setting, oh, so perfect for romantics! Rustic yet intimate surroundings of warm cedar walls, hardwood floors, linens, and romantic mood music are highlighted by soft candlelit tables, fresh flowers, a terrific view, and a blazing fieldstone fireplace! Share elegant luncheons such as "Oregon Bay Shrimp Salad", or "Italian Tortilla Wrap" ($7-13), mouthwatering appetizers like "Thai Chicken", "Mesquite Grilled Shrimp", "Panko Crusted Crabcake", "Wild Mushroom Medley with duck proscuitto and roasted garlic in sherry cream" ($4.75-7.25); and popular dinners like "Oregon King Salmon wrapped in grape leaves with hollandaise sauce", "Raspberry Chicken in pecan bread crumbs", or "Petite Rack of New Zealand Lamb" ($12-23.95). Allow the Wine Consultants to recommend the perfect "food beverage" to complement your meal. Create an interesting "twosome" evening with a special dinner, sunset view, complimentary wine tasting, and winery tours - then create a custom "love basket" from gift shop selections!

Open all year - call for seasonal dining and tour hours / Private parties in main dining room / A non-smoking property / Reservations recommended / Full bar and of course a selection of exquisite Tabor Hill wines!

185 Mt. Tabor Road • 1-800-283-3363 or 616-422-1161
www.taborhill.com

À Deux Adventures

- Harbor Country and Southwest Corner

New Buffalo - Michiana - Three Oaks

Harbor Country Day Spa 616-469-7711

Warren Dunes State Park 616-426-4013

Red Arrow Equestrian Center/Red Arrow Trails

    (stables, hay & sleigh rides) 219-872-2114

Three Oaks Spokes Bicycle Museum 616-756-3361

Zieger Centennial Farm

    (maize and farm tour) 616-756-9707

Union Pier

Heart of the Vineyard Winery &

    Riviera Gardens 616-469-6623

The Wine Sellers, Inc. 616-469-7566

St. Julian Winery of Union Pier 616-469-3150

Bridgman

Tabor Hill Champagne Cellar 616-465-6566

Benton Harbor area

Sarette Nature Center 616-927-4832

Niles and points east

Fernwood Botanic Garden & Nature Center 616-683-8653

Swiss Valley Ski Area 616-244-5635

*"a loaf of bread, a jug of
wine, and thou . . ."*

"Love was as subtly catched as a disease,
But being got it is a treasure sweet,
Which to defend is harder than to get,
And ought not be orphaned either part,
For though 'tis got by chance, 'tis kept by art."
                                              - John Donne

ℒakeshore - South Haven & Van Buren County

"*The Magic Unfolds*"! Imagine! You're floating above Lake Michigan's shore, aloft in a hot-air balloon, and you see it - a port, a "haven" - a duneside jewel! Drop in! You'll discover a peaceful place. You'll discover **Van Buren County**...

Intrepid travelers cruise the shore with Captain Shaul on his 35 foot "Jubilee" charter sailboat, or aboard the luxurious "White Rose" cruise boat - a delight for dinner, sunset, or moonlight tours.

Landlubbers "cruise" the historic former railroad Kal-Haven Trail in Sesquicentennial State Park, on cross-country skis, snowmobiles, and bicycles. Adventurers try downhill skiing, horseback riding, "off-road mini jeeps" and go carts, or even parasailing.

What about those quieter souls? You'll find them strolling about on the new Harbor Walk, from pier to pier, reading the historic signs, picnicking on a beach in the riverfront park, and admiring the lighthouse, or the lake, from a shoreside deck. You might join them in a tour of the Michigan Maritime Museum, a tasting at a nearby historic winery, a harvest at a local berry farm, feeding the deer at Deer Forest, or a performance at the old-barn-style Legend Theatre on the lake.

Or, you might just have a quiet romantic dinner and gaze at a fiery sunset - igniting the flames of desire!

Lakeshore CVB
1-800-764-2836 or 616-637-5252

The Carriage House

AT THE PARK or AT THE HARBOR - SOUTH HAVEN
"the atmosphere of yesteryear ... the comfort of today"

*T*hese two unique bed & breakfast Inn's offer Victorian elegance with all the amenities you expect. Spacious common areas offer a quiet respite, while "The Pub" or "The Pantry" are great for socializing over 5:30 soft drinks, snacks, and hors d'oeuvres.

Each richly appointed guestroom has a fireplace, full private

bath, and TV/ VCR, along with beautiful antique and Amish furnishings. In addition, many have whirlpool tubs, or scenic decks.

At the Park, enjoy one of nine attractive rooms for $95-180. Especially romantic? The Victoria and Bridal rooms. Crawl into a king-size pencil post bed with lace, share a home-baked treat from "Ginny's Kitchen", or cuddle in your private balcony or sitting area.

The bright breakfast rooms will be your morning stopover for a Full Country Breakfast including "Stuffed French Toast with strawberry topping", "Egg Casserole with sausage", or "Oatmeal Pancakes". Scrumptious!

Or, choose to overlook the Black River Marina from one of Carriage House ***at the Harbor's*** eleven luxurious rooms. "Barouche" with corner deck, or spacious "White Chapel" may be your choice for that special night (rates also $95-180).

Breakfast here features an outstanding harbor view to complement such specialties as "Broccoli or Asparagus Quiche", or "Stuffed French Toast with fruit topping". All day treats of cookies, candies, popcorn, and soft drinks will be enjoyed at fireside in the snug Library, the Gathering Room, or on the enclosed Porch.

Only the Harbor location is equipped to host weddings, but keep it small and simple with 25 (adult) guests maximum.

Are you here for a blissful celebration? Let the Innkeepers know if you'd like to order flowers, champagne, wine or candies. In keeping with the theme, perhaps you'd like to arrange a private carriage ride!

Choose *"the Harbor"*, or choose *"the Park"*, you'll truly feel pampered (but try to plan one year in advance to assure your romantic getaway during peak times). Promise a rainbow, promise a weekend, at . . .

The Carriage House at the Park
616-639-1776
233 Dykman Avenue, South Haven 49090

The Carriage House at the Harbor
616-639-2161
118 Woodman Street, South Haven 49090

Inn-spired Activities ———————————

Watch the sunset at the beach; take a sunset cruise or sailboat ride; take a carriage ride about town!

The Seymour House - SOUTH HAVEN

*"an historic mansion on spacious, beautiful
grounds - where your privacy is assured"*

E scape to Seymour House - a brick Italianate mansion loaded with character and charm. Antiques, as expected, are part of the decor, but you can also expect some surprises.The five guest rooms (each with private bath and shower) as well as the 2-bedroom log cabin, are described as "rustic elegance". Each room is individually themed to reflect the essence of the state it's named for. The Michigan Room is nautical, while the popular Arizona Room surrounds its log furniture with Southwest decor, and includes a Jacuzzi® for two. Your choices include another Jacuzzi® room ("Wyoming" style), and two rooms with cozy fireplaces ("Vermont " and "Colorado"). Guest rooms, and cabin, rent from $80-135 depending on the season. Be sure to call 2 months in advance for peak times.

Of course, guests may curl up by the living room fireplace, and enjoy a book, game or movie in the Inn's library, or complimentary fresh-baked cookies, teas, cider and cocoa. But even more delightful are the 14 *outdoor* activities suggested for you on this 11 acre estate. Will you try a relaxing paddle around the pond in the red canoe, skate across its frozen surface, or pick your love some wildflowers along the woodland trails?

Breakfast seating in the formal dining room is enhanced by fresh flowers, and the Inn's ever-changing place settings, as well as a full Gourmet Breakfast combining local fruits, muffins, or breads, with an egg, pancake or French toast entrée and the Inn's house blend coffee (lighter fare on request).

While each visitor is gifted with a memento of their stay, guests celebrating a special occasion will also take home a recipe packet enabling them to reproduce some of the Seymour House specialties, such as "Eggs Santa Fe", or "Bananas Amaretto". Want to treat your sweetie? Select a piece of pottery or photography from the Gift Shop. All are original works of the Innkeepers.

Weddings? Yes - in the foyer, living room, or patio. Ceremony, reception, or anniversary parties - 10 guests max.

For ultimate seclusion and privacy, it's the Log Cabin - with 2 bedrooms, living room with stone fireplace, and fully-equipped kitchen. TV, VCR, BBQ grill, and all linens are provided, but no meals or maid service.

Whether you stay in a Seymour House guestroom, or the Cabin, you'll be sure to say . . . "Alone at last! Let romance blossom!" at . . .

The Seymour House
616-227-3918
1248 Blue Star Highway, South Haven 49090
www.laketolake.com/inns/seymourhouse
email: seymour@cybersol.com
No Smoking please

Inn-spired Activities ———————————

Check out local antique shops, boutiques, and wineries; go horseback riding; ask us for our private list of 15 year-round things to do!

$\mathcal{Y}$elton $\mathcal{M}$anor $\mathcal{B}$ & $\mathcal{B}$ AND
THE MANOR GUEST HOUSE - SOUTH HAVEN

"uncommon luxury for uncommon love"

Lake Michigan's shoreline is graced by this magnificent Victorian mansion, and its Victorian guest house.

The accommodations? Extravagant! Eleven gorgeous, uniquely private rooms in the Manor feature floral themes and elegant traditional furnishings artfully mixed with antiques and lovely accessories. Of course, the finest amenities are included -

private baths and TV/VCR in all, while some have Jacuzzi®, fireplace, or lakeside view.

Relax in one of two fireplace parlors, toast each other at the den bar, or melt away your tensions with soothing music or unique books and videos in the other luxurious lounges. Drift away to the "Widow's Walk" and admire the sunset over the lake, or stroll the incredible gardens and stop for some time in a deck swing.

The Manor Guest House, an "independent ... escape", houses six beautifully appointed suites with fireplace, Jacuzzi®, and private bath.

Though a comfortable wicker porch and genteel parlor welcome Guest House couples, the hideaway nooks and fully equipped suites make this more of a private love nest!

Thinking of booking the honeymoon suite? Congratulations! Ask for the Rose Room at The Manor, or The Dewey Hotel Suite in the Guest House.

The service? Exceptional! Daylong goodies abound in each separate Inn. Snack on homemade chocolate chip cookies, brownies, and lemon bars, or dip into plentiful candy dishes, fruit bowls, popcorn maker, or fridge full of soda and juice.

Depending on the occasion, each guest is individually treated to different amenities guaranteed to make their memory a special one.

While Manor guests look forward to a lavish Buffet Breakfast, and evening hor d'oeuvres, Guest House patrons enjoy a Continental Breakfast delivered to their door for private enjoyment. All the food here is prepared with love and creativity.

Your hosts believe in individual service and assistance. Should you be looking for a hiking trail, a picnic spot, or even a jewelry store, they'll find out and get you there! They'll host your wedding, too - in garden, porch, or parlor (25 guests only), and help to plan your special event. They *"understand romance!"* at . . .

Yelton Manor Bed & Breakfast
and The Manor Guest House
616-637-5220
140 N. Shore Drive, South Haven 49090
web:yeltonmanor.com
email: elaine@yeltonmanor.com
Sorry, no smoking permitted

Inn-spired Activities —————————

Enjoy our area hiking trails and beaches; do a little biking, rafting, or xc skiing; take your sweetie to a jewelry store!

Dining Delights

Hawkshead Inn- South Haven

Dine in the fireside comfort of a Tudor mansion, overlooking the lush green links of Hawkshead Golf Course. Gourmet cuisine ("all your old favorites ... with a delightful twist") is served in an atmosphere of "understated elegance", candlelight, and fresh white linens. You'll enjoy luncheon sandwiches and salads ($5-7), and "Buffalo Rock Shrimp" appetizers, with dinners like Crab Legs, Filet Mignon, fresh Pasta specialties, or famous "Sweet Potato Mash" ($13-27) in the Scottish Pub or Main Dining Room. You may even wish to stay in one of nine romantic Inn rooms!

Closed winters - call for dates / Reservations recommended / Smoking in Pub only / Full bar / Private dining room (with its own fireplace) seats 14

6959 - 105th Avenue • 616-639-2146

Dining Delights

The Sea Wolf Restaurant -
South Haven

Casually elegant dinners in the 75 year-old dining room of Weinstein's Resort. Escape for an evening in this natural country setting. Dine on deck surrounded by the sugar maples and fruit trees, or inside amongst white tablecloths, candlelight, and fresh flowers. Three generations of owner's recipes blend with Seafood features to create a large, enticing menu including "Matzo Ball Soup", "Steak Alaska", "Pasta Jambalaya", and "Seawolf Salmon - with sundried tomatoes and fresh herbs" ($13.95-22.95 including appetizer and dessert). Savor it!

Closed winters (call for dates) / Outdoor dining on deck / Full bar & wine list / Parties are possible / Reservations recommended / Smoking in limited area

176 Blue Star Highway • 616-637-2007

One beach location, two different dining rooms - knotty pine "cottage-y", or dramatic "movie star" theme. Both feature candlelight, flowers, and fine food like breakfast "Fruit Waffles", "Oatmeal Pancakes", or "Skillet Potatoes with veggies & cheese"; luncheon "Salad Nicoisse", "Pita with artichoke hearts, spinach, tomato, feta & fontonella cheeses", and other specialties; or dinners of "Grilled Whitefish", Ribs, Lamb Chops, Steaks, and "Chicken pasta with garlic, cheeses, artichokes & spinach", (breakfast & lunch $6-9, dinner $10-19). Delectable!

Open April - October, but call for holiday availability / No smoking or reservations / Mid-week lunch & dinner, weekend appetizers & cocktails, & smoking o.k. on outdoor deck / Full bar & wine list / Banquet room seats 24, M-F parties also in DR for 40 max / Ask to see 2 nicely decorated Jacuzzi® rooms
51 North Shore Drive • 616-637-6738

À Deux Adventures

-South Haven and Van Buren County

South Haven Area

Legend Theater............. winter 616-639-1486 / summer 616-637-7829
White Rose cruises 616-639-8404
Captain John Shaul ....home 219-272-2918
  (Jubilee sailing charters)..boat 616-637-5656
Chute the Breeze Sunsports (parasailing) 616-637-3600
Adalla Reins (horseback riding)....................................616-253-4529
Magnolia Grill on Idler Riverboat (casual fine dining)...616-637-8435
Michigan Maritime Museum..616-637-8078
Fideland Fun Park (go carts, mini jeeps, etc.).................616-637-3123
Kal-Haven Trail/Sesquicentennial State Park 616-637-5252
Lighthouse Balloon Adventures 616-637-7408
Timber Ridge Ski Area (30 Mi. East) Ski School 616-694-9449
Paw Paw - Coloma
St. Julian Winery 616-657-5568

"the Art Coast of Michigan" -
Saugatuck - Douglas - Fennville

*P*aint yourselves a romantic holiday! Couples visiting this area's coastal villages and rolling farmlands will choose from an artist's palette of delights: Lake Michigan's azure shores; golden sand beaches; blazing orange sunsets; Kalamazoo River's verdant green valleys; sparkling white winter hillsides; rainbow-hued gardens, galleries, and shops; blue ribbon dining; and red hot entertainment.

Practice the art of relaxing with a cruise on the "Star of Saugatuck" Sternwheeler, or the "City of Douglas" cruise boat. Or, better yet, take a ride across the river on Saugatuck's most unusual hand-cranked chain ferry! Stroll the boardwalk or holiday-lighted streets, picnic at the gazebo, or mellow out at much-heralded Oval Beach. Ride the "Interurban", rent a sailboat pedalboat or pontoon, tour the SS Keewatin floating maritime museum. Pick some blueberries, cuddle in a horse-drawn carriage, sip a soda at the Saugatuck Drugstore fountain, sample wines at local tasting rooms, or cider and pie at *Fenneville*'s Crane Orchards.

Satisfy your "art of adventure"! Couples can rent a snowmobile, jet ski or bicycle-built-for-two, climb 279 steps up Mt. Baldhead dune for a glorious view, hike or cross-country ski area state parks and forests, ride a horse, go parasailing, or hop aboard a dune-schooner for a thrilling tour!

Exploring the numerous world-class galleries, working art studios, and art schools of the area is especially fun, since they're tucked into all the village nooks and crannies! Examples of the finest painting, sculpture, prints, ceramics, glass, photography, crafts, jewelry, and furnishings  are available for visitors admiration and acquisition.

Year round festivals and celebrations of the arts offer opportunities to appreciate music, theater, fine cuisine, vintage wines, and the talents of local artists and craftsmen. One of the most popular events is July's Harbor Days/Venetian Nights, with its famous lighted boat parade.

Share an evening's entertainment - at Red Barn Playhouse professional summer theatre, or one of many local nightspots that feature live entertainment for listening or dancing pleasures.

Take a tour to nearby Holland's Dutch Village and visit a 19th century Netherlands town, multi-colored tulip fields and gardens, historic windmills, and a wooden shoe factory.

Perfect the art of shopping in the quaint and sophisticated specialty shops of the Village of *Douglas, Saugatuck*'s streets, alleyways, and dockside Water Street marketplace.

Mix all these colorful pleasures to "create your own masterpiece" retreat!

Saugatuck/Douglas Area CVB
616-857-1701
www. saugatuck.com

Fennville C of C
616-561-5550

Bay Side Inn - SAUGATUCK

"your home on the water"

*T*ired of lace and flowers and antiques? Then this sunny, contemporary waterfront Inn is just for you! Original underwater photography appears throughout the inn, as well as art-photos of scenery, birds, and floral displays. Soft colors and the nautical theme here are reflections of the water's edge - just 16 feet away!

All six guestrooms have a private bath, private deck or balcony, phone, cable TV, and an aura of casual elegance!

While any of the spacious, light and airy rooms are great romantic hideaways, you may wish to plan your cozy stay with a waterfront, or fireplace suite. Perhaps Room Six, with view of Saugatuck Harbor, balcony, king-size bed, and VCR is right for you. Or Room One, the largest, with double length balcony, a view of the Harbor and Kalamazoo River, too (rates $60-185.) Or check into the suites at next door Harbor House (breakfast also included, for $175-225).

Celebrate that special event with complementary champagne. Skol! Ask about Grand Escape, and Wine Lover's Weekends.

Ask your hosts for a pool pass for the Beachway Resort swimming pool, and for discount tickets to the historic and scenic narrated trolley tour which operates at 11 a.m. selected days. Enjoy walk-to shopping, beaches, parks, and entertainment. Watch the boats go by from your balcony, or from the riverside patio hot tub. Or, cozy up in the large, comfortable common area with TV/VCR,  stereo, fireplace and lots of overstuffed seating! Huge windows frame the waterfront for your enjoyment, as you relax with complimentary flavored coffee or sweet treats.

Wake up early, or sleep in a bit, but do plan to enjoy the Continental Plus Breakfast of muffins, breads, bagels, dry cereals, fresh fruit and beverages served Monday-Saturday from 8-10 am. Sunday mornings, (or on a whim!) you'll enjoy a full breakfast which may include "French Toast Casserole" or "Egg and Cheese Strata".

Yes, enjoy this picturesque harbor village, and enjoy this "boathouse" Inn. You'll be lulled into loving, at . . .

The Bayside Inn
1-800-548-0077 or 616-857-4321
618 Water Street, P.O. Box 1001, Saugatuck 49453
www.bbonline.com/mi/bayside
Smoking only on your private balcony, please

Inn-spired Activities ———————————————

Take a swim or Sunday afternoon ice cream tour; do dinner or brunch on a City of Douglas cruise!

The Belvedere Inn AND RESTAURANT

- SAUGATUCK
"the last word in elegance"

S tep into the foyer of this 1913 mansion, and you'll step into a world of stately elegance, eclectic traditional styling, soft music, a gurgling fountain, grand piano, and rich warm woods.

Guests here experience gracious and grand (but not stuffy!) surroundings, yet feel cozy and comfortable enjoying the whole house and five acre grounds and gardens. Play a game of croquet, settle back in the wraparound terrace's white wicker

furniture or ten person Jacuzzi®, watch TV in the common room, or browse in the library.

Once a trysting place for Al Capone, this delightful Inn welcomes overnight and dinner guests year around. Nine rooms transport you to the past with simple traditional decor, original 19th century colors, turned-down beds, and impeccable service. Each room has a different feel - perhaps "Country Quilt",

"Garden", or "Canopy" styling. "Abbey's Room" (the former maid's quarters) offers a more masculine ambiance with lots of light and windows all around. Third floor rooms feature window-box seats under the eves, and a view of the sand dunes.

Couples will feel extra special in the luxurious "Belvedere Suite", with separate sitting room, dressing/workout chamber, two-person shower and Jacuzzi®, fireplace, wet-bar, phone, private view balcony, and spiral staircase. Or, maybe the "Balmoral Suite" with rice-carved bed, sitting room, and complimentary champagne for two with fruit and cheese board. Standard rates range from $95-195, and $295 for the Belvedere Suite, though special packages are available for such occasions as New Year's or Valentine's Day.

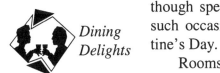

Dining Delights

Rooms include a Full Gourmet Breakfast, served in the Sunroom and including breakfast specialties like "Ginger Pancake with lemon sauce", "Eggs Benedict with tomato slice in place of ham", "Gourmet Cheese & Herb Omelets served with popovers", handmade breads and pastries, yogurt, granola, fresh fruit, fresh-squeezed orange juice, and freshly brewed Belvedere blend coffee or tea.

Reservations are a must for dining in one of the two highly romantic dining rooms (open to the public, also). Fine linen and crystal grace the six intimate tables in the main dining room. A cozy fire reflects on fine wood floors in Winter. The Club Room (originally the house living room) centers around a huge, magnificent fireplace, and is equally perfect for refined, yet comfortable intimate dining.

Guests are invited to bring in their own favorite wine ($6 corkage fee) to complement the contemporary American cuisine. Menus change frequently to best use the available fresh local ingredients. Innovative specialties may include "Grilled Quail", "Tournedos of Beef with shiitake mushrooms and tomatoes", "Breast of Chicken stuffed with proscuitto and topped with roasted red pepper-basil butter", and always at least one vegetarian dish such as "Stir Fried Vegetable with roasted garlic rice cake and orange-cilantro brown sauce" ($21.50-$27).

Everything here is uniquely designed and tailor made. If you wish a special preparation, they'll gladly do it!

Call for dates and information on Wine Maker's Dinners - produced in cooperation with Fenn Valley Winery, and including a trolley tour of the winery.

Catered parties or weddings and receptions are courteously and professionally arranged for 150 (outdoor) or 70-75 (indoor) guests. Since weddings are a frequent event, it is suggested you call several months in advance for room reservations, though last minute cancellations are always a possibility.

Belvedere's dining rooms are closed Tuesdays, and hours vary seasonally. The Inn and Restaurant are open all year.

For your reception, for your escape, or just for dinner - It's truly an experience, it's truly . . .

The Belvedere Inn and Restaurant
616-857-5501
3656 - 63rd Street, Saugatuck 49453
Smoke free interior - ashtrays on outside terrace only

Inn-spired Activities ———————————

Attend the Red Barn Playhouse across the street (it used to be a livestock barn, now it's a professional theater!); tour Fenn Valley Winery; enjoy all of magnificent Saugatuck - the "Cape Cod of the Midwest"!

Maplewood Hotel - SAUGATUCK

"the romance of history,
the romance of now"

*T*his "gleaming tribute to the 19th century" is conveniently located in downtown Saugatuck. Twenty-five foot white pillars grace the front of the restored Greek revival resort hotel. Premier service and accommodations grace the interior.

Fifteen guest rooms are decorated with "exquisite furnishings and antiques" for a uniquely tailored presidential feel, and are constantly renovated. All have private baths, color TV, and phone, though the 8 suites are considered most romantic with original hotel furniture, in-room Jacuzzi® tubs, and cozy fireplaces or sitting rooms. Room 104 is the premier accommodation, and is spectacular. Maplewood hosts will try to honor requests for certain rooms, but can't guarantee, so it's best to call as far in advance as possible.

Rates vary seasonally, depending on the room, from $85-165, and include a Full Gourmet Breakfast served in the formal dining room or on pink wrought iron tables in the favored porch (it's insulated, but unheated, so not used in Jan., Feb. & Mar.) China, crystal, silver, and fresh flowers enhance your enjoyment of fresh fruits, cereals, bagels, toast and one special entrée such as "Asparagus Quiche with hollandaise", "Stuffed French Toast with raspberries, cream cheese, and lemon sauce", or "Baked French Toast with local blueberries".

Be sure to ask about special packages such as "Gourmet Weekends". Celebrate in style here, with a gift of private label wine served on a silver tray with Maplewood signature chiller and corkscrew!

Summer in Saugatuck can be hectic, but Maplewood Hotel offers several more quiet reprieves. Most spacious is the Mitchell Lounge with classic Oriental and Chippendale mauve and green furnishings, fireplace, soft lighting, and a delightful reproducing grand piano. Guests also enjoy the cozy Butler Library's dark paneling and fireplace, and the Saugatuck Room - a glass-enclosed rattan-filled sun porch filled with ferns. A wooden deck wraps the back for sunbathing by the heated pool (mid-May through mid-Sept.), and an adjacent gazebo provides a cool, shaded hideaway. Common areas are always open.

With advance notice and renting of the entire Inn, private parties and weddings can be arranged (within management parameters) for 30-35 guests. If the formal Burr Tilstrom Dining Room, and Parkside Screened Porch are utilized, 42 persons can be seated for catered meals.

You can escape the hectic outside world, but you can't escape the romantic allure of . . .

Maplewood Hotel
616-857-1771 or 1-800-650-9790 (Res. Only)
428 Butler Street, P.O. Box 1059, Saugatuck 49453
Sorry, no smoking permitted

Inn-spired Activities _____

This is a boaters' paradise and an artists' colony, but
we also offer tennis, golf, shopping and canoeing - try them all!

The Park House - SAUGATUCK

"instantly relaxing ...
a place for endless love"

You'll feel comfortable anytime of year in the "livable ambiance" of this 1857 Saugatuck landmark. Yes, the furnishings include antiques and country primitives in keeping with the age of the Inn, but the informal atmosphere is cordial and certainly not "untouchable".

Just a small part of this Inn's time-honored tradition of hospitality is your Full Breakfast, served buffet style and fireside, on the Common Room's plank table, or "gardenside" on the screened porch. Feature items may be "Orange French Toast", of "Missy Potatoes" (you have to try it!), in conjunction with homemade bread and jam, and a mug of special coffee.

Rent one of two Jacuzzi®/fireplace suites, and order breakfast served in bed, or on your private balcony, on antique china! The Suites are perfect hideaways, with TV/VCR and telephone included, for $150 per night. Or "sample the captivating spirit" of the 2 bedroom Loft Suite with sitting room, fireplace, and spiral staircase; or one of five bedrooms with brass, warm woods, and themed and different decor, individual personality, and of course private baths. Three of these include a fireplace - rates vary from $85-150. Most popular? The Lumberman's Room with its large handmade bed and burlap walls! For specific room selection, call as far in advance as possible - a minimum of 2 months is recommended.

For ultimate privacy, consider one of the six cottage accommodations for $115-225 daily or $575-975 weekly. Rose Cottage, with kitchen, grill, and personal hot tub, is right next door and includes breakfast at the Inn and daily maid service. Indian Pointe is contemporary seclusion with a view! Your outdoor hot tub and screenroom overlook the Kalamazoo River and Potawatomie Marshlands. A fireplace, surround sound, and canoe put you in the mood for romance. The Willows (in the Village of Douglas) offers two quiet, yet convenient one bedroom cottages. And, at "a setting like no other in Saugatuck", you'll find Peterson's Mill . . .

The mill pond, creek, and river soothe your spirit, and create the perfect backdrop for the "rustic" ambiance of this restored grist mill (in front) with water wheel, or the historic Brittain House (in back). Each is fully equipped with phone, TV, and spacious yard, and the Back Mill includes fireplace and screen porch.

Sorry, Park House and its cottages cannot accommodate receptions or parties, but they *do* create unusual, unique romantic memories on request. Guaranteeing a very personalized and very special celebration, whether surprise or shared plans, your host can set up a unique event like no one else can. Perhaps a romantic Victorian picnic with antique china, linens, and doilies; or an arrangement of fresh flowers in simple, natural "splendiferous" glory! You need only ask. Or, consider joining Park House for one of its own special packages, or a Grand Escape Weekend.

For a getaway that promises "so much more than expected", and "one step more than anything you asked", call . . .

The Park House
616-857-4535 or 1-800-321-4535
888 Holland Street, Saugatuck 49453
www.bbonline.com
Sorry, no smoking permitted

Inn-spired Activities —————————————

Relax in Saugatuck - it's a Nantucket-style casual area; take a woods or beach walk; enjoy a picnic; be here for a Candlelit Christmas and winter vistas; a one-of-a-kind gift of art or jewelry would be *very* romantic - take your honey shopping!

"Whoso loves
Believes the impossible."
- Elizabeth Barrett Browning

Rosemont Inn Resort - SAUGATUCK

"hold onto your heart!"

*T*he only Saugatuck area Inn on Lake Michigan to stay open all winter, the elegant Rosemont Inn Resort stands proudly atop a bluff overlooking this Great Lake.

This turn-of-the-century Inn is a very popular scene for engagements, garden or gazebo weddings, and honeymoons. So romantic and memorable is their stay, couples return again and again for anniversary celebrations.

Admire the custom-crafted entry with its richly inlaid rose-medallion floor, then get settled in your choice of fourteen

individually decorated guest rooms. Rich, dark woodwork forms a stately backdrop for the simple, traditional furnishings. Many rooms feature gas fireplaces, Jacuzzi® tubs, lake views, or spectacular Winter sunset vistas. Each is newly renovated, with private bath, phone, and four-poster bed. The most requested room is #1, with its private Jacuzzi® tub, and corner fireplace. Rates are $95-235, varying seasonally.

Relaxation is an easy task here, in any of three common areas. The popular and spacious "Garden Area" with its 3-sided fireplace, floral "needlepoint" furniture, cedar walls, TV, and cozy tables, is the setting for each morning's "sumptuous" Buffet Breakfast. Feast anytime between 8:30-10:30 am on a selection of quiches, breads, muffins and croissants, fresh fruit trays, and the Rosemont's homemade granola-yogurt-fruit parfaits, with special coffees. Refrigerator, microwave, and coffee bar are available for guest use, and be sure to indulge in complementary snacks and beverages, hot and cold hors d'oeuvres at 5 pm, and late night handmade treats! Pick up a magazine and saunter out to the adjacent deck; take a dip in the heated pool; stroll past the huge fountain in the English-style gardens; or take an evening walk on the beach.

For a cozy evening respite, snuggle in the "Lakeside Gathering Room" a classy "speakeasy style" glassed-in porch with warming fireplace, and "bring-a-beverage-of-your-choice" bar.

Wind up your busy (or rainy) day with a trip to the contemporary sauna and Jacuzzi® room. Soft music, tile floors, cedar paneling, skylights, and a dressing room/shower area are perfect complements to a mood-mellowing rendezvous corner.

Your hosts can arrange your wedding, private party, a massage, or a balloon ride. Or, they can simply guarantee a relaxing and romantic time to enrich your life - enrich your love, at . . .

Rosemont Inn Resort
616-857-2637 or 1-800-721-2637
83 Lakeshore Drive, P.O. Box 214, Saugatuck 49453
www.saugatuck.com/rosemont

Inn-Spired Activities ————————————

Take a scenic supper cruise; rent a paddle boat or power boat; take in a play; enjoy the Lake Michigan Sunsets; whatever . . . it's an unforgettable combination with your stay!

Twin Gables Country Inn- SAUGATUCK

"furnished with love"

*H*osts at this delightful country-style Inn feel "It's not the place that's romantic, it's the people!", but Twin Gables will certainly inspire your romantic nature. You'll feel instantly at home here, relaxed and comfortable, amid the country stenciling and handmade crafts, maple flooring, and nostalgic embossed tin ceilings and walls. Enjoy your privacy in the large, uncrowded Common Room, or on the screened front porch with its wicker and antique furnishings, and cool summer breezes (a great spot for sunset gazing, too!).

Memorial Day-Labor Day guests will also enjoy the heated outdoor swimming pool, or some quiet time in the terraced gardens. Winter visitors look forward to a soak in the indoor hot tub, TV watching, and a hot cup of coffee or tea beside the wood-burning fireplace.

Fourteen charming and individually country-themed guest rooms all offer private bath and "tete-a-tete" sitting area for two.

Snuggle under your quilt or comforter in the Western-style "Tack Room", the "Cape Cod", "Sunset", or "Governor Van Wagoner" rooms. Your "love nest" may feature handmade furniture, canopy bed, color-coordinated wallpapers, carpet, or hardwood floors, but rest assured each is comfortable and private. Quiet time is requested at 11 pm.

Awaken, refreshed, to a Full Buffet Breakfast including a variety of quiches, huge bowl of fresh fruit, nut breads, and unlimited quantities of private blend specialty coffee.

While room rates vary seasonally from $59-104, Twin Gables also offers private 1 and 2 bedroom cottages by the week ($290-370), or weekend (2 people, 2 nights $230-370) depending on dates and not including breakfast. Antique and country decor cabins are fully furnished including TV, picnic tables, and grills, though you will need to bring all your own towels. Lakeview Cottage is so-o-o-o romantic, with its own cozy fireplace!

Whatever your choice of accommodation, you will want to plan at least 3-6 months in advance, and you may want to inquire about special events at Twin Gables, such as their Renaissance Concert (a "consort of voices"), or the Grand Escape weekends. Any time you stay, your hosts will happily direct you to area attractions and events.

For "that lovin' feelin'", check into . . .

Twin Gables Country Inn
616-857-4346 or 1-800-231-2185 (res. only)
900 Lake Street, P.O. Box 881, Saugatuck, 49453
www.bbonline.com
Smoking in Common Room or Cottages only please

Inn-Spired Activities ———————

Lose yourselves in the marinas, orchards, and wildlife refuges; climb to the observation tower; enjoy picturesque and primitive beaches in any season; ride our bicycle paths, hike the dunes, and walk Oval Beach!

Heritage Manor Inn - FENNVILLE

"the 'Romance Capital'"

*T*hrough the country mist appears an English manor ... not a formal, stodgy relic of the old world, but a peaceful and gracious Inn offering friendly "country hospitality", and "gracious living at its finest."

A stunning marble-floored stone-walled two story foyer leads one direction to the formal parlor with Victorian velvet fainting couch and grand piano. Or, to a more casual Great Room with stone fireplace, oak plank dining table, simple Mission Oak furnishings, beamed ceiling, and another piano for your musical enjoyment.

From the Great Room, enter the Guest Kitchen - fully

equipped for your use to prepare snacks (or a meal), and stocked with popcorn, sweet treats, and beverages; or the adjacent indoor heated pool and whirlpool available anytime for all guests use.

Grill, picnic facilities, volleyball, croquet, and basketball are also available for the very active couple.

Soft instrumental music accompanies you up the grand staircase to one of 14 rooms, eight of which are Jacuzzi® suites with wood burning fireplaces. Some rooms are cozy, while others are quite spacious - all have private bath and tasteful, individually styled country or Victorian decor. Dimmer switches help create that soft, oh-so-romantic mood. Of the Jacuzzi®

rooms, "The Tiffany Suite", with its stone fireplace, is a particular favorite of men; while the Victorian Romance Room is furnished with the ladies in mind, and features a look-through fireplace.

Regular rooms are charming, with an enchanting garden feel. Most romantic of these is the "Brass Bedroom" with its large skylit bathroom, and floor-to-ceiling marble fireplace at the foot of the bed! Or, ask for a Romantic Townhouse getaway and enjoy a sunken Jacuzzi®, and white marble fireplace in your own living room! Rates range from $55-160, and summer weekends fill up fast, so call at least 1 month in advance.

Heritage Manor serves a very large and "Sinfully Delicious" Breakfast, which may feature their famous "Belgian Waffles" and eggs, blueberry muffins, homemade breads and cinnamon rolls, cereals, fresh fruit compotes, and beverages.

For that occasion that "deserves the best", the Manor offers a package that includes a bottle of St. Julian bubbly beverage, flowers, balloons, treats, and a personalized memento. Whatever you ask, the personal touch is here. Your hosts will make any arrangement - no limit - to assure your memorable special occasion or parlor wedding. Ask about other special packages, such as the annual "Christmas Event" where donuts, hot cider, a hayride, and a Christmas tree are part of your weekend event.

There's a special kind of romance here - there's space, quiet, fresh air, privacy. There's a special brand of hospitality you just can't buy - they give it freely at . . .

Heritage Manor Inn
616-543-4384
2253 Blue Star Highway, Fennville 49408
Some smoking rooms available
Smoking permitted in Great Room except during breakfast

Inn-Spired Activities

Take a picturesque Fall hike on Allegan State Forest trails; enjoy theater, cruises, tours; explore "our unique corner of Michigan with its pristine atmosphere & quaint resort towns!

The Kingsley House - FENNVILLE

"roses, lace & candlelight . . .
it brings out the romantic in you!"

*T*his "elegantly Victorian" turreted mansion is centered in the orchard-dotted rolling landscape of Fennville. While the mood here is distinctly formal Victorian, it's "not stuffy", and guests are invited to "really sit on the parlor chairs" and make themselves comfortable amongst the antique furniture and soft floral decor.

Loving attention to detail is evident in every area of this wonderful Inn, from the wicker filled porch with its ever-popular porch swing, to the formal parlor with its fireplace,

books, and board games, to the eight charmingly elegant guest rooms (with private baths) named for apple varieties.

Reserve your room 2-3 months in advance for weekends year-round, especially if you're requesting a particular room. Most popular is "Northern Spy", the third floor honeymoon suite. This cozy, private hideaway features a 2-person whirlpool, electric log fireplace, and private sitting room in the turret. The "Golden Delicious" is also very romantic with its four-poster canopy bed.

The "Empire Suite" (formerly the carriage house), proves a popular winter retreat, highlighted by warm pine paneling, wood burning fireplace, large library with TV/VCR, huge separate sitting area, 2-person Jacuzzi® and private entrance.

Equally private is the former wine cellar - the "Cider Nook" - at the base of the tower. A huge whirlpool for two, 1886 brick fireplace (electric logs), corner bed, and private entrance fill every "nook" and cranny of this delightfully cozy room.

Standard rates of $80-165 (ask for mid-week and winter specials) include a Full Weekend Breakfast highlighted by "Honey Glazed Pecan French Toast", or another of the Inn's specialties. Weekday guests enjoy a Continental Plus Breakfast.

Your stay in any whirlpool suite entitles you to a choice of joining the other guests for breakfast in the dining room, or requesting breakfast served in your room - a perfect treat for your anniversary of honeymoon! Expect more "surprise" treatment for that special occasion, too!

All guests at the Kingsley are treated to tea, coffee, lemonade and iced tea, and have access to a refrigerator, chilled wine, glasses and corkscrew, ice buckets, beach towels, area brochures and restaurant menus. Ask to borrow a bicycle to explore the countryside!

As one of the area Inn's offering "Inn-timate Country Getaways", the Kingsley House co-sponsors packages such as Horse Drawn Wagon Rides, Christmas in Michigan, Mardi Gras, and Mexican Fiesta, plus more. For information, phone toll free 1-888-673-6164, or check www.getaway2smi.com/icg.

Remember, "be yourself", but be romantic, at . . .

The Kingsley House Bed & Breakfast
616-561-6425
626 W. Main Street, Fennville 49408
www. bbonline.com
email: garyking@accn.org
Smoking outdoors only, please

Inn-Spired Activities ——————

Enjoy rafting, beaches, hiking and biking; take a
bottle of wine and a picnic supper for a sunset at a private beach
we know about - ask us!

Clearbrook - Golf Club & Restaurant - Saugatuck

"Come here for romance anytime!" they invite, "we satisfy all appetites - just a drink or dessert, salad or bistro fare, or classic fine dining, accented with fresh herbs from our own gardens". Overlook the golf course or lush gardens from your table in the dining room, the lounge, or on the patio. Order "Fire Grilled Bistro Pizza with arugula, roasted red peppers, mozzarella and housemade pesto", "Caesar Salad for Two - prepared tableside", "Herb Roasted 1/2 Birdie (1/2 chicken)", "Fresh Canadian Walleye", "Lobster

Rissotto - chunks of lobster tossed with Arborio rice, tomato concasse, asparagus, herbs, garlic and cream", "French Rack of Lamb", or "Roasted Veal Chop Saltimbocca" ($8.95-21.95). Great selections! And that's just the beginning! Also featuring Friday, Saturday, and Sunday Brunches, with the "19th Hole Breakfast Platter - Italian frittata, bacon, sausage, redskin potatoes, fresh fruit, muffin, and Cinnamon Vanilla French Toast or Blueberry Multi-grain Pancakes ($8.50), or "Eggs Benedict Clearbrook with cappiola ham and fontina cheese" ($7.95). Delightful!

Closed November - May / Smoking in designated areas / Private parties in dining room or banquet room / Reservations accepted / Patio dining / Full bar and wine list

6494 Clearbrook Drive • 616-857-2000

Dining Delights   *Ida Red's Cottage* - Saugatuck

Some people say this is "the best breakfast in town!" Try homemade specialties like "Banana Nut Crunch muffins", "Whole Grain Griddlecakes", or "Eggs Ondine - 2 basted eggs on sautéed onions, topped with cheese and sliced tomatoes", or a large variety of omelets ($2-6.75). For lunch, how about a variety of pasta dishes, homemade soups, salads and sandwiches, or specials like "Pizza with roasted garlic, portabello mushrooms and herbs", "Spinach-Romaine Salad with red onion, toasted pecans, and blue cheese-yogurt dressing", "Green Bean, tomato and feta salad", or "Turkey Tomatillo Pita with cheese, roasted sweet peppers, and tomatillo salsa" ?($4.25-6.75). Sunny day diners may want to relax at the garden's edge on the patio, or indoors in the "diner" atmosphere. "Please remember, there is no fast food here!"

Closed Monday & Tuesday, and after 2 p.m. / Patio dining / Smokers must open the window!

645 Water Street

Dining Delights   *Toulouse* - Saugatuck

French country cuisine in a beautiful, relaxed setting, or in the garden courtyard patio. Sample the "Tray for Two - house pate and spinach roulade", or "Boursin and muenster with fruit and bread" appetizers. For dinner? How about "Pacific Snapper en croute", "Tournedos and Lobster", "Cassoulet - lamb, sausage, and white beans en casserole", or one of several daily specials ($14.95-21.95) accompanied by an award-winning wine, or "superb dessert creation". Mouth watering!

Open all year / Private Parties in the "Monet Room" / Reservations suggested / Outdoor dining on courtyard patio / Full bar and wine list

248 Culver Street • 616-857-1561

119

Loaf & Mug Winery, Bakery, & Restaurant   -   Saugatuck

Have your breakfast, or a hearty homemade lunch, in the cozy Franklin-stove indoor warmth, or the secluded, tranquil beauty of the garden courtyard. Let the tinkling "music" of a fountain accompany your morning "Eggs Benedict with spinach soufflé and tomato", "Glendawitch - scrambled eggs and cheddar, or ham and Swiss, or spinach and cheddar on a croissant", or "Eggs Sophia - egg pancake with potato, onion, green and red pepper, and side salsa" ($2.75-6.50). You'll love your lunch of "Chicken or Veggie Pita", Daily Soups, "Crab Salad Sandwich", Caesar Salad, or "Tortilla Wrap Sandwich ($3.99-7.35), and wonderful homemade breads. Sweet tooth? Try one of their "beyond delicious" desserts. Pack your picnic basket, too!

Closed December 24 - February 1 / Small smoking section / Outdoor garden courtyard dining / Winery / Bakery
236 Culver Street • 616-857-2974

The Avalon Restaurant - and
Banquet & Conference Center - Douglas

A place for casual gourmet dining, and a "million dollar view" of the Kalamazoo River - "between two great towns - Douglas & Saugatuck". Enjoy happy hour and an extensive lighter menu in the lounge - Prime Rib Sandwich, Steak Sandwich, Pizza, Calamari, etc. for $4.95 & up. In the dining room, try menu delights like "Nest of Capolini - shrimp and artichoke hearts in rich tomato sauce", Seafood, Pasta, Prime Rib, "Cajun Black-ened Top Sirloin with carmelized onions & creamy gorgonzola sauce", BBQ Ribs, Whitefish, and nightly Chef's Specials ($9.95 and up). Tempting!

Open all year / Reservations appreciated / Smoking in desig-nated areas / Full bar / Private parties possible for up to 300 / Live entertainment weekends and special occasions
200 Center Street • 616-857-1441

À *Deux Adventures*

- *Saugatuck, Douglas, Fennville, and Surrounding Areas*

Douglas
City of Douglas - Cruises & Dinners / Ary Lou Calypso
Cruises / SS Keewatin Museum 616-857-2107
Krupka's Blueberry Plantation 616-857-4278
Lakeshore Bike Rental 616-550-1383

Fennville - and Surrounding Area
Allegan State Game Area
Crane Orchards...616-561-2297
Fenn Valley Vineyards & Wine Cellar..................616-561-2396
   or.. 1-800-432-6265

Saugatuck
Best Chance Charters (boat rental)........................616-857-4762
Chequer's Pub (relaxed dining)..............................616-857-1868
Horse-Drawn Carriage Rides (c/o CVB)................616-857-1701
Horse-Fly Farm (rides, lessons, & carriage)...........616-543-4663
Interurban Transit Authority (trolley)....................616-857-1418
Oxbow Summer School of Art...............................616-857-5811
Pumpernickel's Eatery (casual fare)......................616-857-1196
Red Barn Playhouse 616-857-7707
River Rat Rentals, Inc. (pontoons, boats & pedal
   boats) 616-857-1360
Saugatuck Drug Store Soda Fountain....................616-857-2300
Saugatuck Dunes State Park
Saugatuck Dune Rides, Inc....................................616-851-2253
Saugatuck Sailboat Charters..................................616-543-4273
Star of Saugatuck Boat Cruises 616-857-4261
Tabor Hill Wine Port Tasting Center 1-800-283-3363

The Shoreline - Grand Haven & Area Surprises

*S*tarting with a riverside boardwalk deemed by locals as "second to none!", and adding sun-splashed Lake Michigan sandy shores, a noble lighthouse, and a matchlessly intoxicating waterfront musical fountain - you have a recipe for romance unique to the *Grand Haven* area.

Add a little spice to your visit! Perhaps a pinch of cross-country skiing or sledding at Pigeon Creek Park; a sprinkle of

excitement at *Muskegon* State Park's luge run, or West Shore snowmobile trail; a plateful of scenic beauty from the Dunes Platform Overlook at P.J. Hoffmaster State Park, or from the decks of Grand Haven's Harbor Steamer sternwheel paddleboat, or Muskegon's Port City Princess dinner-dance cruise; a cupful of culture at local art galleries, bandshell concerts, and Cherry County Playhouse; three spoonsful of sweetness from local confectioners; just a smidgen of history at Hackley & Hume

Historic Site or Gerald R. Ford Library; a dash of adventure with train rides, color tours, and trips to nearby covered bridges (Ada, Fallasburg, & Whites), windmills, tulip farms, a wooden shoe factory, and fabulous Frederick Meijer Gardens; a generous portion of fun from theme parks, to beaches, in-line skating, ice skating, ice sailing, biking, hiking and picnicking to "flagging down the trolley" for a ride!

Blend to taste for a "grand" and marvelous memory!

Grand Haven - Spring Lake Area CVB
1-800-842-4499
www.grandhavenchamber.org

Muskegon County CVB
1-800-250-WAVE
www.muskegon.org

Holland Area CVB
1-800-506-1299
www.holland.org/hcvb

Grand Rapids/Kent County CVB
1-800-678-9859
www.grcvb.org

Boyden House - GRAND HAVEN

"a place to revive, and create memories "

*P*rominent families from Grand Haven's history have created a backdrop of memories in this big old 1874 house-turned-Inn. Unique architectural features are definitely a part of its charm - a gracious curved stairway (with unique curved window) archways, and beautiful woodwork are all anchored by rich parquet flooring.

Yes, this is a Victorian-style home, but the decor is eclectic, featuring personal collections of the Innkeepers rather than the usual lace and flowers. The downstairs "parlor" is set off by a bay window and natural fireplace, while upstairs the common area centers around a Franklin stove and a painted "rug" on the wood floor. A complete library encourages guests to select a book and relax indoors, or on the rear gardenside deck. Flowers are everywhere, even hanging on the wicker-bedecked porch and private balconies.

Seven cozy rooms (each with private bath) call to your romantic spirit. Room #1, with its canopy bed and private flower decorated balcony, is considered most romantic and especially appealing to the ladies. Room #7 also has a gorgeous, covered and private balcony, but includes a 2-person Jacuzzi® tub. Room #6 features a private deck and whirlpool tub as well. Rates range from $75-120.

Hospitality is premier here. "The guest is #1" is their motto. To insure your enjoyment of Grand Haven, innkeepers will happily direct you to nearby beaches and attractions, and even provide a picnic basket and chairs!

Part of the hospitality at this fun, delightful Inn is the Full Sit-down Breakfast, served in the dining room or on the verandah. Loads of fresh fruit is set out to accompany a different entrée every morning. They're known for their "Blueberry Pancakes", "wonderful, famous homemade muffins", and "Mighty Good Quiche".

Though Boyden House is open all year, you'll want to reserve your choice of rooms 2-6 months in advance for peak times.

"An interesting home, interesting people, and a decent breakfast!" If you're looking for "a *total* B & B experience", call . . .

The Boyden House Bed & Breakfast
616-846-3538
301 S. Fifth, Grand Haven 49417
No smoking please, except on private balconies

Inn-spired Activities ———————————

Visit our *incredible* beaches; see P. J. Hoffmaster Park's Gillette nature area; take a hike!

ℋarbor ℋouse - GRAND HAVEN

*"you'll be . .surrounded by
the feeling of warmth"*

A bit of whimsy, combined with pine floors, soft music, fresh flowers from the garden, and simple traditional decor, set the tone here for casually elegant romance.

Lose yourself in the spacious living room with tinkling fountain, and sparkling fireplace, the charming library (also with fireplace), or the beautiful perennial garden. Or, while away some quiet time on the wraparound screened porch with its welcoming white wicker and scenic view of Grand Haven Harbor, - watch the passing boats, or marvel at the famous musical fountain.

Guest amenities include a European style Buffet Breakfast, served from 8-10. Guests may dine at private tables in the dining

area, on the screened porch, or take a tray to their room for a private tete-a-tete! Treats include cheese, hard-boiled eggs, fresh fruit, breads, scones, muffins, coffee cakes, and beverages.

Access to the pantry/kitchenette area includes refrigerator, sink, ice, lemonade, iced tea and cookies in summer, and hot cider, coffee, and light snacks in winter. Best of all, each guest receives an in-room sample of Harbor House's own homemade caramels to satisfy your sweet tooth! Mmmmm!

Guests who book a major portion of the Inn can schedule a small reception or party. Anniversary or honeymoon couples will be treated with special care. Christmas decor at Harbor House is exceptional, and celebrations for Valentine's Day, and New Year's will include wine, champagne, and hors d'oeuvres.

This English country style Inn is only 11 years old, but looks 100! Victorian era charm and modern conveniences team up to create individually-styled romantic moods in each of the seventeen completely private rooms (with private bath and sitting area). Eleven rooms feature gas fireplaces, whirlpool tubs, and canopy beds. Each floor offers a phone and powder room, while third floor rooms offer a view of Lake Michigan (especially spectacular in winter with snow on the dunes!)

Harbor Cottage, right next door, houses two separate unique accommodations. Select the Riverview Room with screened porch, sitting area with fireplace, whirlpool tub, king bed, phone, and TV/VCR.Or, the Courtyard Suite with fully equipped kitchenette, fieldstone fireplace, phone, TV/VCR, and sleeping room with queen bed and whirlpool tub.

Standard rates vary from $80-180 depending on choice of room/cottage and day. Summer weekends are busy, so plan to book 6 weeks in advance.

The best feature of Harbor House may be its location. You can walk, roller-blade, or bicycle to everything - dining, lake activities, entertainment, and shopping.

"Welcome...relax...indulge"... and let the Innkeepers "pamper your every whim" at . . .

Harbor House Inn
616-846-0610 or 1-800-841-0610
Corner of Harbor & Clinton, Grand Haven 49417

Inn-spired Activities ——————————

Investigate a bike path; cross the street to the river walk; enjoy a casual lunch at nearby Snug Harbor; have a romantic dining experience!

Highland Park Hotel - GRAND HAVEN

"a restful retreat"

*N*ow more an Inn than a hotel, this historic property sits comfortably between "Lovers' Lane", and Lake Michigan, in an area filled with stately homes. Can't you feel it? That nostalgic pull, drawing you to Highland Park and the romanticism of this area . . . to the history, the beauty, and the peace.

Listen to the sound of the waves and admire the sunsets from the quiet garden areas, the upper and lower porches, or from the popular front rooms. Or select a more private middle room. All six guest rooms feature private baths, and an open, airy, uncluttered, and eclectic feeling. Antique furnishings are not to be considered priceless, but rather to be used and enjoyed.

The general ambiance is described by the Innkeeper as "comfortably historic". The service is complete, yet unobtrusive - it "feels like home." The welcome is very personal - a small placard on your door proclaims "These accommodations have been especially prepared for : your name. Anniversary and honeymoon couples can expect special notoriety, or complete privacy - the Innkeeper won't mention it if you don't!

The Breakfast? As relaxed as possible and served buffet style. Guests may eat anytime - early coffee is out at 7:30, and a full repast is put out at 8:45 including such scrumptious specialties as "Baked French Toast with cream cheese", "Potato Quiche", and "Graham Walnut Coffee Cake". Expect to enjoy home-cooked and fresh muffins, coffee cake, fruits, and beverages.

Ask your Innkeeper about nearby romantic spots, such as the rambling old boardwalk along the dune bluff - a great getaway and particularly quiet and peaceful! Or simply relax in the upstairs sitting room with its wicker furniture, TV, refrigerator, coffee maker, microwave, and other amenities. Summer days, enjoy the quiet garden areas, white iron gazebo, and the lower porch with its chirping birds, gently breezes, and porch swing. Take the stairway to the beach, stroll among the old-fashioned street lamps, and admire the lighted pier.

Though you'll want to reserve 3-4 months in advance for those busy summer weekends, you'll enjoy porchside sunsets, sun-filled beaches, and the glories of the Great Lake. Consider, however, a *really* relaxing getaway here in winter - watching the power of the lake, and cozying up to a roaring fire in the downstairs common room! (Ask about winter packages).

Any season at all, you can book a room at "a nice, comfortable, pleasant beachhouse" by calling . . .

Highland Park Hotel Bed & Breakfast
616-846-1473 or 1-800-951-6427
1414 Lake Avenue, Grand Haven 49417
Sorry, smoking only in garden or on lower porch

Inn-spired Activities ———————————

Don't miss the bluff boardwalk!; take a relaxing paddleboat ride, or cruise via sailboat, Harbor Steamer, or a restored Chris Craft; slip into 22 Harbor and listen to some weekend piano tunes!

ℒakeshore ℬed & ℬreakfast -

"charm, style, and ambiance too rich to describe"

*D*rive through the gates and feel you've arrived . . . at your private Lakeshore estate. This is what luxury is all about.! Stay in a restored 4500 sq. ft. mansion on 275 feet of private Lake Michigan beach. *Luxuriate* amid an unparalleled collection of memorabilia from every era of the American Presidency!

From the half-formal, half-comfy Washington Sitting room, admire the ever-changing panorama of Lake Michigan's shore. Even in Winter it's special, when you experience the awe of waves crashing and ice building. Enjoy morning juice and coffee, weekend evening aperitifs, and anytime complimentary beverages, fruit and cookies at the historic hotel bar. Snuggle by the fireplace, view a movie, or enjoy spectacular sunsets on the deck. Outdoors, enjoy horseshoes, the hammock, or the beach. "You'll feel so alone - it's so quiet and private you'll feel that you own it!" Showers, a refrigerator and ice, are available in the beachfront bathhouse, the roof of which provides a sunny patio. Cookout in the shoreline Steakhouse, complete with commercial grill, slate floor, flagstone walls, eating area, and connecting deck.

Ask your hosts about their take-out taxi service! They'll order, pick up, and bring back your full dinner from a fabulous local eatery. Dine in the comfort of "your estate".

Ready to settle in? Each of three private suites (under lock of skeleton key!) is highlighted by private bath, lakefront views, CD player, Jacuzzi® tub, and fresh flowers always. Upstairs, under the eves, find the Lincoln Room. Downstairs, the Ford Suite, and . . . the stunning and *very romantic* Presidential Suite, with its private 770 foot deck. "All you see is water" from the oak 4-poster bed and sitting area. Don the terry robes, and enter your spacious bath with whirlpool tub, and star-view skylight.

Sip a complimentary sherry in your room, and end the evening on a sweet note with candies and chocolates. Perrier®, wine and glasses, lotions and soaps, are but a few of the special touches. No White House guest has been more pampered!

Guest awaken to a full Gourmet Breakfast, served on White House china, and including specialties like "Eggs poached in white wine with crab strips", "Lobster Quiche", "Brandy Cherries Chambord", or "Ricotta and Cream Cheese Crepes".

Rates vary seasonally from $125-275 (book 3-4 months in advance for summer weekends, please). A separate "Guest House", and cozy Lighthouse Cabin, are available by the week only, mid-June to Labor Day. Weekend rates apply off-season.

Off season weddings, inside or out, are hosted with pleasure (40 guests max). Inquire about the many custom services available to make your special occasion more memorable.

Innkeepers hope you'll agree . . . "This one is *really* special - the best there is - it's *the* place to be!"

Lakeshore Bed & Breakfast
616-844-2697 or 1-800-342-6736
11001 Lakeshore Drive, Grand Haven Township 49460
www.bbonline.com/mi/lakeshore/
Sorry, smoking outdoors only

Inn-spired Activities ————————————

Experience day or lighted night xc skiing at very special Pigeon Creek Park; ask us to pack a picnic or box lunch; stroll along the river boardwalk to the lighthouse for a *very romantic* sunset!

Dining Delights

Arboreal Inn - Grand Haven

Get away to the quiet country. Dine in the casual warmth of brick, dark woods, plaids, and 1700s charm of the bar; the intimate homey comfort of the Old Room with fruit still-lifes and wine racks; or the classic Colonial elegance of chandeliers, candelabra sconces, white lace curtains, and fireplace of the popular Blue Room. Monday-Friday luncheon service includes Chef's Specials along wtih Salads, Soups, Hot Entrées like "Tenderloin Medallions", and Sandwiches like "Louis the Fourteenth - shaved prime rib on Russian rye with au jus", or "Sir Walter - shaved prime rib on Rib, Swiss cheese, sauteed onion, & French dressing on onion roll" ($5.25-9.75). For dinner, start with Escargot perhaps, then move on to entrées like "Tournadoes Oscar", "Shrimp, Filet, Crab Legs, "Chicken in brown sauce with tomato, onion & mushrooms", or "Whitefish - either broiled; Grenoble with lemon, capers & butter; or Luzerne with tomato, onion, capers and parsley". Or, be really adventurous (and romantic!) and select order-ahead entrées like "Chateau Briand" ($14.95-30). Enjoy!

Closed Sundays / Smoking in designated areas / Reservations recommended, especially on weekends / Full bar and very extensive wine list / Parties of up to 50 generally accommodated in Old Room

18191 Old Grand Haven Road • 616-842-3800

*"Love is life. All, everything that I understand,
I understand only because I love. Everything
is, everything exists, only because I love."*
- Leo Tolstoy

Dining Delights

The Bil-Mar Restaurant -
Grand Haven

This one has "an extra romantic setting"! Commanding spectacular Lake Michigan views framed by beach gras & windswept sand, Bil-Mar offers evening diners candlelight, linens, Perch, Prime Rib, Filet, Split Crab Legs, and much more ($12.95-28.95). Enjoy perhaps Sandwiches, Soups, Seafood, & Pasta Salads, NY Strip Steak, and lightly battered Great Lakes Perch for lunch ($6-8) in the dining room or on the sun-splashed deck in Summer. Drift on in!

Open all year / Designated smoking areas / Reservations recommended / Full bar & wine list both imports & Michigan / Upstairs banquet room seats 80 for Winter parties only / Entertainment on New Year's Eve

1223 S. Harbor • 616-842-5920

Dining Delights

Piper - Macatawa (Holland area)

Every table here has a panoramic view of beautiful Lake Macatawa. Diners relax in a casual, whimsical atmosphere, and enjoy treats like 10" personal "Wood-fired Pizza" (watch the ovens operate!), "Sausage Gumbo", "Brew Battered Calamari", "Duck Carbonara Linguini", "Panini - Italian Sandwiches", "Woody Hen - roasted chicken breast with garlic, peppers, leeks, spicy sausage & tomato mashers", "Smoked Baby Backs", and "Pipercorn Salmon" ($6-17). Sweet endings include gelatto and sorbet, and "Poncino - cordial flavored cappucino". Yum, Yum!

Dinner served 7 days May - August - otherwise closed Sundays / Smoke free environment / Reservations for parties of six or more only/ Outdoor dining on covered deck with heaters / Full bar & wine list / Banquet room seats 120 - Deck parties for 24

2225 South Shore • 616-335-5866

À Deux Adventures

Grand Haven
Harbor Steamer...616-842-8950
Harbor Trolley............................. (summer only) 616-842-3200
Jet Set (Jet ski rentals) 2 locations 616-846-7472
P.J. Hoffmaster State Park.....................................616-798-3573
Pigeon Creek Park
Studio 206 (Full service Day Spa).........................616-847-0550
Waterfront Stadium..616-842-2550
Holland
Dutch Village Theme Park & Shopping.................616-396-1475
Delft Factory, Deklomp Wooden Shoe Factory,
    and Veldhuis Tulip Farm....................................616-399-1900
Windmill Island Municipal Park............................616-355-1030
Wooden Shoe Factory 616-396-6513
Muskegon
Craig's Cruisers Family Fun Centers - 3 locations
   616-798-4936
Cherry County Playhouse 616-727-8000
    or...1-800-686-9666
Hackley & Hume Historic Site..............................616-722-0278
Muskegon State Park...616-744-3480
Pleasure Island Water Theme Park.....................1-800-692-3391
Port City Cruise Lines, Inc. (Port City Princess)....616-728-8387
    or...1-800-853-6311
West Shore Snowmobile Trail 616-744-3480
Spring Lake - Nunica - Coopersville - Grand Rapids
Paradise Cove Boat Rentals, Inc. 616-842-3713
Moser's Dried Flower Barn.....................................616-842-0641
The Coopersville & Marne Railway Co..................616-837-7000
Frederik Meijer Gardens..616-957-1580
Gerald R. Ford Museum 616-451-9263

Cities by the "Sea" and THEIR NEIGHBORS
Pentwater - Ludington - White Cloud

*N*estled between the majesty of Lake Michigan and the Manistee National Forest, Pentwater and Ludington offer couples a chance for old-fashioned laid back relaxation, and barrels of fun!

Pentwater locals deem it "an undiscovered jewel", "a slower pace ... a quaint village", "more removed ... just feels like family", "not commercial", "New England flavor", and "Pier Pleasure!"

Borrow a bicycle or take a historic walking tour (maps available), and discover small-town delights including ice cream parlors, dockside and deckside dining, jazz on Sunday, a variety of shops, Thursday evening outdoor vil-

lage band concerts, peaceful, shaded streets, and picture-perfect harbors.

Explore the beaches, trails, pier and parks. Cross country skiers, hikers, mountain bikers, and cyclists will look forward to investigating the Pentwater Pathway (Pere Marquette State Forest), Mt. Baldy Footpath (Charles Mears State Park), or Hart-Montague Bicycle Trail State Park.

Looking for leisure? Take a lazy auto tour past Pentwater Lake on scenic Lakeshore Drive, take a picnic to a state park beach, or stroll the nearby Secret Garden.

Looking for excitement? Take a trip to adults only Double JJ Resort for horseback riding, sled dog "mushing", and cowboy barbecues; visit nearby Mears for the thrill of dunescooter rides, jeep, watercraft and bicycle rentals, and parasailing adventures; take a hay or sleighride, trail ride, or bike ride in Shelby or New Era; tour a gem factory in Shelby; or hit the local snowmobile trails!

Ludington locals insist "don't expect us to entertain you - people come here for quiet and relaxation!"

Popular Fall color tours are highlighted by a stop at Pere Jacques Marquette Monument, where a huge illuminated cross

stands vigil over-looking the harbor. Winter visitors glide in solitude and whitewashed splen-dor on groomed cross-country ski trails; watch the "Candelier" make ro-mantic "lights"; skate across a frozen pond; buy their sweeties chocolates; spend a day at the spa; or a night at the dinner theater.

Spring heralds wild flowers, blossoms, and the Scottville Clown Band concert series! Fly a kite, get out your in-line skates, play some putt-putt golf, and visit White Pine Village - "where history becomes real".

And summer , ah summer . . . a lighthouse tour, a moonlit beach walk, a scenic seaplane ride, a peaceful float down Pere Marquette River, a pontoon cruise of Hamlin Lake, a private picnic in undeveloped Nordhouse Dunes. Sunbathe, stargaze, catch a concert in the park, pick some berries, and enjoy Luding-ton's two star attractions - the "Big Lake's" famous car ferry, SS Badger, and its 1/2 mile sugar sand beach!

From the country serenity of *White Cloud*, consider a "backroads adventure" to uniquely beautiful Shrine of the Pines, and Loda Lake Wildflower Sanctuary. Head South to lunch at Grant Depot Restaurant, and its fascinating train museum. Or East to that "village of yesteryear" Loafer's Glory in historic Blanchard.

Nature sets the tone for a casual weekend in this outdoor paradise - winter parks, groomed snowmobile and cross-country ski trails, forest hiking trails, and riverside canoe rentals offer ample opportunities for leisurely pleasures.

White Pine Village

You'll discover a little bit of heaven, and a lot of romance, in the "cities" by the "sea" and their neighbors!

Oceana County Tourism Bureau
1-800-874-3982
http://Tour.Oceana,net

Ludington Area CVB
1-800-542-4600

White Cloud C of C
616-689-6607

The Candlewyck House - PENTWATER

"someplace for sparkin', and
spoonin', and fallin' in love"

*S*tep into "someplace else" - some-
place completely different from home. Put your feet up, lean
back, relax, and experience the pampered care of one of the best
hostesses ever!

Candlewyck's guests have the run of this primitive-country
repro-Americana-style home! "Plant yourselves"in the garden,

on the sunny patio,
or in the sitting area
in front of the fire-
place. "Entertain
yourselves" with
150 movies or over
1,000 books!
(Honeymooners are
encouraged to show
their wedding
videos!), or borrow

one of their bicycles and ride to the beach for sunrise . "Indulge
yourselves" with cheese and crackers, iced tea, cappucino,
cookies, wine or "gooey" evening desserts. An "open refrigerator" policy is the rule here! Fish boil dinners, or Friday night
"soup's-on-the-stove" welcomes, are available on request.

Or, "cocoon yourselves" in one of six suites, each with
private bath, TV/VCR, refrigerator, and sitting area. Three
suites offer fireplaces for cuddlin'! Suites rent for $70-100,
depending on your choice and the day. The "Hunt Club" sets a
lodge mood with Adirondack chairs and hunting and fishing
accessories; "Sailor's Rest" is (what else?) a den of nautical
inspiration (private bath across the hall); or perhaps try the
"Patriot Room". Couples looking for a romantic nook often

select "Hannah's Hideaway", tucked under the eaves and high-lighted by an antique clawfoot tub!

The dining room, featuring a display of your host's hand-made baskets, is the center for family-style adults-eat-together breakfasts. Go ahead, contribute to the restoration of the art of conversation! And, while you're at it, enjoy a fabulous full breakfast including gourmet coffees roasted especially for the Candlewyck (hazelnut is their trademark!), and an entrée item such as "Mary Jo's Seafood Quiche", "Stuffed Strawberry-Cream Cheese French Toast", crepes, or Heart-shaped Waffles!

This ultra-hospitable Inn offers Couples Retreat, Murder Mystery, and Basket Workshop weekends. They're open 365 days, but do accept children, so busy summer months are usually family times. Winter, when town population drops to about 600, is a peaceful time to visit. Call at least 60 days ahead for peak times - by March 1 for prime weekends.

This Inn is different and special - your hostess makes it so. For a winning combination of warm ambiance, solitude, and good food, call . . .

The Candlewyck House Bed & Breakfast
616-869-5967
438 E. Lowell, P.O. Box 392, Pentwater 49449
Smoking outdoors only, please

Inn-spired Activities ———————————

Celebrate our festivals, including Fall & "Christmas in the Village" with concerts, cuisine, candlelight and camaraderie; walk the beach barefoot after dinner, sit on a log there and hold hands!

ℋexagon ℋouse - *PENTWATER*

"truly a halcyon hideaway"

*R*ead poetry to your loved one on the porch! Wrapping itself lovingly around this architectural wonder, the porch provides a very quiet, private place to be alone.

Yes, the Hexagon House is true to its name - its shape offering a unique space for four very special accommodations to be tucked around the top of the clerestory stairway at the center. Each room offers a private bath, and a private outside entrance  to the porch and the outside stairway access. TV or phone is available on request, movie channels and video remote, too. Antiques, some original to this 1867 home, create an old-fashioned ambiance that's true to the era, yet crisp, fresh, and new feeling. The outstanding choice of many honeymoon or anniversary couples is the "Cherub Room", where romance and sweet dreams are guaranteed by the "angels" decorating it!

Rooms are available for $125 (3 nights for $300), by reservation only (no walk-ins). Your hosts like as much advance notice as you can give, but for July and August weekends plan to reserve early in the year. Hexagon House is open mid-May - mid-October.

A very private, separate cottage is set to open in 1998. More rustic, with a Southwest decor, it includes a kitchenette and all linens but no breakfast ($100 per night/$500 per week).

Though not licensed to handle receptions, small wedding ceremonies are joyfully scheduled here. Wedding couples enjoy a champagne breakfast, or other appropriate treats, with their first night's stay. Requests for flowers, champagne, or "your heart's desire" can be arranged and priced by your hosts. They take great pleasure in making special occasions *"special"*.

While you'll certainly enjoy the Victorian parlor, and the comfortable, traditional-colonial style living room/dining room, as well as the huge porch-deck hot tub, you'll want to find Hexagon's own "Secret Garden" - the perfect place for a kiss!

Take your morning coffee to your room, out on deck, or to the beautiful gardens, complete with fountain and bird feeding stations. Breakfast here is served "the way it used to be", with linens, silver, lace, and all the extra nice things. "Orange Frappe" is served each day, with a different fruit blended in, to complement a variety of muffins (try raspberry sour cream!), a fruit course, a hot dish such as quiche or baked French toast, and regular and flavored coffee.

Caution! This unusual Inn may inspire engagements, or at the very least, a romantic experience to remember!

Hexagon House
616-869-4102
P.O. Box 1030, Pentwater 49449
616-869-4102

Inn-spired Activities ————————

Watch the pleasure cruisers and sailboats from Mears State Park beach; let us reserve a porch dining table for you at Nickerson Inn; for a majestic view of spectacular sunsets try the pier or a beach bench!

Nickerson Inn - PENTWATER

"a magnificent obsession - this place - your love!"

*G*one are the stagecoaches which once carried passengers across the channel on a ferry and up the hill to the Nickerson Inn. But the Inn remains, welcoming guests continuously for 84 years. Though recently renovated, the Nickerson retains the grace, charm, and spirit of genuine hospitality that has always been its trademark.

You'll feel at home on the front porch, in the cozy lobby/ sitting area in front of the stone fireplace, in the candlelit dining room, second floor sitting area, or in your private suite or room. Deep, rich colors create a warm; and dramatic backdrop for the

common areas and many of the 10 themed, and different, rooms (each with private bath and soft comforter!). Try "Loggers Run" with its log bed and walls, and "lure of the wild" feeling, or perhaps "Artist's Garden" with a white iron bed and mood inspired by Monet. Perhaps you prefer "Seascape" complete with a ship's wheel bed, nautical accessories, and views of Lake

Michigan, or "Tally Ho"'s paisley decor and draped black iron canopy bed. Whichever you choose, no TV or phone will disturb your peaceful night's rest, available for seasonal rates from $90-100 per room.

Two suites reflect that Lake Michigan beach atmosphere with their whitewashed walls, natural wicker, and fluffy robes. View the sunset over the Lake from your private balcony, cuddle in front of your personal gas fireplace, or soak in your whirlpool tub. Both "Sunrise" and "Sunset" suites are very special romantic hideaways for rates of $170-185 (depending on time of year).

Small wedding ceremonies, receptions, and anniversary parties can be easily accommodated off-season. Your hosts will do their best to comply with any special arrangements you may request - flowers, wine and cheese trays, homemade fudge, fruit or gift baskets, etc. Stop in the lobby gift shop, too.

Plan one year in advance for peak weekends at this popular Inn. Winter is a marvelous time to go - ask about Romantic Getaway Packages, Christmas Tea Weekends, and French Cooking Classes. Anniversary couples booking a stay 14 days before of after their date receive a 1% room discount for every year they've been married!

For breakfast, choose the main dining room, or the screened porch with its "ice cream style" furniture. Homemade specialties vary daily, and are prepared from the freshest ingredients available. *Dining*

Dinner at the Nickerson Inn *Delights* combines "impeccable service" with "superb cuisine" created here fresh daily to delight Inn guests and dinner guests alike. Start with a selection from the extensive wine list, and an appetizer of "Baked Brie in Puff Pastry", "Roasted Forest Mushrooms", "Smoked Lake Trout Mouse", or other Seafood delights for $6.95-7.95. Entrées may include menu offerings like the Inn's specialties - "Duck Lakota stuffed with wild rice, pine nuts, sundried tomatoes and mushrooms, on strawberry sauce", "Quail Chambord ", "Sea

Scallops a la Sherry", "Tournedos Del Rio topped with jumbo shrimp and dijon caper sauce", "Rack of Lamb", "Tortellini Roma with artichoke hearts, sundried tomatoes, mushrooms, chicken breast and cheese/spinach tortellini with basil cream sauce", "Citrus Shrimp with jalapeños, ginger, flash of rum, and mound of pasta", or "Beef Wellington" (plus many others!). Daily specials round out the dinner menu. Prices range from $11.95-24.95. The perfect ending? A dessert of the day, or espresso, cappuccino, latte, mocha, or after dinner cocktail. (The dining room is open weekends only off-season).

Whether dining, or staying the night, you'll enjoy individual attention and that "personal touch".

"The *whole Inn* is so special, you won't wait to get here!" Call . . .

Historic Nickerson Inn
616-869-6731
262 W. Lowell Street, P.O. Box 986, Pentwater 49449
A smoke free establishment

Inn-spired Activities ————————

Enjoy boating, hiking, biking, cross-country skiing, dune rides, our beautiful beaches, spectacular sunsets, and beautiful "dune scapes"!

144

The Lamplighter - *LUDINGTON*

"this is the moment . . .
you've waited for."

Soft colors, soft music, stately antiques, and just a bit of lace grace this very elegant Inn. Carefully preserved historic appeal blends with thoroughly modern conveniences for the perfect luxurious romantic getaway.

Entering, you're struck by architectural details such as the golden oak grand staircase, sculptured porcelain tiles surrounding the living room fireplace, and unusual cast-iron radiators.

Make yourself comfortable in the parlor, or in the living room, for TV watching, quiet conversation, or warming by the fire.

You'll be anxious, though, to settle into your personal space - one of five simple, uncluttered yet splendid, Victorian rooms (each with private bath, phone, and cable TV). For an outstanding experience, consider spending this "magic moment" in one of the two Jacuzzi® rooms. Rates vary from $75-135.

Lamplighter accommodates guests all year, but suggests booking at least one month in advance for summer or fall weekends.

You'll be treated like royalty here, so be prepared for the finest accommodations and service. Arrangements can be made for small, intimate weddings (10-15 people). Anniversary and honeymoon couples may even be treated to a chauffeur-driven ride in the Inn's '36 Chevy! What a way to arrive at dinner, or be picked up from the ferry landing!

Your Full, Gourmet Breakfast will be personally served in the formal dining room, or outdoors (weather permitting) on the gazebo/deck or patio (and with consideration to any dietary concerns). Every attempt is made to feature Michigan products and fresh produce - including items from Lamplighter's own garden. Homemade bakery goods are complemented each day by such treats as "Lemon Fruit Soup with fresh fruit", "Rhubarb Strawberry Cake", "Baked Strata with hashbrowns, ham, portabella mushrooms and fresh chives", or "German Apple Puff Pancake".

Stay for a night, a weekend, or a Murder Mystery Weekend. Seize the romantic moment at . . .

The Lamplighter Bed & Breakfast
616-843-9792 or 1-800-301-9792
602 E. Ludington Avenue, Ludington 49431
www.laketolake.com/lamplighter
email: catsup@aol.com
A smoke free Inn

Inn-spired Activities ————————————

Rent a pontoon boat on Hamlin Lake; cross-country ski or walk the sand dunes in the State Park - you can always find a quiet cove, even in summer!

Schoenberger House - LUDINGTON

*"quiet refinement, and
elegant beauty"*

*S*et the scene for romance at this fabulous neoclassical mansion!

Act I - The Welcome. Your entry into Schoenberger House causes delight and surprise at the awe-inspiring beauty of inlaid parquet floors, fine woodwork, and paneling - different in each room - moiré and hand-stenciled Art Nouveau wall coverings, magnificent chandeliers, five fireplaces, Oriental rugs and design influence, fresh flowers and fantastic plants throughout, unusual artwork, and an overall ambiance of warmth, simplicity and absolute elegance.

Enter each common area and enter a new world - pass from the imposing white oak foyer, to the classic cherry living room, into the American sycamore dining room, and back to the mahogany

music room (tinkle the ivories on one of two grand pianos!). And, finally, settle into the extra special black walnut library - its book room, or its game room with fireplace and window seats.

Act II - The overnight stay. Relaxed (and with a decided air of importance!), you float up the stairs to discover five luxurious European-style impeccable and wonderful rooms. Each has private bath, fluffy down comforter, extra pillows and is airy, light, and stunning, with extremely interesting architectural influences and unusual decor touches. Rates vary by day, room, and season from $120-195. You wander one to the other, and finally settle into the two room suite, sampling the comfortable separate sitting room and the soothing "bedchamber". You step out for a brief respite on the balcony and breathe a sigh of contentment. You feel very special, and very alone - just you two!

Act III - Breakfast. You're seated in the dining room and served (individually) your Continental Plus Breakfast on "especially divine" tableware, unusual flatware and glassware. Enjoy fresh croissants and jams, with imported pastries and bagels made just for Schoenberger House, fresh-squeezed juice, and freshly ground coffee . You feel like the invited guest of a very wealthy, prestigious host! And, it's guaranteed, the breakfast here is so special, you won't miss a full breakfast!

Act IV - The happy ending! After a stay in this extremely warm, enveloping atmosphere, you find yourself planning a perfect winter escape, a musical evening, or looking forward to an arranged catered lunch, dinner, or small wedding (max 16 guests). Planning as far in advance, of course, as possible - particularly if room selection is important - but planning to return for a repeat performance at . . .

Schoenberger House
616-843-4435
409 E. Ludington Avenue, Ludington 49431
Sorry, no smoking permitted

Inn-Spired Activities ————————

We suggest the State Park Beach - one of the most beautiful in the world! It's not just the park, it's the drive to get there!

Summit Inn - LUDINGTON

"it'll sweep you off your feet!"

Ah-oo-gah! You'll be greeted in the driveway by "Tin Lizzie", but you'll be surprised by the thoroughly modern amenities at this "built-for-an-Inn" bed and breakfast.

Simple, classic, traditional decor and deep rich colors accent an all white backdrop throughout this spacious, open Inn. a large and comfortable formal living room is separated from the dining room by a two-way see-through fireplace and set-up bar (bring your own wine or beverages).

Climb a spiral staircase (or use the elevator) for access to the library/ game room, and four guest accommodations. Each large room features private bath, sitting area,  TV, intercom to reach the hosts, and queen bed with fluffy comforter. Lakeside rooms share a 50 foot balcony overlooking Lake Michigan and a four acre property with wildlife feeding area. Deer, red fox and porcupines share the spotlight with passing freighters, the stars, the moon, and *great* sunsets!

Rates range from $100-120 (including tax). Off-season discounts are available, but be sure to book at least 1 month in advance for summer stays.

Weather bad? Or do you simply want to cocoon on this get-away trip? You can stay right here and entertain yourself handily. In addition to the upstairs game room/library, the Summit offers a complete recreational/entertainment area in the downstairs (basement) level. Deep green walls and a cozy fireplace, card tables, pool table, putting practice area, games, cards and puzzles - all here for your relaxing fun. What else? How about a separate TV viewing room, presented theater-style with large screen satellite TV, HBO, and leather chairs with ottomans! The convenient bar/kitchenette is stocked with evening snacks, cookies, pie, shortcake, or other daily treat!

In great weather, wander the grounds exploring groomed private pathways, wooded grottos, and the lakeside lounging area. Since the Inn sits high on a lakeside bluff, beach access is nearby at a park with picnic tables, grills, and tennis courts.

Have your morning coffee, (or carry-out lunch or dinner) on deck or front porch. You may join the other guests at small intimate dining tables for a Full Gourmet Breakfast of fresh fruit, cereal, muffins, beverages, and pancakes, French toast, or "Baked Eggs." Dietary restrictions cheerfully accommodated!

Before you leave, take a turn on the old-fashioned swing, "sized for adults"! If you're celebrating a special occasion, you may even get a spin in "Tin Lizzie"!

Your hosts believe in special treatment and ultimate service. Their goal is "not to imitate any other Inn", but to provide a unique escape at . . .

Summit Inn Bed & Breakfast
616-843-4052 (call 10-6 M-F)
4711 S. Lakeshore Drive, Ludington 49431
No smoking please, except for deck or porches

Inn-Spired Activities

Take in a free summer concert; take a shoreline cruise (available three times a year on the SS Badger; go skating, snowshoeing, scuba diving, or star gazing!

The Shack - WHITE CLOUD

"couples come here to do 'nuthin' ...
except be together!"

*T*he glow of soft candlelight reflects from your private table onto Robinson Lake, as you dine in the warmth of this magnificent cozy log cabin lodge.

You'll appreciate the cozy quietness of any room here, with their handmade log furniture, private baths, TV, and lake or garden view. Perfect for romance, though, are rooms in the Granary. These eight provide ultimate privacy and comfort, hot tubs (some are heart shaped!), rocking chairs, gas fireplaces, and a covered porch where signs encourage you to "Sit Long - Talk Much!"

Twelve rooms in the main lodge also have hot tubs. All hot tub rooms offer VCRs (select a tape in the lobby). Friday and Saturday night guests in these special rooms are served a tray with a non-alcoholic sparkling beverage and candies.

They'll leave the lights on for you, and be sure your room is toasty warm (or cool depending on the weather!), and guarantee your comfort in *any* of their 35 rooms. Rates range from $50-165.

Hors d'oeuvres and a buffet dinner are included with rooms here on Friday and Saturday nights only, but guests are treated *every* evening to a hand-dipped banana split!

Banquets are possible for 100 guests, but Friday and Saturday night events will be set up in the smaller banquet room seating 40. The coffee's out all day, and microwave popcorn, snack, and beverage machines in The Silo can satisfy your "munchie" desires.

Breakfast is a Home Country Buffet, with all the chilled and hot items you'll want to start your day at this private retreat. Summer plans might be a paddleboat ride, strolling the beautiful gardens, swimming, or just relaxing on the porch. On a fine fall Saturday, sign up for a ride on the wagon pulled by Belgian horses, and cozy up to the bonfire for cocoa and cookies. Hiking the wooded trails is always an option, or challenge each other to horseshoes, volleyball, basketball (outdoors), checkers, shuffleboard, or pool (indoors). In winter, cross-country ski and snuggle by the fireplace in one of two very comfy sitting areas. Spring brings maple syrup time. The sap is gathered with the aid of the horses, delivered to the "Sugar shack", and boiled into syrup for sale at the Inn. Try some!

You can do it all at The Shack, or "do nuthin'", but be sure to plan ahead at least 4-6 weeks for a weekend visit any time of year.

The "atmosphere allows pleasant and peaceful feelings to relax you" your hosts comment, and further note, "Yes, there's still a little bit of heaven left on earth" at . . .

The Shack Bed & Breakfast
616-924-6683
2263 W. 14th Street, White Cloud 49349
"Jugville, USA"
Smoke free "Granary" rooms

Ǝnn-Ǝspired Activities ———————

Stay right here and soak up nature, or scoot into White Cloud or Fremont for a casual meal!

Dining Delights   *Gibb's Country House* - Ludington

"Come as you are ... to the "House of Homemade!" Special seasonal menus like "Taste of Autumn", or "Christmas in July" add some spice to the daily fare of fresh "no preservatives", "like Mom used to make" (with a creative twist!) cooking. An extensive menu is complemented by baked goods from the on-site bakery. Luncheon treats like "Chicken Salad Sunrise Sandwich with broiled havarti cheese and pineapple ring" or "Spinach Salad with bacon, water chestnuts, mandarin oranges, and hot bacon dressing" ($3.25-9.95) go along with the one-of-a-kind Gourmet Table - soup, salad, sandwich and dessert bar. Dinners like "Linguine Alfredo", Prime Rib, or other Pasta Specialties ($9.25-19.95) are served in a casual atmosphere. You're invited to try Gibbs "because you love good food".

Open 7 days / Reservations accepted / Deli & take-out service / Private parties arranged for up to 300 / Full bar / Smoking in designated areas / Piano entertainment Wed., Sun., and Sat. eve
3951 W. U.S. 10 • 616-845-0311

Dining Delights   *Scotty's* - Ludington

Ahoy, Mateys! Relaxed, casual, and "simply the best", says this nautical-theme eatery. Weekday luncheon service features homemade Soups, Salads, Sandwich selections, and charbroiled Burgers. Sunday breakfasts feature a selection of Omelets with other standard AM entries. Dinner specialties include Prime Rib, "Aztec Steak with spicy South-of-the-Border marinade and four onion sauté", "Jamaican Chicken", "Chicken Frangelico with wild rice and almonds", and signature "Swordfish Steak", "Renowned Lake Perch", or "Seafood Kabob with grilled, marinated swordfish, shrimp, scallops, & veg." ($8.95-17.95). Great!

Full bar / smoking in designated areas / Parties possible
5910 E. Ludington Avenue (U.S. 10) • 616-843-4033

153

Dining Delights

𝒞. 𝒞ℳ. 𝒮teamers - Ludington

For casual waterfront dining and wonderful City Marina views, try the contemporary nautical charm of P.M. Steamers. Cruise in for a hearty lunch or dinner of "Cobb Salad", assorted Stir Fry, Steaks, Prime Rib, Pasta dishes, and daily fresh Fish, with specialties like "Grilled Fajitas", "Key Largo Chicken with fettucine, light sauce,, 2 cheeses & bacon", "Seafood Papillotte - orange roughy, crab and shrimp baked with wine & seasonings in a parchment bag", Gourmet Pizza such as "The Seafarer with shrimp, artichoke hearts, tomatoes, basil, mozzarella & parmesan", "Crab Cakes with horseradish sauce", or "Nutty Walleye with pecan/sugar crust & dried Michigan cherry sauce" $5.95-18.95). Join them for "Mason County's finest Sunday Brunch", too!

Full Bar / Smoking in designated areas / Parties possible / Appetizer and cocktail service on outdoor deck

502 W. Loomis • 616-843-9555

Dining Delights

Capers Restaurant & Bar - White Cloud

Assorted "Super Stack Sandwiches, Light Entrées, and Soup, Salad, and Sandwich bar, add variety to luncheon here ($2.50-6.95). For an evening's "Great Beginning", try "Shrimp & Crab or Broccoli & Cheese Stuffed Potato", or "Raspberry Chicken Vinaigrette Salad". Dinner's "Enticing Entrées" include "Orange Roughy Oscar with hollandaise", Steaks, Stir Frys, Mexican delights, & favorites like "Dijon Chicken", "Center-Cut Pork Chops", and "Tempting Twosomes" of Steak & Lobster or Steak & Shrimp ($6.95-14.95). Sunday Buffet is $6.95. Finish with a "Sweet Finale" dessert, ice cream drink, or a "Hot Toddy" like "Godiva Café". Special!

Full bar / Smoking in designated areas / Special Event banquet facilities for up to 200 guests

234 Charles • 616-689-1282

À Deux Adventures

Pentwater

AJ's Family Fun Center (mini-golf, etc.) 616-869-5641

Cross-country ski trails (c/o C of C) 616-869-4150

Meers

Mac Wood's Dune Rides 616-873-2817

Sandy Korners Jeep Rentals 616-873-5048

Silver Lake State Park (xc ski & snowmobile) 616-873-3083

The Wood Shed (bike rentals) 616-873-4338

    or 1-800-618-4338

Wave Club Water Sport Rentals, Inc. (Jet boats,

    Para-sailing, Wave Runners, Pontoons) 616-873-3700

New Era - Rothbury

Rainbow Ranch (Riding, hay & sleigh rides) 616-861-4445

The Secret Garden 616-861-4878

Double JJ Resort (riding, sled dog rides) 616-894-4444

Shelby - Hart

Craig's Cruisers Family Fun Centers 616-873-2511

Hart-Montague Bicycle Trail 616-873-4959

    or 616-873-2488

Kay Marie Ranch (trail riding, hayrides) 616-861-5421

Shelby Man-Made Gemstones 616-861-2165

West Shore Snowmobile Trails 616-893-4585

White Cloud - Baldwin - Blanchard - Points East

Grant Depot Restaurant 616-834-7361

Loda Lake Wildflower Sanctuary 616-689-6696

Vic's Canoes (& kayak rental) 616-834-5494

Baldwin Canoe Rental 616-745-4669

    or 1-800-272-3642

Ivan's Canoe Rental 616-745-3361

Shrine of the Pines 616-745-7892

Loafer's Glory 517-561-2020

À Deux Adventures

- Pentwater - Ludington - White Cloud & Area

Ludington

AJ's Action Territory (mini-golf, etc.) 616-843-4836
Beachwatch, Inc. (parasailing) 616-843-9228
Big Sable Point Lighthouse Keepers, Assoc.
(tours - call C of C)...616-845-0324
Candelier™ of Ludington.....................................616-845-9953
Historic White Pine Village 616-843-4808
Kilwin's Chocolates 616-843-7598
Lake Forest Performing Arts Co. (dinner theater - at
Lands Inn & Convention Center) 616-845-7311
or.. 1-800-707-7475
Lake Michigan Carferry - SS Badger 616-845-5555
or.. 1-800-841-4243
.... www.ssbadger.com
Ludington State Park 616-843-8671
Mason County Aviation (rides)............................616-843-2049
Nordhouse Dunes (Manistee Ranger District) 616-723-2211
Scenic Seaplanes (air tours) 616-845-2877
or Cellular...616-357-1557
The Blueberry Patch (pick your own) 616-9561
or...616-843-9619
The Chocolate Shop 616-843-2325
The Great Escape (spa services)...........................616-845-7020
Therapy Too Charters (boat rides & scenic cruises
....616-845-6095
or.. 1-800-845-6095
Trailhead Bike Shop (rentals)...............................616-845-0545
West Shore Community College Cultural &
Performing Arts..............................1-800-848-9722 ext. 3131

156

The Port Cities - Frankfort - Elberta - Onekama & Manistee - with Beulah/Benzonia

Welcome to small-town America at its (surprisingly) romantic best! Once bustling shipping centers, these sleepy Lake Michigan communities radiate Victorian charm at every turn!

Touch on some history and take home a memory from **Manistee** - stroll the gaslit Riverwalk, take a village walking tour

and admire the restored Victorian-style architecture, ride the trolley, tour The Lyman Building Museum, sip Victorian high tea, and take in a production at Manistee's cultural landmark - the lumber-era Ramsdell Theatre. Wait, though! The best is yet to come! Don't miss the Victorian Sleighbell Parade & Olde Christmas weekend in early December, with hot-cocoa open houses, costumed carolers, horse-drawn evening parade units, and chestnuts roastin' by the open fire!

Sneak some private moments at Udell Rollaways National Recreation Area, or seek some invigorating solitude hiking the North Country National Scenic Trail - just 15 minutes East in the Manistee National Forest.

Nearby Bear Lake is home to Rockin' R Stable - "a touch of the old West". With hayrides, sleigh rides (pulled by Clydesdales!), scenic trail riding, rodeos, and even teepee and cabin camping, visitors have a chance to experience the cowboy life. Or, how about a lakeside carriage ride, topped off with a campfire dinner cooked just for you?

Drawn by the beaches, the bluffs, and the lakes, couples flock to sister cities **Frankfort** and **Elberta** for sunfilled getaways. Their days are filled with shopping, swimming, sailing and sand castles; galleries and gliders; planes, hiking, and hang gliding; canoeing and cross-country skiing, picnicking and photography; skating and sledding; lighthouse tours, and lovers' trysting! Their nights are filled with awesome sunsets from Elberta's bluffs or Frankfort's Piers; delightful dining; casual entertainment; huggin' and kissin'!

Visitors will love the Benzie Hills Arts and Crafts Tour, but must include the "not-to-be-missed" riverside studio and nature haven of **Benzonia's** Gwen Frostic, a well-known and talented artist and poet. They'll make a stop for "treats" at The Homestead Sugar House, or gather up a picnic lunch at a local deli (with some Cherry Hut pie!), and head to the shores of Crystal Lake for one of **Beulah's** concerts in the park.

Scenic! Scenic! Scenic! That's the best description of this area, where natural beauty is the finest feature. Summer "top down" drives, or Autumn color tours, wind gracefully throughout. Try the winding forest-lined Lakeshore Drive North from Manistee; follow the shoreline on M-22 through **Onekama** and

Frankfort, and on to the Southern edge of Sleeping Bear Dunes National Lakeshore; take a side trip to serenity at beautiful Platte River Point "peninsula", or the sun-splashed virtually undiscov-

ered beach in Empire; venture North through Benzonia and Beulah on U.S. 31 to admire Mother Nature's reflected glory on gorgeous Crystal Lake; paddle (or float!) two fabulous rivers - the Betsie and the Platte; or simply "cruise" through the drive-in for a nostalgic bit of fun!

Go ahead, lose yourselves! As one local brochure advises, there's "plenty to do - nothing planned!"

Benzie County C of C
1-800-882-5801
email: chamber@benzie.org

Manistee/Onekama
1-800-288-2286

Portage Point Inn - ONEKAMA

*"a special place of charm,
tradition, and nature"*

*P*erched commandingly on a narrow peninsula between Portage Lake and Lake Michigan, historic Portage Point Inn is reminiscent of old-style New England coastal resorts, and oh! so inviting!

Accommodations are varied. If you'd like to experience the quaint nostalgia of the main hotel, expect comfortable rooms,

but a bit less privacy due to noisy hall traffic. Privacy *is* served here, however, in four other ways: Terrace House suites; new and nicely done townhouse-style 1 bedroom condo units that have lakefront views and fireplaces; 1-4 bedroom cottages (all available by the week only in summer); and adorable one bedroom "Dollhouse Cottages" (by the night or week). Nightly summer rates range from $115 to 225 for rooms or one bedroom suites/ cottages. Ask about off season rates. Condos and townhouses are available all year.

Portage Point is well away from any hustle-bustle, and an excellent place to get re-acquainted. Endless miles of uninhabited beach beckon lovers. Sailing, or cruising the two lakes by speedboat, pontoon, or waverunner can be easily arranged at the front desk (hourly or day rentals). Landlubbers can relax at lakeside pool or Jacuzzi®, or rent coaster or tandem bicycles for a peninsula picnic outing. Don't miss spending a few precious moments, or hours, on the magnificent porch watching the world float by. Enjoy the spacious gameroom with bar and sandwich grill, which also features live entertainment and dancing on key summer weekends. Winter getaways invite a spin on snowmobiles (rentals also available), cross-country skiing, snowshoeing, or a day of nearby Alpine schussing! Warm your toes by the fireplace of the multi-purpose lobby Fireside Room. Psst! Also a great place for a cozy, intimate meal for two in the off-season!

Dining Delights

For that romantic Summer sustenance, select your meal from seasonally changing menus in the dining room. Serving breakfast, lunch, and dinner 7 days in summer, but only weekends off-season, this kitchen may offer such dinner choices as "Louisiana Bourbon Steak", "Lime Chicken", or "Pasta Alfredo" for $11.95-17.95. Luncheon specialties? Try Pizza, or "Chicken Salad with dried cherries". Mother's Day - October look for Sunday Brunch with an omelet station and carving station.

Weddings and receptions can be arranged to suit your tastes, but cannot be scheduled during busy July & August. Imagine your ceremony on the perfect white-pillared porch!

Imagine your lakeside rendezvous at the perfect . . .

Portage Point Inn
616-889-4222 or 1-800-878-7248
8513 S. Portage Pt. Drive, P.O. Box 596, Onekama 49675
Sorry, smoking prohibited indoors (except pavilion bldg.)

Ꙃnn-spired Activities ———————————

Summer is spectacular, but don't forget Winter fun - xc ski at Crystal Mountain or Big M, or natural areas; snowshoe, snowmobile, ice skate; share Fall color on the peninsula!

The Birch Haven Inn - FRANKFORT

"the things we cherish . . ."

Will include this wonderful hilltop Victorian Inn. Adorned with antiques and fresh flowers always, and filled with the strains of soft music, Birch Haven is exactly that - a haven for romantics! Here gracious hospitality and "soothing ambiance" combine to provide a true spirit-lifting getaway!

Whether you're most comfortable in Mary's Room, with its unique curved radiator; or the Canopy Room (queen-sized canopy bed, of course!); the Garden Room, overlooking the formal gardens, fountain and gazebo; or the Tower Room, with its sunset views (Sept. to June) - you'll find yourself at home in any season.

Your reservation, made at least 3-4 months in advance for peak seasons (one year for holidays), will guarantee your room at a rate of $80 per night.

A separate, very private accommodation, the Carriage House - with 2 bedrooms, kitchen and living room - is also a favorite for couples to enjoy for $400 per week (June-Sept.), or nightly with a 3 night minimum on long, off-season weekends.

In those daylight hours, guests will notice the magnificent glass etchings - a talent of the owner's Father. They'll also enjoy

TV/VCR and movies in the formal guest parlor, and a refrigerator stocked with juices and sodas in the upstairs sitting room. On a fine summer afternoon, sit with your sweetie on the porch swing or outdoor rocking chairs. Ask your hosts for directions to a secret spot for lovers - an uncrowded beach. They can direct you to beautiful views, great picnic spots, and fabulous hiking trails, too! After dark, listen for the foghorn - the almost eerie reassurance that someone is looking out for you will lull you gently to sleep.

Your anniversary will be a magical moment if you'd like to indulge in a package including dinner at a favorite local restaurant. You may even be treated to champagne in your room if you share your secret!

Breakfasts here get rave reviews. Served family-style in the formal dining room, this "hearty & sumptuous" meal may be centered around "Grand Marnier French Toast", or "Sausage Soufflé" with fresh fruits, breads, and beverages.

For a bit of continental intrigue and old-world hospitality, engage your hosts in a conversation (if you can) in German or Spanish. They speak both fluently! If not, don't worry. Even in English, the hospitality is a true art at . . .

The Birch Haven Inn
616-352-4008
219 Leelanau Avenue, P.O. Box 411, Frankfort 49635
Smoking outdoors only, please

Inn-spired Activities ————————

Ski Crystal Mountain or Sugar Loaf; go rafting on our 2 nearby rivers; try hang gliding!; check our nearby wineries; walk the beach - just 2 blocks away!

⊙he ⊙rookside ⊙nn and - BEULAH
⊙he ⊙ℋotel ⊙rankfort - FRANKFORT

"ultra-romantic"

*A*ccommodations at these sister Inns were designed *just for two!* Lose yourselves in your personal

suite - each with king-size mirrored canopy water beds, Polynesian spa, sitting area, and cozy wood-burning stove. Each of twenty Brookside suites is uniquely designed to feature local artisans. Themes vary from garden, to nautical, to country styles. Hotel Frankfort's eleven suites are a bit more formal, with mostly Victorian decor. Each property also offers even more luxurious havens, which add sauna, steam bath, loft, or French tanning solarium to the basic amenities. Special pampering services, or champagne and flowers, are available with advance notice - ask for a quote.

Rates of $185 to $250 (depending on the luxuries you desire!) include a complete dinner for two (selected from the full menu), and your choice of breakfast. Taxes and gratuities are included - alcoholic beverages are not.

164

While evening meals are elegant at Hotel Frankfort, dining at the Brookside is very special for Inn guests, and dining-only guests as well. Request seating "brookside" - on the tree-shaded streamside deck - or "fireside" in *Dining Delights* the softly-lighted antique-filled dining rooms. You'll love the house salad with its creamy parmesan dressing! Aside from the usual scrumptious entrées, such as Pasta, Seafood, Steaks, and Lamb, you can order such specialties as fresh Lobster and Trout you select from live tanks, or various German dishes. Or, perhaps you'd like to try Brookside's very unique "Stone Cooking"! Your choice of chicken, shrimp, sirloin, or baby lamb chops is served to your table *raw,* along with a flat stone heated to 700 degrees, for you to cook each morsel to perfection right in front of your eyes! (Sorry, live tanks and stone cooking not available at Hotel Frankfort.) Dining only? Expect to pay $10-20 for standard dinners, $24.95 for stone cooking.

These two restaurants, and their bakeries, are famous for their apple dumpling and chocolate fondant desserts, too! For a very special evening entertainment treat, spend some time in the candlelit wine cellars, sampling German wines only available from the Inns.

Breakfast choices ($3-7 dining only, included with room) include "Eggs Benedict", Omelets, and Fruit Pancakes, as well as simpler fare, and fresh bakery goodies.

For luncheon, $4-5 buys ample servings of Pastas, Salads, or Sandwiches. Try "Gwen's Favorite - cream cheese, olives, walnuts and seasoning on sourdough", or a "Grilled Dilly - ham & Swiss on dill bread".

After dining, be sure to browse in each Inn's Gift Fair to select an "I care" surprise for your love! Then share a walk on nearby Lake Michigan beach, or cross

the footbridge to Brookside's gardens. Just picture your wedding ceremony among the beautiful floral and herbal displays. Each Inn specializes in customized wedding receptions and anniver-

sary celebrations. Floral arrangements are coordinated by their on-staff designer.

For a very special ending to this romantic adventure, consider a hot air balloon flight. Available all year (weather permitting) at dawn and dusk, these aerial "I love you"s vary from 1 1/2 to 3 hours, and are highlighted by a champagne toast for $150 per person.

You'll want to plan ahead for a getaway at either of these unusual properties. For weekends, call 1-3 months in advance, midweek 1-3 weeks. Special packages change monthly - ask for details, but remember . . .

"One night is never enough!" at . . .

The Brookside Inn
U.S. 31, Beulah 49617

or

The Hotel Frankfort
Main Street, Frankfort 49635

For either Inn, call 616-882-7271

Inn-spired Activities ——————————

There are many wonderful sights, and special things to do in this area, but be sure to save lots of time to enjoy our amenities - this is the ultimate!

Chimney Corners Resort - FRANKFORT

"the old-fashioned summer cottage -
refurbished, and special!"

*T*he Latch String is out . . . come right in!" That's the welcome heard May to November at this 300 acre retreat, since 1935.

Positioned on Crystal Lake, one of Northern Michigan's clearest and most beautiful inland lakes, the resort offers beautiful vistas, and restful, calming fields and forests. The property adjoins Sleeping Bear National Lakeshore, with its mile of hiking trails, windswept dunes, and peaceful Lake Michigan beaches. Stressing a quiet vacation,they provide no phones or TVs, but guests are welcome to use rowboats and paddleboards, tennis courts, shuffle-board, tetherball, swimming, basketball, and volleyball facilities. Sailboats and power boats may be rented (or a hoist for your own boat), but Jet Skis® are not allowed to disturb the peace and beauty of the lake.

While Chimney Corners offers many larger cabins for families and groups, couples will find an appealing selection of remodeled 2 bedroom cottages and one room apartments. Most have fully equipped kitchen facilities, all have decks or screened porches, and all include fireplaces for those nippy nights, and romantic moments! Small and cozy favorites are West Hills, Hillside, Silverwood, Highview (larger with

lake view), and the Lodge Apartment. Lots of space between cottages assures your privacy. Renting by the week from $330 to $1175, or daily from $55 to $85 (depending on season), the units are best reserved one year in advance (though last minute weekends may be available May-early June and in Fall).

Lavish Buffet Breakfasts are available daily in summer, (weekends off-season), at the charming Beach Dining Room. Luncheon snack bar and soup-salad-homemade-bread buffet may also be on the agenda - check with your hosts for a schedule. Weddings are always possible - please ask for details.

"Treat yourself to a restorative" getaway at . . .

Chimney Corners Resort
616-352-7522 (best time 8-4, M-F)
1602 Crystal Drive, Frankfort 49635
www.innsandouts.com
Smoking outdoors, please

Inn-spired Activities ——————————

Attend the Sail Inn cabaret-style dinner theater; find a quiet spot at Platte Plains, Empire Bluffs, or the Old Indian Trail;   visit Pt. Betsie Lighthouse; take a romantic evening stroll in downtown Frankfort - get some ice cream and admire the Victorian mansions!

Dining Delights

The Glenwood Inn - Onekama

This old-fashioned "beachhouse" with its screened porch welcomes couples for casual dining year-around, but winter is most romantic - a quieter, more private experience. Whet your appetite with "Spinach Artichoke Dip", "Brick Oven Cheese Bread", or a salad with the fat-free house lime ginger dressing. Whet your whistle with a selection from the *very* extensive beer list, the modest wine list or full liquor menu. Culinary Institute of America chefs serve up "Grilled Chicken Pesto", "Potato Crusted Whitefish", "Beef Wellington", "Almond Battered Shrimp with cherry mustard sauce", or "Flamingo Chicken - flamed tableside with a special blend of liqueurs", along with other nightly features ($8-20). Everything is homemade from scratch - even the pastries. Bon Appetite!

Reservations recommended in summer / Private parties, yes-call for details / Full bar + beer & wine list / A No Smoking property
4604 Main Street • 616-889-3735

Dining Delights

The Manitou - Frankfort

This small, casual dinner house specializes in Great Lakes Whitefish, Trout, Sautéed Perch, Choice Steaks, Rack of Lamb, BBQ Ribs, Crab & Lobster ($11.95-30 average price $15-18). A special "Early Bird" menu is available for guests dining 4:30-6 pm. Look for homemade soups and pies "to die for", but get here early or expect a wait! Relax and enjoy.

Open daily May - mid November / Flexible limited smoking area - basically non-smoking / Extensive beer & wine list - no hard liquors / Dining on screened patio / Private parties up to 40 people (not in July & Aug.)
M-22, 9 mile N. of Frankfort - 3 miles S. of Platte River
616-882-4761

 *Dining Delights*   *Cabbage Shed* Waterfront Pub-Elberta

This funky old former cabbage warehouse serves up lots of fun, along with "fine food & generous drinks", in a rustic building on Betsie Bay. For starters, how about "Crab Rangoon" or "Wings of Fire"? Feast on slow roasted "Beastly Beef", "Cajun Prime", broiled "Great Lakes Walleye, "Basil Pesto with toasted almonds on linguine", or famous "Two Breasted Chicken" among other surprising menu delights and specials ($7.95-13.95). Guests are encouraged to rouse themselves from a fireside chair, or bayside deck table, to join the live music and dancing, "sing along, take a chorus on the kazoo, pluck the washtub, or beat out the rhythm on the old washboard"! Get "hooked on the Cabbage Shed"! (Ostentatious tipping is o.k.!)
Open all year / Smoking in designated areas / Full bar, wine & beer lists, tropical drinks & world's best martini! / Entertain.
On beautiful Betsie Bay • 616-352-9843

 Dining Delights   *Northern Delights Cafe* -Benzonia

For casual dining and a "bite of culture", try this sparkling little gem of a cafe. Cooking classes, 4 course Tuesday Wine Dinners, Sunday afternoon Wine Tasting & Art receptions, World Food Tours, and Saturday Nite Concerts, complement a variety of healthy menu options like "Black Bean Burrito", "Wild Mushroom Ravioli", "Thai Chicken Curry", Fresh Fish, Wild Game dishes, and Middle Eastern specialties. From energetic & lively lunches ($3.50-7), to quiet, candlelit dinners($8-16), "It's not just a way of eating, it's a way of living"!
Open May-Oct. except Mondays (Oct.-May for special events and catering) / Smoking on outside deck only / Beer & wine, including microbrews & organic beers / Reservations accepted, and a must for special events / Private parties for 65 max
1058 U.S. 31 (top of the hill) • 616-882-9631

À Deux Adventures

- Beulah, Elberta, Frankfort, Manistee, Onekama & Area

Beulah
Crystal Lake Adventure Sports (watersports rentals)
....616-882-4301
Crystal Lake Marina (boat, watercraft rentals) 616-882-9636
The Cherry Hut..616-882-4431
The Homestead Sugar House 616-882-7712
Elberta
Crystal Re-Sources Wellness Center (massages &
  hypnotherapy)..............................616-325-2888 or 616-325-2842
Highland Sailing Charter.....................616-590-7791 or 616-924-5993
Slo-Mo-Sean Charters (cruising & adventure)...............616-352-5019
  or...616-947-3186
Frankfort
A & W Drive-in..616-352-9021
Kilwins Confectionery Shoppe 616-352-6107
Northwest Soaring Club of Frankfort............................616-352-9160
Manistee
Orchard Beach Aviation (plane rides)............................616-723-8095
Ramsdell Theatre..616-723-7188
Sleeping Bear Dunes (park headquarters).......................616-326-5134
Trolley Tours (Manistee Cty. Transportation)................616-723-6525
Victorian Teas & Tours...616-723-6286
Water Bug Tours on the River.......................................616-889-3378
Bear Lake - Benzonia - Honor - Lake Ann - Thompsonville
Rockin' R Stable...616-864-3539
Benzie Historical Museum 616-882-5539
Gwen Frostic Prints 616-882-5505
Sail Inn Restaurant 616-882-4971
Vacation Trailer Park (canoeing) 616-882-5101
  or 1-800-482-5101
Riverside Canoe Trips 616-325-5622
Chain-O-Lakes Pathway (xc ski)................................1-800-882-5801
Crystal Mountain Ski Resort 1-800-YOUR-MTN
  or... www.crystalmtn.com
Betsie & Platte River Snowmobile Trails 1-800-882-5801

Leelanau Peninsula - "LAND OF DELIGHT"
Glen Arbor - Leland - Northport - Suttons Bay

If dune-swept "Cape Cod" shores, and quaint New England-style fishing villages are your idea of romantic, don't miss the Leelanau Peninsula!

Awesome Sleeping Bear Dunes National Lakeshore anchors the Southwest corner of the mitten's "little finger", and provides a perfect destination for romance. Discover secret picnic alcoves, hike to Sleeping Bear Point, laugh your way up the 150' Dune Climb, rent a canoe or cross country skis, wander the trails and boardwalks, or seek a vantage point on beautiful Pierce Stocking Scenic Drive. Do the Dunes!

Dazzling sunsets and Autumn forests set tiny **Glen Arbor** on fire. In winter, the Great Lake beaches are "a study in black & white - a stunning contrast", set off with a touch of color at South Manitou lighthouse. In summer, since the area's abuzz with activity, lovers seek the solitude of forest havens, and the hidden beaches of a sparkling inland jewel - Glen Lake.

Three communities stand out as representatives of the

peninsula's waterfront paradise. Leland, Northport, and Suttons Bay each have their own unique signature appeal, but share the ambiance of mast-filled harbor scenes reminiscent of those East coast seaside paintings.

Leland is perhaps the most old-word charming, with the Leland River cutting and curving through the town, and with it's unique "Fishtown" district filled with shanties, shops, and dockside dining. This is the departure point for cruises to the

Islands - North Manitou's 15,000 acre wilderness (a rugged two day trip), and South Manitou's simple solitude (plan a picnic, or schedule a tour, for an afternoon escape!). Shoreline cruises, with cash bar, are scheduled four evenings a week - or plan an on-board private party.

Wind slowly up scenic M-22 under cover of natural forest archways, past sun-dappled clearings peppered with wild flowers, and private beaches like Good Harbor at Pyramid Point. Destination *Northport,* the tip of the peninsula. In this most remote and rural harbor town, you'll find an irresistible "step-back-in-time" quality, highlighted by streamside water wheels, quaint shops and galleries, and lovely lakeside parks. Pack a picnic and head up to  the Grand Traverse Lighthouse Museum in Leelenau State Park. Seek out secluded Cathead Bay beach - a one mile hike to supreme privacy!

Take in a bandshell concert! Rent a mountain bike or cross-country skis to navigate those orchard-dotted roads and hillsides! Stop at an herb farm for garden tours and tea! Visit a winery for samples of liquid peninsula art! Follow the glistening shoreline to *Suttons Bay . . .*

Still picturesque, with a more suburban feel, this Southeast peninsula jewel invites the casual couple to boutiques and galleries galore, marinas, parks and beaches, and the scenic 15 mile Leelanau Trail - just perfect for hiking, biking, and skiing.

The sparkling water - a reflection of romance. The lush countryside - a multi-seasonal escape. The peninsula - "land of delight!"

Leelanau County C of C
616-256-9895
www.leelanau.com/chamber

Glen Lodge - GLEN ARBOR

*"a jewel . . .sparkling
on the lake"*

On the shore of one of the world's most beautiful lakes you'll find it - the Lodge of your dreams!

Each of three suites is furnished in "Up North" lodge style, with cedar wainscot, wallpaper and accessories effectively coordinated to carry out the theme. Each also boasts a spectacular view of Glen Lake. The Center View suite is most requested, perhaps because it has a romantic fireplace to settle down in front of on those crisp, cool evenings. Each suite has a fully furnished kitchen, lakeside great room, outdoor firepit and grill, and a notebook chock full of great suggestions for area things to do, hiking guides, menus, and useful visitor information.

While no weddings are hosted at the Lodge itself, ceremonies can be arranged at nearby Old Settler's Park. A beautiful setting anytime, the park offers a gazebo for outdoor weddings, or an indoor chapel for inclement weather. Spend your honeymoon (or anniversary) at Glen Lodge, however, and you'll be treated to wine and a lovely personal card in your suite.

The beautiful vistas of Sleeping Bear Dunes National Lakeshore, the beaches of Glen Lake and Lake Michigan, the serenity of this heavenly lodge. You owe it to yourself to kick back and take in a sunset for $85 per night off-season, and $650-750 per week during summer. Reserve 3-4 months in advance, though, for peak times.

Fall in love all over again at . . .

Glen Lodge
Lodge 616-334-4656 Office 810-695-2050
7953 S. Glen Lake Road, Glen Arbor 49636
No smoking in Lodge, please

Inn-spired Activities ————————————

Enjoy beautiful Glen Lake, the Dunes, and all the Peninsula!

The Legend of Sleeping Bear

According to Chippewa Indian legend, a mother bear and her two cubs, to escape a raging Wisconsin forest fire, attempted to swim across Lake Michigan to safety. As they neared the shore, the exhausted cubs lagged behind. The mother bear climbed a huge, solitary sand dune to keep vigil. The cubs perished, but she can still be seen, waiting and watching, in the form of Sleeping Bear Dune. Her cubs, sadly, are seen just offshore in the form of North and South Manitou Islands.

The Homestead - GLEN ARBOR

" 'America's freshwater resort' -
simply irresistible"

A heady perfume fills the air - the scent of the inland "sea", the aroma of tree-sifted breezes, the flower of romance. A rhapsody sounds - of gently lapping waves, of splashing waterfalls, of birds' song, of laughter. Dazzling images appear - sunsets melting, stars twinkling, water shimmering, eyes glowing with love. And the aura enfolds - sun-warmed sand, crisp snow, hot blazing bonfire, tender embrace.

Welcome to The Homestead - wilderness haven of sensual pleasures! Dozens of delightful discoveries await: Lake Michigan's dune-draped shores; Crystal River's cool, canoeable currents; Sleeping Bear's wooded wonderland; Leelanau Peninsula's peaceful panoramas; The Homestead's swimming pools, clay court tennis, shops, sauna, whirlpools, fitness and hiking trails, golf, exercise room, cross country ski trails, downhill ski runs, massage services, sailboats and canoes, snowshoe and bicycle tours, kayaking and tubing, bonfires, ice skating, sunbathing, nature walks and yoga, kite flying, Lifetime Skills© lessons (in golf, tennis, sailing, skiing and snowboarding), crafts, star-gazing, and just plain fun. Whew!

Do it all - or do nothing at all - just "lose yourselves in the surroundings", and re-discover romance!

Wander the woods or beach and drink in the "remarkable" natural beauty. In summer, enjoy a sunset toast at Cafe Manitou or a picnic lunch *Dining* from Cavanaugh's market. In winter, a *Delights* cocoa break at CQ's Cabin, or a fireside snack at Whiskers. Treat yourselves to an intimate, informal Northern Italian dinner at Nonna's Ristorante - inside timber, fieldstone, and open-fireplace warmth, or outside "au-natural" ($8-20). Or, to an intimate overnight rendezvous in your private accommodation . . .

The Homestead offers several tranquil and appealing lodging options: 77 private-entrance Fiddler's Pond Guest Rooms - Standard rooms, or Deluxe with fireplace and tub-spa ($69-150); 14 ultra-romantic Suites in Little Belle, with sitting area, wet bar, fireplace, and 2-person spa tub ($89-200 depending on dates); private one bedroom condominiums - in quaint Fiddler's Pond, on a ridge overlooking Lake

Michigan, on Crystal River's banks, or on a private beach - for seasonal rates of $120-388 nightly (weekly rates and larger condos available), or in brand new Stony Brook Lodge, with spectacular Lake views, for $191-355.

Be sure to ask about "Just for Two", and special holiday getaway packages. The Homestead begins accepting summer reservations in early February, and winter reservations in early September (resort is open early May to late October, and mid-December to mid-March).

Resort regulars eagerly await the mid-summer 1998 re-opening, after renovation, of the original "Homestead" Inn, which will offer a small number of "premium" rooms ($120-300) and one bedroom suites ($210-375). The Inn provides the only hotel-style accommodations right on the water.

There's always something new to look forward to at The Homestead. This is a place of "transformation" - theirs, and yours "from stressed-out to mellow"!

So . . . energize! fantasize! *Romanticize!* at . . .

The Homestead
616-334-5000
Wood Ridge Road, Glen Arbor 49636
Some smoking accommodations available

Inn-spired Activities ——————————

Rent kayaks, river tubes, and bicycles to explore; go stargazing at the Leelanau School Observatory; wander the National Park trails and wooded hillsides for magnificent vistas of Lake Michigan; watch an unforgettable-in-any-season sunset from our grounds, or from Sleeping Bear Point, Glen Arbor beach, Good Harbor beach, or Otter Creek beach (Empire); come for the glorious color in Autumn!

"And what's romance? Usually, a nice little tale where you have everything As You Like It, where rain never wets your jacket and gnats never bite your nose and it's always daisy-time.

                         - D. H. Lawrence

The Sylvan Inn - GLEN ARBOR

"a gem of a place ...
in a gem of an area"

Y our hosts believe "The romance is in the experience of merely being here. Taking hikes and being the only ones on the trail; enjoying beaches, sunsets, lakes, and forests; sitting on the porch at 10 pm and listening - to the dead quiet. There's something really magical about this area."

"Relax - get on Glen Arbor time!"

"There's a certain *feeling* about this Inn that's very special" they say. Original plank flooring sets the tone for the Americana-style common areas. Guests relax, as well, on the outdoor patio,

 and white-wicker filled wrap porch. It's country living at its best!

This is y*our* Inn, and your hosts will do what they can to make your stay a special one. It's very informal and relaxed, with a great deal of fun and laughter. Guests get involved here (if they wish), and wrapped up in the spirit of it all.

Believing that "the magic of our Inn is the surroundings", your hosts will become "tour guides extraordinaire". They know all the beaches, trails, and restaurants, the biking tours, cross-country ski and showshoe trails, on the entire peninsula. Whatever *your* idea of twosome activities may be (there's lots here!), they can tell you all about it. "Your discoveries are endless!"

Remember, the Inn is closed and November, and mid-March to June 1. You'll want to call extra early for weekend visits in July and August or Color Tour especially if you want to reserve one of the seven rooms or suites with private bath ($90-125. Seven shared-bath rooms start at $60).

Each room is light and airy, with lots of pillows, fluffy comforters, antiques, iron or brass beds, and a traditional/country "Laura Ashley" sort of feel. Summer breezes and ceiling fans cool your room and its sitting area (with TV and phone - though feel free to unplug both!)

The demi-suite features cupola-skylight, sitting room, and kitchenette. Two extra large rooms have a private entrance, but #3 is the favorite - it's the only room on the same level as the common whirlpool and sauna. Most requested, though, is the very private and exquisite top floor "Penthouse" Room. With its vaulted ceiling, and a deck overlooking Lake Michigan, it's a wonderful place for star-gazing!

Wake to a Continental Plus Breakfast, served in the parlor (or take to your room). Fresh fruits, muffins, croissants, mini-breads, and beverages will start your day deliciously!

Plan to visit soon - "It's such a neat place for people to be!"

The Sylvan Inn
616-334-4333
M-109, P.O. Box 648, Glen Arbor 49636
Smoking outdoors only please

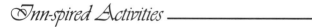

Enjoy a canoe trip on scenic Crystal River; hike our nature trails, and chill-out on our fabulous beaches!

Aspen House - LELAND

"'s wonderful, 's marvelous"

*N*o stress here! Only a candle-lit barn for your nightly "welcome-home!", and the comfortably intimate ambiance of "old world charm". . .

This restored 1880s farmhouse welcomes guests all year to its 3 grand guest rooms, and spacious "overstuffed" living room. Traditional and elegant, but not *too* formal decor "wraps you in absolute comfort". A cozy fireplace, clock collection, library of books, and cold-weather afternoon tea, set the tone for your relaxation. During Winter months, this common area is lighted by the soft glow of kerosene lamps. *Warning!* This setting may inspire you to "pop the question"! It's been known to happen here.

Reserve 2-3 months in advance for peak weekends, and select the large downstairs Pine Room with sleigh bed, love seat, private entrance, and deck with Adirondack furniture; the Victorian, with antique Belgium furniture and Battenburg lace accents; or the honeymooners' favorite Aspen Room in French country decor, with garden views, and a 2-person spa tub. Family collections, down comforters, private baths, and soft terry robes grace each guest room. A very comfy common sitting room is situated between the upstairs suites. Lose yourself in these light and airy spacious suites, complete with soaps, lotions, and love potions!

Standard rates of $100-125 include day-long coffee, tea and refreshments in the pantry, and evening snacks and desserts, as well as a Gourmet Breakfast served on different antique dishes every day. Sample "Artichoke or Spinach and Swiss Cheese Crepes" with fresh homegrown herbs, "Crustless Quiche", "Asparagus Baked Eggs", or "Grilled Parmesan Vegetables" complemented by "Herb & Onion Potatoes", Fruit Soup (in season), homemade bread and scones, and beverages.

On request, your hosts will prepare a light soup or stew meal for Friday evening, and a special Saturday dinner (off season only). Want a picnic? Want to borrow some snowshoes? Just ask. Ask, too, about walking and hiking trails, local activities and dining, and a private beach location and some kindling wood for a bonfire and a peaceful sunset moment!

A maximum of fifty guests can be accommodated for your outdoor wedding and reception or party. Advance warning is required, of course, for this, and for special treatment to celebrate your anniversary or occasion. Gift Wrapping and Herb Classes, and Holiday packages are available, and any type of custom package can be arranged.

Join the revelers, the "relaxers", and the wildlife, for a true romantic getaway, at . . .

Aspen House Bed & Breakfast
1-800-762-7736 or 616-256-9724
1353 N. Manitou Trail West, P.O. Box 722, Leland 49654
www.laketolake.com
email: aspen@netonecom.net
Smoking outdoors only, please

Inn-spired Activities ———————————
Visit our four wineries, and restaurants; enjoy beauti-
ful beaches, and hiking and nature trails; go to Sleeping Bear Dunes, Leland's historic Fishtown, and fabulous Interlochen!

Snowbird Inn - LELAND

" 'Leelanau's Grand Lady' ...
above all else, a romantic place."

*T*his "visually romantic" Inn, situated on a peaceful 18 acres of rolling meadows, is known for its "country serenity", individualized service, and "bountiful breakfasts"!

The broad veranda and beautiful gardens will appeal to you hopeless romantics, as will the cozy interior - filled with antiques, fresh "Snowbird" flowers, and whimsical, quirky little odds and ends to delight and amuse you. Your hosts are continually upgrading, so you will always be surprised!

Though the area is loaded with things to do, you may just wish to enjoy the gardens and orchards or walk the scant 1/4 mile past the secluded pond to the private access beach behind the Inn. Walk the beach, enjoy the beautiful island view and sunsets, and just be alone.

Return to the Snowbird and bury yourselves in romantic music and books in the cozy, inviting library. For your "snackin'" pleasure, find the bottomless cookie jar, or one of the many candy dishes placed throughout the house, and request coffee, tea, cocoa, iced tea, or raspberry lemonade to go with.

Best room choices for a "rendezvous" would be "Thelma" with its pink moiré, floral decor, and twinkling Victorian Christmas tree "nightlight"; or the Pearle, downstairs and done in rich colors (each with private connecting bath). To assure your choice, be sure to call in Winter for busy July and August weekends. Current rates are $115-140, but ask about off-season weekend packages that include a dining out experience Friday, and "dining in" Saturday evening.

Custom romantic packages, or very small weddings, can be arranged, and picnic lunch baskets packed for you. Snowbird hosts try to respect guest privacy, but will recognize your special occasion, if you wish, with a privately served porch breakfast, or a complimentary dessert treat at a local eatery. (The Inn is closed mid-to-end of December - call for availability).

Breakfast is served in the formal dining room, or on the porch in appropriate weather, at your pre-arranged hour. Four separate courses may include the favorite "Angel Puff - a soufflé-style egg/cheese dish", "Seafood Spinach Quiche", "Blueberry Creamcheese Muffins", or "Granny Smith Apple-Pumpkin Bread", along with homemade yeast breads, pancakes, waffles, French toast, and fruit. "You won't need lunch!"

You can *Be Pampered ... or Be Left Alone*, at . . .

Snowbird Inn Bed & Breakfast
616-256-9773
473 N. Manitou Trail, P.O. Box 1124, Leland 49654
www.leelanau.com/snowbird

Inn-spired Activities ————————————

Take a spectacular Fall Color Tour; in summer, take a sand chair, a towel, a book and each other to Good Harbor Beach or the dunes & find a little sand nook of your own; in winter, go to the beach - it's wild & gorgeous! Go to the lighthouse, walk around, explore those places you never see!

The Highlands - LELAND

"privacy blends with peaceful harmony"

A gently flowing multi-level rock fountain spills into a meandering stream. Delightful sun-splashed gardens frame the cedar-sided, contemporary Inn. Tucked back into a peaceful cul-de-sac "forest" of white pine,

guests here will "feel they are all alone in the world".

Four private rooms have a separate entrance from the main house. Each mini-suite features a different rich and elegant decor, ranging from contemporary to old-fashioned appeal. Rooms are large and comfortable, with full, private bath, sitting area, and kitchenette complete with wet bar, microwave, small refrigerator, packets of coffee and tea, and wine glasses. You needn't budge from your haven!

Breakfast, a leisurely buffet-style Continental repast featuring muffins, coffee cakes, fruit and beverages is set out in the Great Room from 8:30-10:30.

High ceilings and a massive stone fireplace give you that "ski-lodge" feeling, though the more traditional furnishings are comfortable and charmingly eclectic, and accented with interesting contemporary artwork.

Following a full day of adventure, relax in the loft sitting area, or in your quiet suite ($95 nightly rate). Please call for availability, and reserve 1-2 months in advance for weekends. The Highland is currently open May 1-November 1, but that may change, so please call.

Your hosts will assist with arrangements for your small wedding or reception if you are unfamiliar with local services.

"If you seek a beautiful peninsula, come to Leelanau.
If you seek...romantic...accommodations, come to . . ."

The Highlands
616-256-7632 or 313-292-5503
612 N. Lake Street, P.O. Box 101, Leland 49654
Smoking outdoors, or on the deck, only

Inn-spired Activities ————————

Walk to Fishtown and downtown Leland; walk out on the dunes, and enjoy a sunset at Pierce Stocking Drive; take a sunset cocktail cruise; experience our miles of beautiful beaches, unique shops, and wonderful scenic drives; stop by the Harbor Bar in Omena, and stare out at the water!

Whaleback Inn - LELAND

*"Northern exposure with
Southern Hospitality"*

Soft music and a roaring Winter fire greets you, a fishing lure collection delights you, and local products, art objects, and mementos tempt you in the registration area of this historic lodge's main building.

Former guests say "everything is perfect" at this charming lakeview Inn. Reserve a cozy Country-Victorian style room, or a "Log Room" with handcarved log bed (each one is different and can be ordered for your home) and private deck. Or perhaps you'd prefer a private Efficiency Unit with separate bedroom, dressing area, kitchenette, knotty pine paneled living room, and cozy fireplace (wood is furnished!). Rates vary from $59-159 with seasonal minimum stays.

All accommodations at the Whaleback have simple, but warm and lovely decor, private bath, a screen door, and a custom-made mattress and boxspring ("You've never slept on such a comfortable bed!").

To assure each guest's peaceful and pampered stay: The Inn is known for its quiet time - from 10 pm to 7 am; bedding is hung on the line and pillow cases starched and ironed; fresh-cut flowers adorn each room in summer, and are planted around windows to spread sweet scents; and your hosts spend a lot of time with you (more in Winter!) to acquaint you with the area.

Reservations will be made for you at local eateries (Whaleback patrons enjoy special treatment!) or appointments will be set up with one of 2 on-call masseuses, or for your private time in the "adults only" sauna and spa room (locked and cleaned after each guest). Let your hosts know you're celebrating a special occasion, so they can arrange a fruit basket with local wine and cheese!

For your additional enjoyment, take advantage of the private 200' Lake Leelanau beach, docks, and waterfront sundeck; "white wicker" porch, benches, swings, lawn furniture, and sand volleyball court. Or, settle into the Inglenook Room - the lakeview common area (open 24 hours) with fireplace, card table, and kitchen. Help yourself to coffee, hot chocolate, tea or ice anytime. Popcorn, pizza and candy bars are on the honor system. Read and relax, or even cook a minimal light meal. Winter guests can try out the new snowshoe trail through the forest in back.

On pleasant Summer days, and off-season weekends, a Continental Breakfast of fruit, yogurt, cereals, beverages and homebaked goods is served on the porch overlooking the lake. Surely a relaxing way to start your day!

Relaxation, beauty, and romance . . . a winning combination for romance, at . . .

Whaleback Inn
616-256-9090 or 1-800-WHALEBACK
M-22, P.O. Box 1125, Leland 49654
www.leelanau.com/whaleback
email:wbi@wfn.net
Smoking in designated areas on grounds only

Inn-spired Activities ————————————

Take the trip to Manitou - swim in a quiet, secluded cove; tour our wineries; take a box lunch or cheese and crackers and enjoy the sunset anywhere on Lake Michigan!

North Shore Inn - NORTHPORT

"for 'a love affair to remember'"

*E*ven the food will make you fall in love with this sensational Inn! Handmade hors d'oeuvres and aperitifs from 4-6 pm welcome you in style - as if the comfortable ambiance of a spacious Colonial-style home, and its fabulous, peaceful shoreline location aren't enough!

You never know what unique gourmet delights you'll sample here as a part o the delicious Full Breakfast, but it will definitely be memorable. "Cherry Pecan Scones" may complement your entrée, along with muffins, coffee cake, sausage, bacon, and even edible flowers on your fruit plate! Guests may return 5-6 years later and still be talking about their last repast!

May-October you can admire the million-dollar view from the common room's huge bay window, the English perennial gardens, the sand beach, or the decks and patios. Music lovers may play the grand piano or Hammond organ, while movie lovers may watch a collected classic on the VCR. Play a game, take a refreshing swim, or simply watch the boats and swans drift by!

Your privacy is assured in any of the four deluxe sound-proof rooms/suites - each appointed with private bath, its own unique fireplace, and an engaging view of Grand Traverse Bay. Spend your tranquil interlude in the Heritage Room - Americana style with handmade quilt, fully-equipped kitchen, and private patio and courtyard; the Bayshore Room - a warm retreat with walnut walls and bookshelves, carpet of deep forest green, English chintz, and private screened porch; the Wedgewood Suite with private sitting room, canopy bed, and blue & white seclusion; or the Country Rose Room with its brass bed, rose pattern quilt, and private balcony. Awaken to the gentle lapping (or wildly crashing!) waves, the singing birds, and to morning coffee delivered to your room.

Honeymoon or anniversary couples will delight in fresh flowers and complimentary in-room champagne, so be sure to tell the Innkeeper when you reserve. And, be sure to reserve your room up to one year in advance, though you *may* be able to find a spot by calling after January 1. (Rates from $135-145).

Remember, you're the guest! "Hire no gardener, hire no cook, hire no maid - it's all here!" at . . .

North Shore Inn
616-386-7111
12271 N. Northport Point Road, Northport 49670
Smoking outdoors only, please

Inn-spired Activities ——————————————

Bring your bikes; we'll loan you a blanket for a picnic in the park; peruse the Peninsula shops; stroll through the marina and up the charming, safe Main Street for ice cream or hot bakery cinnamon rolls on the banks of the creek!

Old Mill Pond Inn - NORTHPORT

"a magical place . . ."

"**C**ome with a sense of adventure - this is not a run of the 'old mill' place!", says the innkeeper. This very unusual, but very special, Inn is overstuffed with so many architectural features and collectible items you'll never see them all in one visit!

Guests come from all over the world to experience the host's unique brand of hospitality-with-humor, and to appreciate the lovingly arranged furnishings, whimsical eclectic decor, original folk art, and magical lighting effects in each room. Guest comfort and pleasure is most important - you can put your feet up anywhere, you can set things anywhere, and you can curl up anywhere! Melt into the warmth of knotty pine paneling, Oriental rugs, and overstuffed sofas. Seek out private spaces in so many corners of the house. Bring back your local wine and cheese to enjoy on the patio, or wrap-around screen porch with its white wicker and tiny white lights. Admire the statuary, majestic fountain, and twinkling lights in the enchanting formal

gardens (and equally enchanting informal peren-nial gardens). Play the grand pi-ano; plan your gar-den wedding, complete with harp and flute; stroll the grounds; over-look the pond; and be together. Of the five rooms at the Old Mill Pond, only two offer private bath, plus the third floor room with 1/2 bath (and cooling skylight and fan). Couples don't seem to mind, however, and frequently request the unusually deco-rated "Wedding Room", or the other room with its massive canopy bed. $75 for a share-bath room, and $95 for private bath, includes a Full breakfast - served on the screen porch in good weather or the formal dining room if weather worsens. Breakfast fare is more traditional, though interest is added with fresh herbs. Meat dishes are served on the side, for those with dietary concerns.

You'll want to reserve your room at least 2 months in advance for weekends (Inn is open May - Oct.), though there's always a possibility of last minute space availability.

Feel the history, find the humor, feel the power of love . . . at . . .

Old Mill Pond Inn
616-386-7341
202 W. 3rd Street, Northport 49670
Smoking on porches or in garden only

Inn-spired Activities ———————————

Go to Peterson Park and catch the sun setting into the lake and lighting up the bluffs; discover our delightful shops, boutiques and galleries, and lovely beach walks; this village has a slow pace that'll knock your socks off!

Century Farm - SUTTONS BAY

> *"it's captivating, it's bewitching,*
> *it's love..."*

*A*nd, it's a beautifully restored and maintained 100+ year old farmhouse-turned-Inn! Have your in-room decanter filled with wine or water - your choice - and settle into one of the main farmhouse rooms. Perhaps the Lincoln Room with its imposing bed, deep blue accents, and presi-

dential memorabilia - sharing a bath with the Folk Art Room with its aged brass bed. For more private trysts, why not choose the Cottage Room - airy, refreshing, and filled with vines and flowers; the Manor Suite - so spacious; or the Great Lakes Suite - with private deck (and private breakfast served on deck - weather permitting!) Each of these exhibits stylish classic period decor, and offers private bath facilities. The ultimate in romantic hideaways here would have to be the newly opened Stone Cottage, and Log Cabin. Stone or hand-hewn log walls, warm wood accents, wood-burning stoves, and clawfoot tubs provide cozy (though up to date) reminders of what life used to be - down on the farm!

Century Farm is a wonderful getaway in any season, at rates of $75-125, but be sure to call for reservations a minimum of one month in advance for busy Summer weekends.

While away the afternoon in the comfortable living room or library, tinkle a tune on the disc-piano, or soak away your cares in the outdoor back-deck Jacuzzi®. Ski or hike the pasture trail across the creek bridge, or borrow a Century Farm bicycle for a leisurely country tour.

Experienced kayakers may inquire about kayak rentals. Marriage minded couples may inquire about arrangements for outdoor weddings, and catered receptions (200 guests max).

Every guest at Century Farm enjoys a Full complimentary Breakfast with fresh fruits, homemade breads, quiches, espresso, and a variety of beverages.

No phones, no TV, just pure "down home" relaxing, at . . .

Century Farm Bed & Breakfast
616-271-2421 or 1-800-252-8480
2421 Jacobson Road, Suttons Bay 49682
Sorry, no smoking indoors

Inn-spired Activities ————————————

Enjoy our local beaches, shops and restaurants; go sightseeing, boating, biking, skiing or just relax; go on a wine tasting expedition, and finish with some of our area's fine dining!

Dining Delights

Le Bear - Glen Arbor

... "Relaxed atmosphere, fun foods, cocktails, beautiful scenery, and romantic sunsets" - all for your personal pleasure! On the waterfront at Sleeping Bear Bay, overlooking the Manitou Islands, and inviting you to enjoy breakfast, lunch, and dinner specialties like "Personal Skillet", "Grizzly Bear Omelet", "Lemon Pepper Chicken", "Five Layer Veggie Lasagna", "Shrimp Coconut", "South Manitou Trout with shrimp, tomato, pepper and cilantro lime butter", or "Stuffed Chicken Breast with goat cheese, herbs, and apple cream sauce" (am $3.95-7.95, mid-day $5.95-8.95, pm $7.95-14.95). Homemade breads and pies, late night snacks and carry-outs, and "Teddy Bear" picnics on their beach. It's Bear-ly believable!
Open 7 days / Outside dining on the deck / Banquet room seating 250 / Full Bar / Occas. entertainment, bands, dancing
5707 Lake Street • 616-334-4640

Dining Delights

La Bécasse - Burdickville

"French Country" is the theme in this cozy, off the beaten path entry into the Northern Michigan world of fine dining. It's purely *country* in location, sitting alone in the woods on a quiet side road near Glen Arbor. It's highly *French* in cuisine - skip the formality, but add the artful sauces, herbs, and wine glazes. Sample "Acorn Squash Timbale" or "Salad of Chevre & Dried Cherries", before your entrée of perhaps "Grilled Escalopes de veau", "Venison with red wine sauce", or "Chicken Breasts with basil mousse in croustades of potato ($17-25). Add a bottle of French wine for a *real "flavour de Francé". Ooh, la la!*
Open May - Oct. / Full bar and wine list / Smoking section available / Private parties possible
9001 S. Dunns Farm Road • 616-334-3944

Dining Delights *Leelanau Country Inn - Maple City*

Unlock the secrets of the sea at this quaint country-cottage restaurant! Fresh, fresh seafood and fish are flown in daily to highlight an extensive menu so creative and freshly prepared it's changed and printed daily! Start with "Pan Fried Alligator", signature "Swiss Onion Soup", or a Specialty Salad. Dining delights may include "Skate Wings Almondine", "Whole Stuffed Lobster Leelanau", "Innstyle Beef Stroganoff", Prime Rib, "Apple Stuffed Chicken with cherry glaze", or "Broiled Boston Scrod with lemon pecan butter sauce", and much, much more ($9.95-28.95). Let your hosts know it's a special occasion - you'll be pleasantly surprised! Plan an evening on the porch, or in a cozy dining room, plan your wedding in the garden, but plan to stop in soon!

Closed Sundays - call for seasonal hours - last seating 9 pm / Reservations a must / A non-smoking property / Full bar & wine list / Private parties more flexible off-season / Six European-style shared-bath bed & breakfast rooms available upstairs $45 M-22/ 8 mi. S. of Leland • 616-228-5060 *or 1-800-COOK-441*

Dining Delights *Kejara's Bridge - Lake Leelanau*

"Feed your senses!" at this charmingly small "deli-style coffee-house" and gallery. Featuring local Native American artwork on display, scheduled live acoustic music, natural deli foods like "House Salad with feta cheese, red grapes, walnuts and romaine", or "Chicken Walnut Salad Sandwich with dried cranberries and celery on a whole wheat kaiser roll", fruit smoothies, juice and coffee drinks. Take some to go, or dine in and soak up some culture!

Call for hours, entertainment schedule, and for take out service / A non-smoking property
202 W. Main Street • 616-256-7720

*Dining
Delights*

The Bluebird - Leland

Relax in the Early Bird "diner" for breakfast and lunch of Omelets, waffles, skillets and specialties ($3.25-5.25), Whitefish Sandwich, Reuben, Fajitas, and "Raspberry Chicken Salad with fresh vegetable and fruit" ($3.95-5.25). Or, find the casual evening comfort of the separate Blue Bird bar with Sandwiches, Baskets, "Cherry Chicken Salad Sandwich", or "Black Bean Navajo Taco in Indian fry bread" ($3.50-6.95), and the dining room for meals like "Good Harbor Chicken with dried cherry chutney", "Filet Mignon Au Poivre with cognac cream", or "Pecan Crusted Rainbow Trout" ($10.95-18.95). Sunday brunch includes appetizers, salads, desserts and pastries, breakfast dishes, carved roast beef and ham, and other lunch creations.

Open all year / Smoking in designated areas / Full bar in Blue Bird / Private parties possible
102 E. River Street • 616-256-9081

*Dining
Delights*

The Cove - Leland

Soak up the sunshine or sunset on the riverfront patio, deck, or in the Sunset Dining Room. Order up a bottle of "Summer Sunset" wine, and "cruise" into fabulous casual dining amongst nautical splendor. They'll cook your own fresh-caught fish, or serve up fresh Whitefish specialties like "Campfire Whitefish - baked in foil", or "Parchment Baked Lemon-pepper Whitefish". Try "Grilled Fresh Veggies and cheese", "Chicken Salad in a melon half", or "Chicken Monterey Sandwich" for lunch ($5.95-7.95); "Seafood Pie", Filet, Prime Rib, or Pasta dishes for dinner ($11.95-15.95/menu changes yearly). The perfect ending? Their "Key Lime Pie". Service, food, and view! Spectacular!

Closes in October-early May / Smoking in designated areas / Just Call ahead for parties/reservations / Full bar & wine list
111 River Street • 616-256-9834

Dining Delights   𝒯*he* 𝒪*verlook* at Leland Lodge - Leland

Overlook the golf course and the lake from the casual contemporary dining room, or hillside deck. Settle back for a refreshing beverage, "Sandwich Wrap", "Oven Roasted Turkey Sandwich" (roasted here), or other luncheon option ($4.95-5.95). Ask about a picnic basket lunch! Start your dinner with "Toasted Ravioli" or "Fishtown Dip - a secret recipe warm whitefish dip". Then try fresh Whitefish, "Stir Fry or Fajitas", Ribs, Veal, Chicken, Steak or Pasta specialties like "Portabello Mushroom Ravioli (8.95-14.25). Enjoy!

Closed in March - open 7 days Mem. Day to Labor Day / Reservations accepted for large groups only / Smoking in limited designated areas or on deck / Banquet room seats 150-200, total max seating for parties 350 / Full bar and wine list
565 Pearl Street • 616-256-9848

Dining Delights   𝒯*he* 𝒞*Riverside* 𝒮*nn* - Leland

Arrive by boat, car, or on foot - you'll find this renovated Inn set alongside the peaceful Leland River, offering "Riverside" dining on the deck or in the dining room. Breakfast, lunch, and dinner guests alike enjoy a casual atmosphere and "innovative" menu selections like "Riverside Benedict with smoked gouda", "French Toast made with Stonehouse cherry-walnut bread and Sugarbush maple syrup", "Quiche du jour with fresh fruit", "Grilled Portabello Sandwich", "Chicken Caesar Salad", "Bronzed Whitefish", "Riverside Jambalaya", "Sundried Diavolo with linguine", or "Rotisserie Chicken" (breakfast $4.50-6.25, lunch $4.25-6.25, dinner $12.50-21.95). Relax - Riverside!

Open all year - call for hours / Smoking in designated areas / Full bar and world-class wine list / Private parties possible / Reservations accepted / Eight cozy B & B rooms avail. upstairs
302 River Street • 616-256-9971

Fresh table flowers, scenic Michigan photos, fresh "from scratch" quality gourmet food, smooth jazz, daily menu surprises, a roaring fire or screen-porch garden view seating - "everything combined will make for a great experience". Perhaps a luncheon of "The Northporter - chicken salad with dried cherries, walnuts & celery on lettuce & tomato", or "Parmesan Crusted Whitefish Sandwich with red pepper remoulade & daily side salad" ($5-7); or dinner of "Broiled Whitefish with tomatillo salsa", "Grilled Salmon with sweet red pepper beurre blanc", or "Vodka Penne pasta with shrimp, vegetables, & portabello mushrooms" ($10-18). September, October, & November - a *great* time for quiet dinners just for two!

Open all year / Check for closed dates and entertainment schedule / Reservations recommended / Private parties in separate back dining room / Full bar & wine list / Smoking areas
115 Waukazoo • 616-386-7611

 Dining Delights　　*Woody's Settling Inn*- *Northport*

This is the place where "life is serious, but food is fun!" They "concentrate on foods & their preparation" ("you can't eat the decor!"), and "recommend everything". A very casual atmosphere serves up food treats like homemade Soups, Tabouleh Salad, Sandwiches, and "Grilled Tuna Steak Sandwich" for lunch ($4.50-8.95). Dinner menu of Chicken, Grilled & Broiled Fish, Prime Rib, Steaks, "Crab Cakes", "Flaming Cheese", "3-Soup Sampler with Italian Bread Stix", or "Cherry Smoked Chicken", and "BBQ Ribs" ($9.95-14.95). "Real cooking...quality food...reasonable prices".

Closed most major holidays / Smoking in designated areas / Outdoor dining on deck / Full bar and wine list
116 Waukazoo • 616-386-9933

Cafe Bliss - *Suttons Bay*

Come here for a "dining experience - not just to eat!", and a wonderful combination of romantic ambiance, gourmet recipes, and healthful fare. Starting with fresh, natural ingredients, Vegetarian and Ethnic dishes, and adding Seafood, Fish, and Fowl for: late breakfasts featuring "Rio Grande Breakfast Burrito", "Florentine Eggs Benedict", and "Stuffed Vanilla French Toast" ($4.75-6.95); luncheons including "Dijon Chicken Salad", "Salmon Roasted in Parchment", or "Kedgeree- curried brown rice with tofu, spices and salad" ($5.25-8.95); and dinners like "Pan Fried Walleye", "Chicken Stir Fry", or "Linguini Brasilia with sundried tomatoes, mushrooms, and garlic sauce" ($10.95-14.95). Take out for picnics, too!

Closed Nov. -Memorial Day / A non-smoking property / Private parties possible / Full Bar / Reservations helpful
  In Uptown Suttons Bay on M-22 • 616-271-5000

Dining
Delights

Hattie's - *Suttons Bay*

You'll love the fresh contemporary atmosphere and scrumptious gourmet cuisine here. The menu changes frequently, but you might find totally addictive dishes like "Mushroom Ravioli with morel cream sauce", "Tequila Lobster - medallions with lime/butter/tequila sauce", "Grilled Venison with tart cherry BBQ sauce", or "Grilled Duck with mustard & bourbon" ($16-30). The chef recommends you try "one of each, but start with dessert!" Or, stop in *just* for a sweet treat. Ask about early pre-theater dining, to be followed by a first-run or foreign film at charming Bay Theater. Original!

Open all year - 7 days in summer / Reservations recommended / Limited Smoking area avail. / Custom planned private parties possible / Full bar and extensive wine list
  111 St. Joseph • 616-271-6222

À Deux Adventures

- Glen Arbor, Leland, Northport & Suttons Bay

Glen Arbor - Maple City - Empire
Good Harbor Grill (breakfast, lunch) 616-334-3555
Leelanau School Observatory 616-334-5890
Schoolhouse Cafe (breakfast, lunch, dinner) 616-228-4688
    take out 616-228-6692
Southwest Seaplane (air tours) 616-590-4438
Outrider (horseback riding, hayrides) 616-326-5150

Leland
Good Harbor Vineyards 616-256-7165
Manitou Island Transit (cruises) 616-256-9061
Sugar Loaf Resort (skiing) 616-228-5461
    or 1-800-968-0576

Lake Leelanau
Key to the County (casual fine dining) 616-256-5397
Northport - Omena
Baypointe Resort (wave runner rentals) 616-386-5491
Grand Traverse Lighthouse 616-386-7553
Stormy C Services (inflatable & jet ski rentals) 616-620-2829
Willowbrook Ice Cream Parlor/Restaurant 616-386-5617
Leelanau Wine Cellars 616-386-5201

Suttons Bay
Busha's Brae Herb Farm 616-271-6284
Geo Bikes (bike & xc ski rentals) 616-256-9696
Hose House Deli & Historic Fire House (lunch) 616-271-6303
The Ice Cream Factory 616-271-6788
The Leelanau Trail .... 616-946-7650 Ext. 148
L. Mawby Vineyards 616-271-3522

Grand Traverse Bay -
Traverse City & Old Mission Peninsula

*H*ow perfectly romantic! Spend a day on the Bay! Fair weather frolics are abundant and inviting here. Ahoy, Mateys! Consider sailing the clear blue waters aboard the "swashbuckling" schooner Malabar, or skimming the waves in a more contemporary craft - the Nauti-Cat cruising catamaran. Take charge of your own water adventure with rented paddle-

boats, jet skis, rowing skulls, sailboards, sailboats, ski boats or houseboats.

Prefer "sailing" with a birds'-eye view? Try parasailing, paragliding, paramotoring, airplane tours, soaring, or a Sunrise Sweetheart champagne flight in a hot air balloon! What sensational ways to celebrate your years together, or "pop the question"! Up, up, and away!

Landlubbers relish the tranquil splendor of the bay from shoreline parks, bicycle and walking paths (ample parking at the West End Beach or the State Park on the East side). Spiking up through the center of the bay is spectacular Old Mission Peninsula - with fragrant Spring cherry blossoms, golden beaches, sparkling inlets, and glorious Fall color displays. Do you hear a picnic calling? Several nearby delis and take-outs will be pleased to pack your basket!

Off-the-bay adventures abound with hiking, cross-country skiing, shopping, horseback riding, hayrides and sleighrides, snowmobiling, canoeing, and guided tours of scenic spots, wildlife, and historic locales. Treat yourselves to quiet country drives, roadside fruit-stand stops, and Autumn color tours. Have a fun-filled afternoon of wine tasting or investigating local micro-breweries, and visit the only horsedrawn cider mill in Michigan.

Spent your "day on the bay"? Spend your night on the town! Dining and dancing are just the beginnings of evening excitement around Grand Traverse. Close by Interlochen Center for the Arts offer year-round concerts and performances by talented amateurs as well as big name headline entertainers. Summertime concert-goers revel in open-air outdoor sunset shows at the lakefront amphitheater. Take a linen and crystal pre-show "tailgate" picnic!

Live entertainment happens in local clubs and lounges, at Northwestern Michigan College's Dennos Center, at the Old Town Playhouse,   and the soon-to-be re-opened Michigan Ensemble Theatre. Jazz legends "get the beat" at Kodiak Supper Club & Saloon (and lots of other area spots), while college students "cabaret" at Dill's Olde Towne Saloon's summer "Golden Garter Revue". Put in your requests at numerous piano bars, sing-along at karaoke bars, take a "trip" on the Grand Traverse Dinner Train, and pick up a copy of *Traverse Area Entertainment Guide,* or the *Traverse City Express* for all the current "happenings".

See it, hear it, inhale it, taste it, feel it - the beauty of the bay!

Traverse City CVB
1-800-TRAVERS
616-947-5075
www.traverse.com

Bowers Harbor BED & BREAKFAST -
OLD MISSION PENINSULA
"your enchanting cottage-by-the-bay"

Set on the Old Mission Peninsula at Bowers Harbor, and boasting 200' of private sand beach, is a delightful 1870s farmhouse Inn.

Getaway from it all in Summer - swim, wade, walk the shoreline, or hike nearby trails. The neighboring marina offer

transient slips for your boat, or launch your jet skis just around the corner. Build yourself a bonfire on the beach, or settle on the fieldstone porch, get a bottle of wine, and enjoy the very best part - the sunset!

The view is equally mesmerizing in Winter, especially as you curl up by the living room fireplace after cross-country skiing or a Peninsula wine tasting excursion.

The three fresh, crisp, and spotless upstairs guestrooms share a private entrance. Room 3, with sitting area and attached private bath, overlooks apple and cherry orchards, beautiful in any season, and a perfect backdrop for the blue and white wicker furnishings. The Marina View room (#2) is smaller, with a private bath across the hall and soft peach floral decor. You'll love Room #1, with plenty of space, private sitting area and attached bath, and a fabulous Harbor view!

Waken to a Full Gourmet Breakfast. Chef's choice entrées may include "Eggs Benedict", with all your favorite accompaniments and beverages.

For luncheon or evening meals, bayside bistro and elegant dining options as well as a picnic-friendly park are within walking distance. Or, enjoy one of the other Peninsula or nearby Traverse City eateries.

Room Rates are $100-130 per night all year (no extra charge for peacefulness!), but be sure to reserve at leat 3-4 months in advance for the busy weekends. Do plan ahead, but plan to set your romantic spirit free at . . .

Bowers Harbor Bed & Breakfast
616-223-7869
13972 Peninsula Drive, Traverse City 49686
Smoking outdoors only, please

Inn-spired Activities ————————————————

Take a hike or cross-country ski nearby Pyatt Lake; appreciate the sunset together!

Château Chantal - OLD MISSION PENINSULA

"the winery, the lodging, the setting . . . cé magnifique!"

*T*ake a slow drive up the long and winding Rue de Vin. Suddenly, you're in the vineyards of France, and arriving at your private chateau - your "Old World Retreat". Actually, you've arrived at Old Mission Peninsula's imposing Château Chantal - home of quiet elegance, unsurpassed views, the finest wines, and classic hospitality.

You'll feel at home instantly here - the entrance and Great Room are much like a comfortable living room, with fireplace, and grand piano, overlooking the terrace and vineyards. During Summer, winery tour groups descend to the cellar for an explanation of the "science and magic" of the wine-making process. Whether it's in the tasting room (Great Room) or on the terrace, after a tour or during a special event, tasting the Château's selection of fine wines, sparkling wines, or unique "ice wine" will be a truly sensual experience.

This is a superb setting for weddings and other special occasions, which can be arranged on a limited basis. Ask for details.château Chantal also hosts Wine Weekend Seminars, weekly Jazz at Sunset (Thursday evening in Summer, Fridays in Fall), Harvest and Nouveau Release gatherings, and various holiday events. But there's more . . .

To make this an *exceptional* experience for two, why not plan a stay in one of the Château's Bed & Breakfast rooms. Be sure to reserve at least 6 months in advance for: The Rose Suite with its floral theme, and views of the sunset and the vineyards; The Pensée Room - upstairs on the sunrise side, with a stunning handmade quilt that's the focal point of a pansy flower theme; or The Merlot Room, with its oh-so-appropriate grape theme. (Future expansion plans are underway for 12 more suites - call for availability). Rates vary from $105-135.

Romantics who overnight here are served a Full Gourmet Breakfast, and enjoy the use of the tasting room at anytime. Waken to "Eggs Morney", "French Vanilla Almond Waffles", or other entrées to highlight your morning.

Amour! Amour! There's no need to travel to Europe for a "taste" of traditional European-style romance. Find it at . . .

Château Chantal
"Your Retreat to the Old World"
616-223-4110
15900 Rue de Vin, Old Mission Peninsula
Traverse City 49686
www.chateauchantal.com
email: ruedevin@pentel.net
Smoke free interior

Inn-spired Activities ———————

Take a Tall Ship cruise; take the horse and carriage ride in downtown Traverse City!

The Grainery - *TRAVERSE CITY*

"where hearts and warm memories merge"

*T*his is a *wonderful* place to escape! Follow your journey, or your day's activities with some mood-adjustment time in the Country Common Room, where afternoon desserts, snacks, and tea are served. Or, wander the 10 acre grounds of this "Gentleman's Country Inn", enjoy the pond, two golf greens, or the outdoor hot tub.

Your romantic rendezvous may be spent in one of two antique-filled Country Victorian rooms (each with private bath);

in The Enchanted Cottage - a secluded cabin that includes TV, phone, fridge, robes, and French doors to your private deck; or in one of two Carriage House suites, each with its own Jacuzzi® tub and cozy fireplace stove. Whichever you choose, you'll get a great night's rest - it's so peaceful and quiet you'll hear the frogs croaking and the fountain tinkling!

For only $65-75 (rooms), $75-105 (cottage), or $130 (suites), you'll get more than you bargained for here, as your hosts believe in making guests "totally happy with their experience". Guests become friends - almost family - and receive whatever they may need and want. Cottage and Carriage House accommodations even include intercom access to the main house!

Part of the marvelous hospitality is your home-cooked Gourmet Country Breakfast, served in the Pondview Breakfast Room, with outdoor "entertainment" provided by deer, turkeys, ducks, cranes, and the resident blue heron!

Be sure to plan ahead, for you won't want to miss the unmatched serenity, unmatched romantic ambiance, and unmatched service of . . .

The Grainery Bed & Breakfast
616-946-8325
2951 Hartman Road, Traverse City 49684
Search for them on the world wide web
No smoking, except in designated areas

Inn-spired Activities ————————————

Take in a performance at Interlochen; go to the Dennos Museum for special events, exhibits, and entertainment; enjoy our beaches; explore our historic district. Romance is still alive in Traverse City!

"It's unthinkable not to love . . ."
-*Lawrence Durrell*

𝒯all 𝒮hip "𝒞Malabar" - *TRAVERSE CITY*

"a floating bed & breakfast -
this 'protector of the sea'"

A Tall Ship Company representative says "There's something about sailing that awakens *all* your senses - you become more alive, more aware." And definitely more romantic!

Start with a 2 1/2 hour Sunset Sail, complete with a picnic-style meal, aboard this traditionaly rigged tall ship sailing vessel. Beer, wine, cocktails, and soft drinks are available on board this comfortable 105 ft. schooner. Prepare for a spectacular sunset, or, at the very least, a picturesque sampling of life on West Grand Traverse Bay. Certain nights, musicians entertain and delight you with ballads and sea chanteys (sing-along songs of the sea).

Overnight in one of eight cozy and rustic windjammer-style staterooms while docked at the end of Malabar's 800' pier. Snuggle into your built-in bunk, or (in appropriate weather) bring a sleeping bag and pad to cuddle on deck under the stars! While your bright, comfortable cabin is private, and contains a washbasin, you will share toilet facilities with other cabins in your section. Modern restroom and shower facilities are available on shore in the Tall Ship headquarters building. (Not normally the most romantic arrangement, but this unique and captivating experience is worth the small inconvenience). Rates of $175 double include a guarantee that the gentle, hypnotic motion of the ship on the gently lapping waves will lull you into a most restful slumber.

Greet the sun, rising impressively over Old Mission Peninsula, with coffee on deck while your Hearty Breakfast is being prepared by your "pirate" chef in the galley. Beverages, oatmeal, breads, and fruits, are complemented by an "anchor" dish such as pancakes, crepes, or egg specialties.

Your hosts post this "WARNING: This overnight experience is for those slightly more adventurous who would enjoy something new (and old) in the way of truly unique lodging!" Landlubbers, if it's not for you, consider taking just a two-hour lunchtime or afternoon sail, and taste the air. If you're an "old salt", and you find yourself yearning for an even longer stay at "sea" inquire about 3, 5, or 6 day journeys aboard the sister ship "Manitou".

The ultimate in precious wedding memories is created aboard the Malabar. Formal or casual ceremonies and receptions, for up to 45 guests, are customized events perhaps including catered hors d'oeuvres, cakes, box lunches, or elaborate meals. The beauty of the Bay and the uncommon traditional mystique of the ship reduce the need for extensive floral displays and decoration. A musical group may enhance the mood - perhaps nautical or classical melodies. Whatever your tastes and personalities, your celebration will certainly be a magical event!

So, you've planned to sail, and here you are - adrift in feelings of love. Adrift on . . .

Tall Ship Malabar
Traverse Tall Ship Co.
616-941-2000
13390 S. West Bay Shore Drive, Traverse City 49684

Grand Traverse Dinner Train -

Traverse City

All aboard! For a supremely romantic "sentimental journey", and an elegant dinner experience, too! Board one of four luxurious dining cars for a four-course luncheon with entrée choices like "Charlevoix Whitefish Salad", or "Breast of Chicken with raspberry cream" ($40 per person); or for a fabulous five-course dinner with selections like "Garlic Roasted Prime Rib", "Breast of Chicken stuffed with smoked duck and apples, with morel mushrooms and mustard-cider sauce", "Farm-raised Rainbow Trout with peach salsa and orzo", or "Tri-color Pasta with roast vegetable stuffing, and spinach-ricotta custard" ($55 per person). Enjoy a leisurely trip with lush spotlighted country scenery, and

special occasion trips like "Dinner with Winemakers", "Fall Color Excursions", or "Murder Mystery" trains. For wedding and parties, rent an entire car seating 56 guests, or the entire train for groups up to 224. For an event, an occasion, or just a brief escape . . . You're invited to "Come Choo-Chew!"

Trains run all year - call for available dates / Smoke free dining cars / Full bar and local wines / All tables seat four

Board at the historic depot, 8th & Woodmere
624 Railroad Place • 616-93-DEPOT

Dining Delights *Minervas, Park Place Hotel - Traverse City*

Sail away to the Mediterranean! Cool marble and an open, airy feel transport you to a world of menu delights like "Chicken Oriental Salad", "Mediterranean Pizza or Pasta" , "Spicy Spaghetti and Chicken Breast", "Lemon Luau Stir Fry with chicken, vegetables, peanuts and rice", "Bayou Burger", Rotisserie Chicken, "Cajun Pork Chop", or "Steak and Mushroom Broccoli Stir Fry" (lunch $4.95-8.95, dinner, $5.75-18.95). Yes!

Open all year / Smoking in designated areas / Full bar / Preferred seating policy - please call / Banquet facilities in Historic Park Place Hotel / Happy hours & early bird specials
300 E. State Street • 616-946-5093

Dining Delights *Windows - Traverse City*

Location! Location! Location! This restaurant seems to hang over the edge of Grand Traverse Bay with magnificent waterfront views from each table. It's an atmosphere of pure class, with first class service, and classic fine cuisine like "Crab Puffs", and "Mussels Provencal" for appetizers ($6-10); Daily Cajun, Vegetarian, and fresh Fish features, plus a bi-annually changing list of entrées like "Veal Champignon - medallions with a trio of mushrooms in brandy cream", "Le Duo - rice-stuffed Quail and Petite Filet", or "Marinated Duck" ($20-30), as well as famous desserts, a Prix Fixe early menu, and special events like "Mardi Gras". Marvelous!

Open all year - check seasonal hours / Smoke free / Private parties possible - call for details / Outdoor dining on deck / Full bar and very extensive wine list
7677 West Bay Shore Drive • 616-941-0100

Trillium Restaurant - Acme

A *top floor* bi-level contemporary glass-tower setting with stunning views of Grand Traverse Bay and millions of twinkling lights! *Top flight* candlelight service, coupled with *top shelf* cuisine featuring lighter fare mid-day treats of "Paninis (Italian Sandwiches)", "Nicoisse Sandwich with tuna, and anchovy vinaigrette", or Pastas with wild mushrooms and fresh sauces ($7-12); Salads; Wood-fired Pizza; and dinner entrées like "Steamed Salmon wrapped in a banana leaf on jasmine rice with tropical salsa", "Veal Chop with preserved lemons and rosemary", "Filet with fig sauce on wild mushrooms and spinach"; or "Whitefish in Italian Salsa" ($18-30). Go straight to *the top!*

Open all year for Dinners / Lunch daily June - Sept. / Smoking in designated areas - Cigar Room on 17th floor / Reservations recommended / Full bar and wine list / Parties possible for under 20 / Call for entertainment and dance schedule

Top floors in the Tower - Grand Traverse Resort
6300 U.S. 31 North, Grand Traverse Village • 616-938-5455

 Dining Delights *Bowers Harbor Inn* -Old Miss. Pen.

Crystal and linen, low lights, and an intimate corner table, combined with a waterfront sunset! Wow! This popular restaurant is newly remodeled, and now features fine aged beef like Prime Rib and a "28 oz. Porterhouse", in addition to the favorite "Fish in a Bag", and "South African Lobster", or specials like Veal, Duck, "Steak Diane", or Pasta dishes, all flavored with fresh herbs grown on the property. ($19-20 up to $50-60). Try the "Baked Smoked Whitefish Dip" appetizer. It's excellent, and rumored to be an exotic aphrodisiac!

Open all year / Smoking in designated areas / Reservations recommended / Parties and Celebrations Welcome / Full bar and extensive wine list / Fri. & Sat. entertainment in Summer / More casual dining in the adjacent "Bowery"

13512 Peninsula Drive • 616-223-4222

Dining Delights

Boathouse - *Old Mission Peninsula*

Exquisite Edibles invites you to ... "enjoy splendid sunsets, service, and special fare in our beautiful, casual beachside bistro on beautiful Bower's Harbor." Enjoy the sun, the sand, the surf, and "original...dining experiences" like "Boathouse Salad with dried apricots, cherries, toasted walnuts, red & yellow peppers, sprouts and raisin vinaigrette", and new menu items, to "break the dining monotony", like "Indonesian Duck", "Mediterranean Stuffed Peppers", and "Blackened Swordfish with Creole seafood cakes"(lunch $5.95-8.95, dinner $8.95-14.95). A place to dream, to dine, to launch a romantic encounter . . .

Open all year / Smoking in designated areas / Full bar and wine list / Reservations recommended / "Charming" Sunday Brunch / Outdoor dining on deck
14039 Peninsula Drive • 616-223-4030 • www.foodguys.com

Dining Delights

Old Mission Tavern - *Old Miss. Pen.*

A unique combination of fine food with fine art is the concept here. Outdoors - an English cottage garden, and a sculpture courtyard; indoors - Bella Galleria studio and gallery, adjacent to the cozy Pub, and light, bright Garden dining rooms. For casual luncheons - a variety of Sandwiches, wonderful homemade Soups, Salads and Pasta ($4-6). for more elegant, candlelit dinners - Steak, Prime Rib, Pasta, fresh exciting specials, or perhaps their "Chicken Artichoke" house specialty ($10-20). Groups of 50, or only two, are invited to dine, to browse, to fall in love . . .

Open all year / Smoking in pub / Full cocktail service / Private parties in gallery (max 50) / Reservations accepted
17015 Center Road • 616-223-7280

À Deux Adventures

- Traverse City, Old Mission Peninsula & Surrounding Area

Aqua Dog Boat Rental 616-938-2826
Bay Breeze Charter Sailing 616-941-0535
Bowers Harbor Vineyards 616-223-7615
Break 'n Waves, Inc. (watercraft rentals) 616-929-3303
Cathie's Tote and Dine® (take out) 616-929-4771
Chateau Grand Traverse (www.ectwines.com) 616-223-7355
Cherry Capital Aviation, Inc. (air tours) 616-941-1740
City Opera House (events & party facilities) 616-922-2070
Dennos Museum/Milliken Auditorium 616-922-1055
Dill's Olde Towne Saloon 616-947-7534
Exquisite Edibles (take out & delivery) 616-941-4529
Grand Traverse Balloons, Inc. (hot air ball. rides) 616-947-RIDE
Grand Traverse Limousine .... 616-946-LIMO or 1-800-350-4502
Grand Traverse Parasail 616-947-3938
Grand Traverse Tour & Travel (area tours) 616-947-TOUR
Hitchpoint Cider Mill 616-264-8371
Interlochen Center for the Arts 616-276-6230
Kodiak Supper Club & Saloon 616-941-4142
Lakeshore Carriage Tours 616-267-5795
Mackinaw Brewing Company 616-933-1100
Nauti-Cat (catamaran adventures, cruises) 616-947-1730
   www.nauti-cat.com or 1-800-743-1400
North Country Guide & Tour 616-929-2642
North Peak Brewery 616-941-7325
Old Mission Peninsula Cellars 616-223-4050
Old Town Playhouse 616-947-2443
Omelette Shoppe & Bakery .... 616-946-0590 or 616-946-0912
Organized Adventures (tours) 616-933-3279
Peninsula Cellars 616-223-4310
Pirates Cove Adventure Pk. & Family Bike Rental 616-938-9599
Ranch Rudolf (canoeing, riding, hay & Sleigh rides) 616-947-9529
Ruby's Water Sports Rentals 616-938-1100
Michigan Ensemble Theatre (State Theatre Bldg.) 616-929-7260
Traverse Bay Parasail 616-929-PARA
T. C. Carriage (horse-drawn carriage rides) 616-633-0753
T.C. Hangliders/Paragliders 616-922-2844

Bay Country - South - "Chain of Lakes"
Torch Lake area, Alden, Central Lake, Ellsworth

Year-round recreation and uncommonly beautiful natural splendors draw visitors to this Northern Michigan resort region. Local residents proudly share their "seasonal spectaculars" - Spring wildflowers, Summer sunsets, glorious Fall colors, and sparkling Winter hillsides.

So what's on the summer activities menu? Fun festivals, tennis, antiqueing, tours, shopping, and the Schussy Cats Dinner Show. Biking, hiking and picnicking in nearby Grass River Natural Area, Skegemog Swamp Pathway, Jordan River Pathway, Coy Mountain, or Shanty Creek. Oh, did we forget to mention boating, swimming, sunbathing, and strolling those marvelous beaches?

Winter here is "snowtime" for being stuck indoors when cross-country and downhill skiing, snow boarding, snowmobiling, ice skating, tubing, sledding, sleigh rides, and tobogganing are all close by!

Any season is the best season to surround yourself with tranquillity and loveliness. Explore . . .

The first link in the chain - bayside **Elk Rapids.** Home to both Elk Lake and one of Grand Traverse Bay's largest harbors, it's a watersports paradise that's "just North of the tension line!" From the "Ol' Bathing Beach" to the winter ice rink and Elk

Lake ice boating, from County Day Park gazebo to the shoreline sanctuary of Palmer-Wilcox-Gates Preserve, from South Arrowhead Park's Elk River boardwalk to downtown's quaint shops, from fabulous sunsets to "Stone Circle Gatherings'" (unique outdoor campfire entertainment), from brewery to cider mill, there's always a chance for a "multitude of memories".

If you're "tuckered" - "untuck" in *Alden.* It's a small "tucked-away" village on the Southeast shore of breathtakingly beautiful Torch Lake - "where the rainbow stores its colors". All of the marvelous delights of nature combine with sleepy small town charm, unique shops, museums, parks, and fine dining for a grand escape. Should you happen to be nearby on a summer's Thursday evening, drop in for an "Evening Stroll" - when street entertainers serenade your shopping adventures!

Scenic drives and calming countryside bring visitors through shopping meccas and historic villages like *Bellaire, Central Lake, Torch Lake, Eastport, and Ellsworth,* and on to Bay Country - North . . .

Elk Rapids C of C
1-800-626-7328 or 616-264-8202

Bellaire C of C
616-533-6023

Central Lake C of C
616-544-3322

Alden (information)
616-331-6787

"Love is made by two people, in different kinds of solitude. It can be in a crowd, but in an oblivious crowd."
- Louis Aragon

Bridgewalk Bed & Breakfast -

"a place you discover - then make your own"

*H*uge stately maples shade this peaceful, relaxing yard. A brook meanders lazily through - you simply must cross the footbridge. You simply must enter this country-Victorian heaven!

Mid-June to mid-October, the Bridgewalk welcomes lovers young and old for a brief visit to a gentler time. Its simple yet

gracious "appointments" are accented by antiques and family heirlooms throughout. Innkeepers encourage you to explore, to "peak" into all the nooks & crannies, and even drawers. Be sure to ask for the fascinating stories behind each discovery!

Guests, perhaps, will settle into hammock, grape arbor, garden, or brookside deck. Couples can be found on a cooler evening (even in summer) warming by the living room fire, admiring the unusual coffee table - a rare antique slave cot! A mellow tune - a mellow mood - resonates through the music room and all these large, airy, high-ceilinged rooms with their elegant woodwork. Guests may play the grand piano - or the antique Victrola.

For that romantic interlude - the Willow, Cherry, Maple, or Evergreen Room, or perhaps the Garden Suite, invite you. Brass or iron beds, charmingly elegant individual decor, private bath, and an old quilt from the owner's collection, are but a backdrop for the focal point of *each* room - the sound of the babbling brook!

Anniversary and honeymoon couples here can expect a special treat, but every couple gets a "morning surprise" - a coffee tray (tea, too)! Be sure to call for reservations (rates $85-95) at least one month in advance, more for the Garden Suite. September is an ideal month to visit. Qualified couples may want to inquire about Bridgewalk's unique Couples Get-Away Weekends for Expectant Parents.

Guest comment endlessly about the Inn's low-fat but plentiful Full Breakfast, served on deck overlooking the brook in good weather. Expect unusual items, not found in restaurants, on the menu. Innkeepers make their own low-fat Cherry Pecan Sausage, Fruit Soups, Scones, Muffins, and Buschiotti to complement entrées not usually repeated. Your dietary restrictions are accommodated.

Need a respite? Take the first step to . . .

Bridgewalk Bed & Breakfast
616-544-8122
2287 S. Main Street, P.O. Box 399, Central Lake 49622
Sorry, smoke free

Inn-spired Activities ————————————

Visit Antrim Creek Nature Preserve; do the Alden Stroll; see spectacular fireworks; go mountain biking, skiing or windsurfing; we know all the best places for biking, sunsets (over either Torch Lake or Lake Michigan), or beach fun - all quiet and undiscovered!

The House on the Hill - ELLSWORTH

"one of the Midwest's best known secrets"

A golden harvest moon rises over the tiny village of Ellsworth. And smiles. This sleepy little berg is home to one of Northern Michigan's finest getaways - The House on the Hill.

Atop a knoll this great lady perches, wrapped in a magnificent porch, and overlooking St. Clair Lake and wooded hillsides. Floral baskets drip from her eves, cool breezes waft through her windows, and wicker rockers decorate her grand, covered front veranda. She's not just another Inn, another rented room, she's like home - but better!

She welcomes you to her sunroom for TV/VCR, stereo, games, books, and complimentary wine and soft drinks each evening (take them outdoors on nicer days), or to her all-purpose room for coffee, tea, ice, or a refrigerator raid for soft drinks, microwave popcorn, or cup-o-soup. In winter, her social hour will most likely find you in the hosts' quarters with woodburning stove and large screen TV. You're also invited to enjoy the "back 40" for hiking, xc skiing, or nature walks.

House on the Hill is the ultimate hostess. Her rich jewel tone decor, and seven private, spacious main house rooms treat you to line-dried sheets, "lightable candles", carafe ice water, lotion, powders, soaps, and surprises to make your stay memorable. She includes those "special touches" in the three Carriage House rooms - the more rustic "American-style" hideaways that back up to a gurgling Artesian creek, and a wilderness scene. Private back deck, ceiling fans, gas fireplaces, electric blankets, quilts, and even umbrellas enhance this special section. Rates vary from $125-150, Main House or Carriage House.

As mornings grace the hill, she invites you to share in her "Candlelit Breakfast Bounty", served on different linens and china each day in dining room or sunroom. Special homemade butters - orange, apple, honey, pecan, walnut - adorn the homemade muffins, and add some "spice" to specialties like "Dr. Seuss Breakfast (green eggs & ham!)", "Tipsy French Toast", "Eggs Nest with Chachouka (ask your hosts!), homemade salsas, and local meats on the side.

The House on the Hill's Innkeepers believe in personal service, too, and will likely remember your personal likes and dislikes (with aid of computer database!). Ask about special packages with local "walk-to" gourmet restaurants, canoeing, boating, and picnic plans, and their secret hideaway beach spot!

Just ask - they'll tell you "You can't do all these beautiful things and come back to a motel - you need a place with character!" You need . . .

The House on the Hill
616-588-6304
9661 Lake Street, Ellsworth 49729

Inn-spired Activities ———————————

It's only 15 minutes to picturesque Charlevoix; take a Fall color tour; enjoy our Winter wonderland; walk to five-star dining, or visit some great local pubs for relaxing, less expensive dining; rent a small boat with 5HP motor from our elderly neighbor, and putt through the wilderness waterways!

Hidden away on the tranquil swan-studded shores of St. Clair Lake, this award winning contemporary restaurant features "Modern American Cooking", thoughtful special attention, a magical setting, and a daily-changing menu of fresh and local products. Your light summer luncheon may include "Chilled Cucumber Dill Soup", "Grilled Quail with mixed greens, asparagus and roasted red peppers", of "Thai Pasta Salad with shrimp, scallops, calamari and crab" ($16-22), set off with Raspberry Lemonade, or wine by the glass. For dinner? One daily menu included "Grilled Figs with duck prosciutto", or

"Shrimp and Crab Gazpacho Cocktail", followed by fresh herb and flower garnished "Cannelloni - herb crepes with spinach,, chevre, lemon, walnuts, and fresh tomato sauce", "Shiitake-crusted Venison with onion risotto, fruit relish, and smoke peppercorn duck", and "Cowboy Beef Tenderloin with beef jerky sauce, barbecued Vidalia onions, baked beans, grilled vegetables, chili onion rings, and peppered corn bread"! ($29-41).

Serving dinner all year - closed Monday in Winter / Lunch served in summer only / Smoke free / Reservations always recommended / Full bar and excellent wine list / Ask for special events calendar / Outdoor dining on deck / Inquire about very small lawn weddings or private parties

9502 Lake Street • 616-588-7971
http://members.aol.com/tapdining
email:tapdining@aol.com

"Michigan's Country Inn" makes everything right here, and offers an ever-changing menu, influenced often by the Provinces of France, and adapted to the seasons using fresh local vegetables, fruits, and fish. "Michigan Cuisine" creations include starters like renowned "Pecan Stuffed Morels", "Tomato Basil Soup", or "Grilled Venison Sausage" ($3.50-11.50); and entrées like "Rainbow Trout stuffed with wild rice, bacon leeks and fresh dill Buerre Blanc", "Duck Magret with dried cherry rice pilaf and blackberry sauce", or very popular "Rack of Lamb with hazelnut crust and lingonberry port sauce", ($19.50-32.50). Daily dessert specials always include signature "White Chocolate Brownie" ($4.50-8.50). Whatever they feature - whatever your choice - these dining "gems" always blend beautifully with a selection from Rowe Inn's extraordinary wine cellars. Sample some at monthly "Sunday Wine Brunches" (Nov.-

June), or special events and "Great Wines Dinners". Excellent wines and marvelous food in an intimate, informal, knotty-pine atmosphere. "Indulge yourself" your host invites, "This is *the best place* for it!"

Open year round - call for seasonal hours / Reservations always recommended - plan one week to 10 days in advance for choice summer weekends / Full bar and over 1200 wines in stock (retail sales by bottle or case as well as dinner accompaniments / Smoke free / Private parties during off-peak times only

6303 Country Road 48 • 616-588-7351

 **Dining Delights**

ᘗpencer ᙅreek - Alden

Intimate dining on the shores of Torch Lake! Great service, a complimentary "starter" treat, and award winning French food like "Artichoke Bisque", "Smoked Salmon and Potato Tart", "Roasted Halibut with sundried tomato and macadamia crust", "Seared Veal Tenderloin with artichoke, roasted garlic, prosciutto, and parmesan potato croquette", or "Seared Arctic Char and Pan Braised Lentils with citrus, asparagus puree, and leek polenta" in addition to Beef, and Pork specialties seasoned with herbs, and served with fresh local vegetables and fine wines (dinners $20-30 incl. appetizer & salad). Unconventional!

Open April - October / Reservations recommended / Full bar and wine list / Private parties possible / A non-smoking property
5166 Helena Street • 616-331-6147

À ᗤeux Adventures

- Chain of Lakes area - Bay Country South

Alden - Bellaire

Alden Depot Museum .... 616-331-4274 or 331-6583
Grass River Natural Area 616-533-8576
Schussy Cats Dinner Show & Shanty Creek
   Ski Resort 616-533-8621
   www.shantycreek.com or 1-800-678-4111

Central Lake

Camp Hayo-went-ha (xc ski).............................616-544-5915
Moore's Acres (hay and sleigh rides)....................616-599-2260

Elk Rapids & surrounding areas

Elk Rapids Historical Museum 616-264-5147
Hitchpoint Cider Mill...616-264-8371
Jordan River Pathway...616-582-6681
Stone Circle Gatherings...616-264-9467
Traverse Brewing Co. LTD 616-264-9343

Bay Country - North - Charlevoix - Petoskey - Harbor Springs & Points North

*A*ny one of these bayside resort communities is a splendid place to drop anchor!

Charlevoix "the beautiful" enjoys frontage on two beautiful waterways - Lake Michigan's Grand Traverse Bay, and Lake Charlevoix. Art galleries, pubs, and shops and, oh yes - miles of multi-colored petunias! line the main street and harbor areas.

Numerous beaches, parks and marinas offer ample opportunities for all the favorite water sports, as well as hiking, cross-country skiing, and catching a "million dollar sunset"! Favorite spots for nature addicts (and tranquility seekers!) are Mt. McSauba dunes recreation area, and Fisherman's Island state park. There's lots more excitement to be found at local festivals, museums, concerts, garden tours, ski resorts, cider mills, fruit and herb farms, and recreation centers. But don't expect too much luxury - Charlevoix is laid-back, casual, and informal fun!

Uniquely Charlevoix: unusual fairytale-like architecture, the brainchild of Earl Young, sparkles throughout the town. Romantic carriage-ride tours and driving or walking tours show them off perfectly; Memorial Bridge on U.S. 31 provides unique summertime entertainment as visitors watch it open each half hour to allow the passage of boats through the Pine River Channel; a novel cable-operated ferry service - the Ironton Ferry - takes 4 cars and a few foot travelers a scant 575 feet across the narrow South arm of Lake Charlevoix - a delightful ride!

Travelers to Beaver Island depart from Charlevoix by plane or ferry boat for day or overnight trips. "America's Emerald Isle" offers "unspoiled...unhurried...unmatched natural beauty", spiced with history and adventure. Rent a mountain bike or jeep (or bring your hiking boots!) for exploring.

One of Hemingway's reputed haunts is quaint, historic **Petoskey** - home of "Gaslight Village" shopping district, and historic Bay View community, as well as peaceful parks, beaches, and harbors.

Craving culture? In addition to local restaurant and pub entertainment, McCune Arts Center offers plays and musical performances, Concerts in the Park take place at the gazebo on Summer Tuesdays and Fridays, or check with the Bay View Association for its schedule of lectures, recitals, and concerts.

Looking for adventure? Boat, bicycle, canoe, and rollerblade rentals are abundantly available. So are tennis courts, riding stables, skating rinks, hiking and cross-country ski trails.

Hungering for relaxation and romance? Be a beach bum! Get sun-fun and sunsets and hunt for Petoskey stones (fossilized corral) at Petoskey State Park. "Have a sandwich with your sunshine!" at Flat Iron Deli, Roast & Toast Cafe, or Bear River Brewing Co. For some "take-out titillation" try Symons General Store, Sprockett's, or the Grain-Train Co-op. Stroll through historic BayView, or on the waterfront. Take a Gaslight Carriage Tour, or wagon ride through sugar bush. Pack a picnic and pack your "pumpkin" off to Sunset Park - sit by the waterfall, dream by the stream, look out on Little Traverse Bay, and make whoopee!

Been there? Done that? Then spend some time in the loveliness of **Harbor Springs**! It's a day-long adventure just waiting to happen in the galleries and shops of this quaint harbor village. Then, of course, you could opt for a more relaxing day amid the sun-splashed beaches, parks, piers or nature preserves. Maybe even visit "Bob" the cat, and spend a couple hours in his owners' Between the Covers bookstore!

Just for fun - glide the local cross-country ski trails; rent a kayak, mountain bike, or roller blades; ride a horse or snowmobile; take in a dinner show with the Young Americans at Boyne Highlands.

Just for thrills - "schuss" or snowboard down a local slope; "whee!" down a sledding hill; take a "Barnstormer" air tour; explore the winter ice caves!

Just for *magic* - picnic at Thorne Swift in the dunes; snuggle in a sleigh ride; take a sunset sailing cruise; toast 'neath the huge downtown Christmas tree; motor up Lakeshore Drive to "points North" . . .

No more beautiful Fall color can be found than M-119's coastline "Tunnel of Trees" Shore Drive, leading you to lunch by the fireside at fascinating Legs Inn in tiny Cross Village.

No more fabulous secluded beaches decorate Lake Michigan than those at Cross Village, Sturgeon Bay, and Waugoshance Point in Wilderness State Park.

This is Bay Country - this is romance!

**Petoskey/Harbor Springs/Boyne Country VB
and Petoskey Regional C of C**
1-800-845-2828
www.boynecountry.com
Charlevoix CVB / Charlevoix Area C of C
1-800-367-8557 / 616-547-2101
www.charlevoix.org
Harbor Springs C of C
616-526-7999
www.harborsprings-mi.com

Charlevoix Country Inn - CHARLEVOIX

*"a little ray of sunshine,
a little beam of love"*

Sit yourself down on the porch, the upper balcony swing, or in front of the parlor fireplace and soak up the view! This cozy country-style Inn wraps itself warmly around a magnificent panoramic view of Lake Michigan!

Welcome to the "gracious hospitality" of a 102 year old lakeside "summer cottage" that retains its cottage-style decor and adds simple country touches like gorgeous quilts and whim-

sical accessories to create a peaceful "at home" appeal.

Eight rooms and two suites offer private baths, queen beds, and old-style comfort. Book your choice 2 months to 6 weeks in advance for busy festival weekends. The Inn is open mid-May to mid- October. Consider reserving "Country Charm", a spacious haven with clawfoot tub/shower and teal, rose and pink highlights for its view of Pine Lake Channel and the garden. Or "Island View", a light, cheery, soft and delicate pastel floral hideaway with its own "commanding" lake view and interesting angles. Your "fella" may appreciate the more masculine feel of the "Bicycle Room" instead. Suites feature full kitchens and living rooms (and great views!) for that totally private escape.

Rates will range from $80 to $135, and vary seasonally, with off-season and extended-stay discounts. Honeymoon or anniversary couples receive champagne and a person congratulatory note. All guests enjoy a sweet-treat of chocolates in their quarters.

Plan some time from 5-7 pm, in the light and airy parlor/ sitting room, to enjoy the complimentary beverage, wine and cheese social. Go ahead - play the piano. It's slightly out of tune sometimes, but fun anyway!

Greet the morning over low-fat and healthy selections from the Breakfast Buffet - fruit platter or fruit salad bowl, cereals, fresh-baked breads and muffins, toast and beverages. Or, indulge yourself with a serving of the daily specialty - like "Featherbed (an egg dish)", French Toast, "Zucchini Pie", "Breakfast Burrito", or low-fat "Egg Muffin".

Watch the passing boats, watch the sunsets, and watch your love grow! at . . .

Charlevoix Country Inn
616-547-5134
106 W. Dixon Avenue, Charlevoix 49720
www.rust.net/~dgoulait/inn.html
Sorry, no smoking except on porches

Inn-spired Activities

Enjoy some of our long list of annual events; walk around town to appreciate the petunia-lined streets, galleries, shops, and Earl Young homes; take a wilderness adventure trip to Beaver Island; you'll love Charlevoix - it's a haven for water sports enthusiasts and nature lovers!

The Inn at Grey Gables -CHARLEVOIX

"tempting your appetite for love . . ."

*E*verything is fresh and new at this completely renovated Inn (formerly Belvedere Inn). From fresh white wicker on the front porch, through the raspberry and cream living room and expanded dining area, to the seven rooms and suites, you'll delight in the soft, rich and warm French country decor.

The full face lift includes an eclectic combination of furnishings - warm wood pieces, painted wood and wicker, overstuffed chairs, bedding accents, and artwork to accent perfectly.

Sit for a moment, or more, and enjoy the peace of the front porch, the cool quiet of the living room with its unusual ceiling medallions and paddle fan, the collection of games for guests' pleasure, or a complimentary evening dessert. Give your hosts 24 hours notice, and you will enjoy a private dinner, served in your room and catered by the next door eatery "Grey Gables Inn" (same owners). Also with advance notice, arrangements can be made for any special celebration, reception, or wedding - even simply in-room flowers, champagne, fruit baskets, cheese trays, etc. Your wish is their command!

Downstairs rooms - the Pine Room with pine floor and furnishings and decor in blue, and the Summer Room in florals - are newly done and delightful. Upstairs, the soft pink and white decor wraps around you and invites you perhaps to the Oak Room, the Rose Room, the Magnolia Room, or even Abigail's Room. Couples might most enjoy the Hanley Suite, which offers a separate sitting room for those private moments. Rates vary seasonally from $60-150 (Each room/suite includes private bath - check out the dual shower heads!). Be sure to ask about Valentine's, New Year's, and Winter specials. Inn at Grey Gables welcomes guests all year except in November. Be sure to inquire about "perks" for guests at this Inn - dining discounts at Grey Gables Inn or the Weathervane, and special rates and discounts at local shops and attractions.

Don't forget Breakfast! An ample repast is served in the dining room at individual intimate tables, or on the newly opened adjacent porch. Look for "Buttermilk Cinnamon Bread", or scones, with "Stuffed Apple French Toast", or perhaps "Baked Peach French Toast". Only a few of the possible different daily breakfast entrées to tempt you.

Be one of the first to sample the delights of . . .

The Inn at Grey Gables
616-547-2251 or 1-800-280-4667
306 Belvedere Avenue, Charlevoix 49720
Smoking outdoors only, please

Inn-spired Activities ——————————

Charlevoix is something for everyone! There's boating, skiing, hiking, antiques and art; avoid the hustle and bustle - sit back and enjoy the beauty!

MacDougall House - *CHARLEVOIX*

"ceud mile failte - (Gaelic for):
one hundred million welcomes!"

Spend some time in this warm, comfortable, informal Inn, and you'll discover a tranquil, stress-free getaway designed just for you!

No need to worry about arriving at a strange house - Innkeepers will meet you in the driveway at MacDougall House! You'll be ushered into the cozy living

room/dining room and offered a cup of coffee or tea while you orient yourself or warm by the fireplace.

As you're shown to your room, you'll realize the focus here is on "comfort and hospitality - not expensive decor". The simple decor isn't fancy, but the five rooms are pleasant, homey, and very inviting, each with private bath and ceiling fan, and sharing a private guest entrance. For a special occasion, why not try a room with sunroom between bed and bath?

Open all year, this cheery Inn has the best rates in town - $58-98. "Best Breakfast, too!" proclaim your hosts. The Full, Family-style repast includes private recipe lower-fat granola, cookies, and coffeecakes to go along with the Inn's own brand of low-fat sausage (made locally to MacDougall specs), beverages, and maybe "Morning Glory Muffins", "Pecan-Apple Pancakes with pure maple syrup", or low-fat "Stuffed French Toast". Their signature Scottish shortbreads, from an old family recipe, are always set out to nibble on.

Feeling guilty about your A.M. indulgence? Walk petunia-lined streets to downtown shops, or Lake Charlevoix's shoreside park. Or, take the three minute "hike" ("if you walk slow!") to Lake Michigan beach for a jog or swim. Your hosts will happily pack a picnic lunch, too!

No guilt? Relax in a wicker rocker on the front porch, watch the birds (or cars) go by, and admire the beautiful floral displays on the grounds.

Innkeepers here "pay close attention to the privacy and the needs of guests." With advance notice, they will plan an in-room treat of wine and flowers for your "Occasion", and can make arrangements for a sampler pack or basket from local merchants, and dining parties or packages in conjunction with local restaurants. If your group rents the entire Inn, special breakfast parties, receptions, or weddings can be arranged (20-30 guests max). Say your vows under the rose-trellis arch in the garden!

For that very special brand of Scottish hospitality, reserve at least six weeks in advance at . . .

MacDougall House Bed & Breakfast
616-547-5788
109 Petoskey Avenue (U.S. 31 North), Charlevoix 49720
Smoking outdoors only, please

Inn-spired Activities ————————————

Take an architectural tour; hike the State forests and Jordan Valley; take a seat in Stafford's Weathervane to watch the boats go in and out; walk to the beach for a "million dollar sunset!"

The Gingerbread House - PETOSKEY

"making people feel special"

Y ou get a lot of "warm fuzzies" at this charming homelike Victorian Inn. Situated on the edge of Little Traverse Bay, in the heart of historic BayView, Gingerbread House welcomes guests May - October.

How would you like: friendly conversation; early a.m. coffee on the buffet or in your room; fresh flowers and candies in each room; a card for your birthday; flowers, card, wine, and a breakfast tray in your room for your honeymoon; and lots of hugs on departure!?

How would you like: a quiet "place of refuge", and romance; a "place to escape the stress of everyday life"; a "homelike atmosphere" 1/2 block from the beach; a cozy entry sitting area, (with telephone) and porch for a warm welcome and simply relaxing; a comfy, foam-topped bed; insulated walls for privacy; a private bath, private entrance, and view of the bay in each room or suite?

Wouldn't you appreciate a Breakfast Experience where the mingling is fun even if you *don't* eat breakfast? You may get surprised with "Filled French Toast" or "Gingerbread Pancake", but you can expect all-you-can-eat fresh fruit, home-baked muffins, coffee cake or cinnamon rolls, yogurt, special recipe granola, and beverages in everyday variety and plenty. Special dietary requests, or favorites, can be prepared if you only ask. (Ask about their cookbook, too!)

Wouldn't you enjoy a cool, airy, yet cozy room to curl up in and renew your love? Choose Suite #2 with bay-view sitting area, country kitchenette, and light,bright blue and white decor accented by a hand-painted wall. Or Suite #3, with delightful rose garden effect, kitchenette, breakfast nook, and window seat. Room #4 - Ribbons & Bows - opens out on the front porch. The Honeymoon Suite (Suite #1) would be your choice for that special time. King bed, private lakeview veranda, and sitting room, are outstanding features in this flowers, lace, and soft, soft colors hideaway. Standard rates are $80-120, but be sure to ask about Fall, Mid-week, and Weekly rate specials. Reservations are accepted all year, but do call one year in advance for July and August weekends.

You'll love it! So reserve some of their "warm hospitality", and spice up your love life, at . . .

The Gingerbread House
616-347-3538
205 Bluff, P.O. Box 1273, Bay View 49770
Sorry, no smoking permitted

Inn-spired Activities ————————————

Go swimming - the beach is only 1/2 block away; walk along the waterfront; shop the Gaslight District and nearby antique emporiums; enjoy Concerts in the Park and at Bay View; hike the great local trails - especially the nature trail at Bay View; take a tour of scenic Lower lake area - Lake Shore Drive, and Thornswift Nature Preserve; take in a sunset over the bay; allow yourselves three days minimum to enjoy our area!

Stafford's Bay View Inn - PETOSKEY

"the 'grand dame' of Michigan's mitten"

*T*he same "Old World" charm that graces New England's stately resorts is evident at Stafford's Bay View Inn. One of Petoskey's premier hotel/restaurant properties, the Inn has so much character you can almost feel its atmosphere wrap around you as you enter. This rare combination of historic ambiance, quaint yet modern accommodations, and friendly service, is carefully designed to give guests a total experience best described as "comfortable elegance".

All of the Bay View's 31 "bed chambers" are individually styled with Victorian era decor and private baths. Trillium Bayside rooms allow garden views, while Cherry Blossom Suites offer a separate sitting room. Also available are reasonably priced and cozy Primrose Rooms, or luxurious Forget Me Not rooms featuring sitting areas with fireplaces, and whirlpool spa tubs. All rooms include complimentary wine and a Full Breakfast (except during Winter midweek, when rates are quoted with Continental Breakfast). Rates average $79-210 depending on the season - no minimum stay required - inquire for open Winter dates.

Dining at Stafford's Bay View Inn is special. The Roselawn Porch dining room is known for its sumptuous family recipes and pampered services. Dinner specialties may include fresh Whitefish (a standard menu item), "Pecan Chicken", or "Cherry Pepper Steak". Among the luncheon selections are unique features such as "Chilled Cherry Soup", and "Chicken Salad Flower". *Dining Delights* Menus change yearly, with dinner prices averaging $16.50-24, and lunch choices $6-10.50.

Sunday Brunch has been a big event at the Inn for 30 years. Served 10 am - 2 pm May through October for $16.95, this well-known feast was voted "Best in the State" by a AAA Michigan magazine poll. A menu listing varied fruits, bakery selections, fish, chicken, vegetable and egg dishes is usually highlighted with ham, turkey, and "Eggs Benedict". As always, the central attraction is Stafford's specialty - a unique "Northern Michigan Tomato Pudding". A more modest breakfast buffet is available at other times.

Weddings, receptions, and special events will be graciously arranged by the Inn's catering manager.

While Stafford's Bay View Inn does not schedule regular entertainment, they do host special activities throughout the year, including jazz weekends and summer "chautaquas" - lectures, travelogues, concerts, recitals, and theater productions. Or, you could simply relax and enjoy the wicker-furnished sunroom, warm and cozy lobby fireplace, or a stroll along the bay. That same romantic New England ambiance will steal over you as you settle into an Adirondack chair on the lawn for a bayside sunset viewing or afternoon refreshment. Croquet, biking, sailing, swimming, or a quiet garden rendezvous could add some spice to your romantic experience at . . .

Stafford's Bay View Inn
616-347-2771 or 1-800-258-1886
613 Woodland Avenue, P.O. Box 3, Petoskey 49770
www.innbook.com
email: stafford@freeway.net
A totally smoke-free environment

Stafford's Perry Hotel - PETOSKEY

*"old-world sohpistication and
new-world spirit"*

*A*nother of the Stafford family's first-class Inns anchors Petoskey's famous Gaslight District. If you prefer a more traditional hotel-style accommodation, this is a grand choice. Though "elegance" is the key word describing the look, "casual", "comfortable" and "homey" best describe the feel here.

Perry Hotel's capable staff is at your comand from the moment you cross the huge wicker-filled porch and enter the

softly lit traditional-style lobby. Your welcome? A blazing fireplace, huge vases of fresh flowers, deep, jewel-tone decor, and friendly smiles.

Each individually styled room exudes pure class! And all the amenities - TV, phone, private bath, and Continental Breakfast. Even a hot tub/spa awaits your enjoyment. Choose a Rose House, Cushman, or Park House room, or perhaps an Imperial or

Arlington room with a view of the bay, and maybe a private balcony. Rates range from $65 to 180, varying seasonally. Unique packages, and special off-peak rates are available, so be sure to ask.

Dining Delights

The Perry Hotel offers dining options including afternoon appetizers and beverages in the Salon; Pizza, beverages and lighter meals in the Noggin Room Pub; and a multi-national menu in the exquisite H.O. Rose Room. Sample breakfasts of "Michigan Scramble with peppers, morel mushrooms, leeks, potatoes and cheddar cheese", "English Walnut Pancakes", or "Cherry French Toast" ($6.50-7.95); luncheons like "Chicken Champignon with creamy wild mushroom sauce" "Buffalo Burger", Seafood Chowder, Quiche of the day, or "Spinach and Smoked Chicken Salad" ($3.50-8.50); and dinner entrées like "Rack of Lamb a la Diable", "Bay Street Pasta with herb vinaigrette, artichoke hearts, vegetables, feta cheese and walnuts", "Filet Mignon with sauteed greens and port wine sauce", or Whitefish served grilled with smoked salmon butter, broiled with citrus butter, or sauteed with wild mushroom sauce ($16-26). Summer "al fresco" meals are offered on the cool front porch. Of course, weddings, banquets and receptions are possible anytime, but plan early.

Weekend dining is enhanced by the addition of soft piano renditions in the formal dining room, and lots of fun is happening when the Pub offers live jazz and folk music.

Oh! Don't forget to check out the downstairs gift shop for that special romantic memento. And, check into this fine, old hotel for that special romantic memory!

Stafford's Perry Hotel
1-800-456-1917 or 616-347-4000
H. O. Rose Room dining reservations 616-348-6014
Bay at Lewis - Gaslight District
Petoskey 49770
Smoking accommodations and dining areas available

Terrace Inn - PETOSKEY

*"striving to be known as the
friendliest Inn in Michigan"*

*E*nchanting in Winter, and radiant in
Summer, this captivating "hidden jewel" is steeped in history
and the traditions of classic hotel service.

Though massive, the comfortably furnished lobby retains a
cozy, warm atmosphere with the help of a glowing brick fireplace, fresh flowers, hemlock paneled walls, and a pianist tinkling out appropriate tunes four evening each Summer week.
Small tables invite you to enjoy a moment of intimate conversation, or one of Terrace Inn's games, in this "Grand Parlor". And

then, the wide
porch beckons
for a lazy sum-
mer afternoon
of relaxing.

If you're
searching for a
more active
getaway, you
may wish to en-
joy the benefits
of "belonging",
briefly, to a pri-
vate association. Terrace Inn Guests enjoy all "members-only"
recreational and cultural privileges of Bay View, the historic
community which surrounds the Inn: private swimming beach
with lifeguard; two tennis courts; sunfish sailing and lessons;
golf privileges at Petoskey/Bay View Country Club; Sunday
evening Vesper programs; 165 acre forest with great hiking
trails; drama and musical theater productions; browsing in the
excellent Bay View library.

Guests also may enjoy the complimentary use of the Inn's bicycles and snow shoes. The downstairs "rec room" offers cable TV, ping pong, and additional games.

Bay View homes are uninhabited in Winter, so the area presents perfect quiet lighted lanes for cross-country skiing, January Saturday night sleighrides, and Fall carriage rides. Guided historic tours can be arranged, as well as old-fashioned picnic basket lunches.

Special events highlight the Inn's calendar. Cooking and Wine Tasting, Murder Mystery, Dixieland Jazz Festival, Country & Swing Dancing, and Victorian Dinner Theater weekends are merely samples of the fun to be found!

A wide staircase and hallways lead to rooms filled with uniquely simple, traditional decor, original Inn antiques, ruffled curtains, soft carpet, and "true Victorian ambiance". (No in-room TV or phone - pay phone in lobby). Room 214 is most requested - a bright, spacious haven filled with light.

Rates vary from $49-103, depending on day and season, and choice of standard or deluxe room. Inquire for packages. Call 3-4 weeks or more in advance for Summer weekends.

Gifts of chocolate, mints, and lace sachet greet celebrating couples. Flowers, champagne, or other requests can be arranged by your hosts.

Hotel guests partake of a Continental Breakfast buffet, offering fresh fruit, toast and jams, fresh pastries, dry cereals and beverages from 8-10.

Your Terrace Inn experience will be enhanced by a leisurely dinner in the *Dining Delights* sunlit dining room, open to the public and Inn guests in Summer Tuesday-Saturday, and for Sunday noontime buffet. (Off-season dinners Thursday-Saturday, and November 1-June Saturday evening buffets only). Though this early 1900s dining room is quite inviting, many Summer guests choose to dine on the porch. The menu features moderately priced "Classic Country Inn Cuisine" with Northern Michigan specialties like "Planked Whitefish", "Chicken Hemingway in basil cream sauce", "Pasties", Pork Roast, and Pasta entrées ($9.85-15.95). End with Gourmet Ice Cream, or a dessert specialty of the day.

Weddings are grand and joyful at Terrace Inn, be they held indoors or out. Arrive for the event via specially arranged horsedrawn carriage! Many brides make a grand entrance up the rear staircase and onto the porch. Receptions and parties of 100-150 guests are easily scheduled. Bay View is a dry community, so you will be required to hire your own bartender and supply your own alcoholic beverages if you wish.

A wedding, a party, a dinner, a stay - once you've tried it, you'll feel a wistful longing to return to . . .

Terrace Inn
616-347-2410 or 1-800-530-9898
1549 Glendale, P.O. Box 266, Petoskey 49770
www.freeway.net/terracei
email: terracei@freeway.net
Smoking on porch only - except when dining

Inn-spired Activities ⎯⎯⎯⎯⎯⎯⎯⎯⎯⎯⎯

Go horseback riding, sailing, or birdwatching; take a hike through fields of wildflowers; enjoy the Fall colors; enjoy plays, concerts, dinner theater, and art exhibits put on by Crooked Tree Arts Council, Bay View Assoc., and the Young Americans; spend some quiet time in Bay View's great library, or museums; cross-country skiing is beautiful here - within Bay View and in the woods on nearby trails - you'll see lots of deer!

ℋighland ℋideaway - HARBOR SPRINGS

"where fantasies come true"

*T*his spectacular setting for romance beckons specifically to couples 365 days a year. Though the overall aura is one of light, airy, eclectic chic with treasured collectibles as accents, Summer visitors and Winter visitors will encounter two completely different "faces" - a changing decor, and a changing character make each visit a *unique delight!*

Though Harbor Springs and surrounding areas offer myriad activities to entertain and amuse you, your hosts at Highland think of the Inn as a destination in and of itself. You'll no doubt agree when you discover the bright Morning Room with its blazing fireplace; the Solarium with its in-

toxicating views, games and fireplace; the Library with TV/VCR and area videos; the Workout Room with music, private indoor hot tub (use by appt. only!), and personal trainer available; and the "Grand Promenade" that wraps around the house with multi-level decks, a large outdoor spa, and sauna.

Snuggle into the Solarium to watch the skiers at nearby Boyne Highlands, the sunset, or the stars, and enjoy hot and cold hors d'oeuvres, aperitifs, mulled spiced wine, apple cider, hot cocoa, "hot tatas", holiday wassail, iced tea, cookies and fruit.

Book a stay for New Year's Eve and experience an evening buffet, and the fabulous fireworks display presented by Boyne Highlands.

A huge "can't-eat-it-all" Buffet Breakfast includes specials like "Sunday Morning Waffles with warm apples or cherries and whipped cream", or "Cheese Filled Spicy Croissants" with fresh fruit, eggs-to-order, muffins, pastries, hash browns,, bacon or sausage, and maple syrup from their own trees!

For that "oh-so-pampered" holiday, your hosts provide a reasonably priced "menu" of special services you can plan -various massage services (provided by a licensed professional), local dining reservations, flowers, fruit or food baskets, or even tarot/astrological readings. For that extra-sensual experience, order the "Affaire 1 Àmour", with intimate hot tub interlude, "Sunglow" wine, chocolates, and satin sheets!

Weddings on the grounds, buffets, and special events/parties (up to 60 guests) are a wonderful idea here.

Book 4-6 weeks in advance (6 months to 1 year for holidays and local regatta) to reserve one of five historically-named rooms (with private baths and cable TV). Settle into a fireplace room or featherbed room for $72 all inclusive (except for any gratuity you wish to add). Special occasion rates will be quoted individually.

Inn hosts encourage you to "leave the outside world, and renew your relationship", at . . .

Highland Hideaway Bed & Breakfast
616-526-8100
6767 Pleasantview Road, Harbor Springs 49740
email: highland @racc2000.com
Smoke free and phone free

Inn-spired Activities ——————————

Go sailing on a day or sunset cruise; cross-country ski at Wildwood, Bay View, or Nubs Nob lighted trail; the snowmobile trail starts 450 yards from our door; ride a horse - or an old-fashioned bi-plane!

Kimberly Country Estate -

"the ambiance of a private club in a gracious plantation home"

*T*reat yourself to affordable oppulence! This is a distinctive getaway - with all the grandeur of a noble Colonial plantation, all the tranquility of a secluded country estate, and all the magnificence of a perfectly co-ordinated, professionally designed decor.

Relax in the comfortable refinement of the living room, or on the terrace, to enjoy the breathtaking views - a flowing stone waterfall spills into the pond, gorgeous floral displays decorate

the landscape, and golfers dot the hills of neighboring Wequetonsing's manicured course.

A grand piano, impressive stone fireplace, books, games, and TV in the pub-style library, a slate pathway and bonfire pit, and an outdoor pool with pool towels, provide ample "at-home" diversions for each and every guest. Wine, beverages, and hors d'oeuvres provide refreshment during "hospitality time" between 5 and 6 pm.

Guests sleep well in this peaceful setting, on top-quality *ironed* sheets and pillow cases, amid fresh flowers, beautiul appointments, and all the comforts of a gracious Inn - including evening sherry and chocolate truffles! Each of seven rooms and suites has a private bath and phone, and some have canopy beds, sitting rooms or areas, and fireplaces. Rates vary from $155-300. From richly "primitive" or deep-colored and cozy, to ultra-elegant, whichever you select you'll get a taste of the life that inspires poets and romantics!

Couples gravitate to the airy, light, yellow and blue comfort of Le Soleil with canopy bed and sitting area; the traditionally elegant Lexington Suite with 4-poster and fireplace; or the large and sumptuous Veranda Suite with fresh, light garden appeal, Jacuzzi® tub, fireplace, hand painted floor and mural, and upper veranda access. To die for!

Make your way to the dining room, or the terrace in great weather, for a Deluxe Continental breakfast of fresh fruit, cereal, muffins, beverages, and perhaps a helping of "Baked French Toast".

Honeymooners and anniversary couples, be sure to ask about special arrangements for baskets of fruit, cheese and crackers, champagne, etc., and complete packages.

Love's perfect hideaway awaits, at . . .

Kimberly Country Estate
616-526-7646 or 616-526-9502
2287 Bester Road, Harbor Springs 49740
Sorry, no smoking permitted

Inn-spired Activities ————————————

Have a patio lunch and incredible view at Little Traverse Bay Golf Club; or stop in at Dudley's Deck for lunch and cocktails; ask us to arrange a picnic basket lunch for your enjoyment at Goodheart Beach of Petoskey State Park; shopping in Harbor Springs is always a pleasure; go sailing on beautiful Little Traverse Bay!

Veranda at - HARBOR SPRINGS

"all the comforts of a fine home"

Y ou'll feel as if you're in the garden all year when you visit the Veranda! Traditional styling, bright floral decor, and antique furnishings are highlighted by the oils and watercolors of nationally known artists. New in 1996, this Inn just oozes charm!

Ease into cushiony comfort in front of the living room fireplace, confer at a table for two, select a video to enjoy, sit and sip a complimentary lemonade or iced tea on the sunny enclosed veranda. It's oh, so nice!

Victorian hospitality - "Southern-style" includes a Full buffet-style Breakfast. Guests may eat their selections of fresh fruit, homemade muffins and biscuits, or special features such as "Peach French Toast" anywhere they like. Cookies, coffee and tea are out all day, and guests have access to a refrigerator with ice maker for their snacks.

249

flowers, champagne, and other special touches. Just ask about special services or small wedding arrangements.

A favorite of here (each with ter view, and bucket, and some balconies) is the Suite" - a room with just perfect for popular for ro- is the suite offer- rate sitting room To assure the five rooms private bath, wa- convenient ice with cozy private "Honeymoon captivating turret Jacuzzi® tub - romance! Also mantic getaways ing its own sepa- (rates $95-185). your selected ac- commodation will be available, book 6 months in advance for summer weekends, and 1 year prior for Regatta or July 4th weekends.

Just like they would in the South - enjoy a slower pace in a friendly neighborhood, and "spend hours rocking on the porch . . . daydreaming about tomorrow", at . . .

Veranda at Harbor Springs
616-526-7782
403 E. Main Street, Harbor Springs 49740
A smoke free bed & breakfast

Inn-spired Activities ————————————

Take a walk around our safe, comfortable town and through the marina and piers; get a picnic lunch from Guerney's Sandwich Shop, go to the park, and watch the boats; explore the ice caves; enjoy our wonderful climate, and our gorgeous ambiance in Winter; "There's only one Harbor Springs - it doesn't get any better than this!"

ℭtafford's ℭWeathervane - Charlevoix

A shining example of Earl Young's unusual architecture. Offering a waterfront view on the Pine River; luncheon treats like "Great Lakes Chowder", "Pine River Salad with chicken, pasta, vegetables, and spinach", "Baked Spinach Pie", and "The Boathouse Sandwich with turkey, ham, tomato, two cheeses, and hollandaise sauce" ($3.25-8.95); and Weathervane Dinner Classics like "Chicken Boursin in raspberry sauce with boursin cheese", "Veal Chop Piccata" and "Rack of Lamb" along with Lake Michigan Fish, Seafood, and premium Steaks ($15.50-23.95). Enchanting!

Open all year / Reservations accepted / Smoking in designated areas / Outdoor dining available / Full bar / Occasional Entertainment such as Friday night guitar/jazz singer

At the Bridge, Downtown • 616-547-4311

ℭhe ℭrey ℭables ℭnn- Charlevoix

Charlevoix's finest dining since 1936 in one of four very romantic and intimate Victorian dining rooms (one with fireplace). Dine elegantly on "Cherry Spinach Salad", "Pan-roasted Norwegian Salmon", "Apple/dried cherry-Stuffed Pork Chops", Prime Rib, BBQ Ribs, "Steak au Poivre Filet", "Cider-Whiskey Chicken", "Rack of Lamb", or "Pasta Provencal with vegetables only, or add shrimp or chicken" ($12.95-29.95). Everything fresh from scratch and homemade - even their famous scones, desserts, and balsamic dressing. Outstanding!

Open 7 days / Full bar & wine list / Reservations suggested for summer & weekends / Parties in banquet room or restaurant / Piano bar / Dancing & entertainment Winter weekends & Wed.- Sat. in Summer

308 Belvedere Avenue • 616-547-9261

Dining Delights   *Andanté* - Petoskey

Intimate candlelight and linen dining in a remodeled house, with a spectacular view of Little Traverse Bay. Though the "gourmet eclectic cuisine" changes seasonally, and at the Chef's whim, you might find such appetizers as "Butternut Squash Bisque with apple smoked bacon and roasted pine nuts", or "Andanté Caesar Salad made with locally smoked whitefish and toaste brie cheese croutons", or entrées like "Fresh Whitefish wrapped in golden shredded potato crust with roasted red pepper buerre blanc sauce", "Herb Encrusted Rack of Lamb with cabarnet demi glace & sauteed wild mushrooms", or "Medallions of Beef" ($29-38). For a sweet treat, try "Dark Chocolate Pudding Cake with caramel cognac sauce & ice cream". Unconventional! *Open 7 days June 15-Labor Day, Tues.-Sat. off season / Full bar & wine list / Reservations suggested / Smaller parties possible*
321 Bay Street • 616-348-3321

Dining Delights   *Arboretum-* Harbor Springs

The menu treasure chest includes such jewels as "Wild Game Mixed Grill - (changing daily)," "Whitefish Roulade - stuffed with smoked trout, spinach, wild mushrooms, ricotta, and topped with hollandaise", "Penne Pasta with fresh vegetables, herb vinaigrette, roasted hazelnuts & feta cheese", "Double Breast of Chicken in citrus, herbs & tequila", "Entrecote Capella - strip steak chargrilled with roasted garlic, butter & yellow bell pepper sauce", House Specialties "Planked Whitefish" and "Marinated Rack of Lamb", or "Peanut Butter & Jelly for Two with Dom Perignon (for $100)!" (dinners $15-25 + market, and Lite Entrées for $8-10). A reputation for "great food, friendly service, and moderate prices". *Open nightly in season - Wed.-Sat. off season / Reservations appreciated / Smoking in designated areas / Parties possible*
7075 S. Lakeshore Drive (M-119) • 616-526-6291

Waterfront dining at its elegant best, featuring "Chilled Cherry Soup", "Baked Goat Cheese Salad", "Spinach Pasta Roll", "Red Pepper Portabella", or "Grilled Smoked Salmon Sausage" for starters ($3.50-8.95), and entreés like "Wild Mushroom Shrimp with carrots, red peppers, and white wine on pasta", "Black Currant Veal - medallions with boursin cheese on barley & wild rice", Broiled, Grilled or Sauteed Whitefish, "Grilled Lavender Duck with savory stone fruit sauce, duck sausage and barley/ wild rice", and "Taste of the Pier - three specialties including rack of lamb, jumbo shrimp, and chicken dijon (for two $55) (other dinners range $18-28). Renowned!

Open all year / More casual dining in The Chart Room & Outdoors on Dudley's Deck / Reservations accepted / Full bar & wine list / Parties possible /Occasional Piano Entertainment

102 Bay Street, downtown • 616-526-6201

Dining Delights

The New York - Harbor Springs

Comfortable but classy, with an architecturally interesting interior, and a waterfront view. Serving breakfast choices like Belgian Waffles, and "Maryland Eggs - crab cakes with poached eggs, hollandaise, and red pepper puree" ($3-6.50); luncheons like "Smoked Whitefish Chowder", Sandwiches, "Thai Chicken Salad", and "Pasta New York with chicken, wild mushrooms, and chive-cream sauce" ($5-8); and dinner choices such as "Cioppino - fish & seafood in spicy tomato broth", "Wolverine Pork Loin stuffed with wild rice and dried cherries", "Medallions of Beef on Crabcakes with bernaisse", Steak, Duck, Whitefish, Salmon, "Vegetarian Lasagna", and more ($11-22). "An outstanding meal in comfortable surroundings."

Open all year except for "Spring Vacation" - call for hours / Full bar / Reservations recommended in summer especially

101 State Street - Corner of Bay Street • 616-526-1904

À *Deux Adventures*

- *Charlevoix, Petoskey, Harbor Springs & Surrounding Area*

Charlevoix

Boyne Area Sailboat Charters ....1-800-582-7470 or 616-582-3200
Boyne Mountain (skiing)............ 1-800-GO BOYNE or 616-549-2441
Cedar Valley Farms, Inc. (carriage for hire, tours, rides)
.... 616-547-7352 or 547-4698
Charlevoix Council for the Arts 616-547-5590
Classic Charters of Charlevoix (sailing) 616-547-2195
Fisherman's Island................................... 616-547-6641 or 547-2101
Friske Orchards (& cider press) 616-588-6185
Harsha House & Depot Museum.....................................616-547-0373
Island Airways..616-547-2141
Mt. McSauba Ski Area 616-547-3267
Shanty Creek & Schuss Mountain (skiing) 616-533-9621
    www.chantycreek.com or 1-800-678-4111
The Beaver Island Boat Co. (ferry rides) 616-547-2311
Ward Bros. Boats, Inc. (rentals).....................................616-547-2371

Petoskey

Adventure sports (bike & scuba rental)..........................616-347-3041
Bahnhoff Sport (bike & blade rental)..............................616-347-2112
Bay View Association 616-347-6225
Bear River Brewing Co. 616-348-8467
Bear River Canoe Livery..616-347-9038
Bliss Meadows Farms (wagon rides) 616-537-2406
Boyne Area Sailboat Charters ....1-800-582-7470 or 616-582-3200
City Park Grill (dining) 616-347-0101
Flat Iron Deli 616-347-5190
Gaslight Carriage Tours 616-347-7301
High Gear Sports 616-347-6118
Little Traverse Bay History Museum..............................616-347-2620
Petoskey State Park & Wildwood Hills Pathway............616-347-2755
Roast & Toast Cafe 616-347-7767
Sprockett's CarryOut Cuisine...616-439-0445
Symons General Store 616-347-2438
The Grain Train Bakery & Deli......................................616-347-2381

À Deux Adventures

- Charlevoix, Petoskey, Harbor Springs & Surrounding Area

Harbor Springs

Andrew J. Blackbird Museum...616-526-7731
Between the Covers (bookstore) 616-526-6658
Boyne Highlands Resort (ski, snowboard, & Young Americans
    Show).. 1-800-GO-BOYNE
    or 616-526-3000
Classic Yacht Charters 616-526-2372
County Wide Services (snowmobile rentals) 616-347-8822
Dudley's Deck at Stafford's Pier....................................616-526-6201
Gurney's Bottle Shop (deli) 616-526-5472
Harbor Springs Gourmet (deli)......................................616-526-9607
Kiwanis Park sledding hill 616-526-5847
Legs Inn (Cross Village) 616-526-2281
Little Traverse Bay Golf Club..616-526-7800
Little Traverse Conservancy...616-347-0991
Municipal Skating Rink & warming hut 616-526-5810
Nub's Nob Ski Area 1-800-SKI-NUBS
    or 616-526-2131
Nut Meg's Food & wine (deli) 616-347-0712
Sogonosh Stables (riding, hay & sleigh rides) 616-526-5766
The Outfitter (kayak & roller blade rentals)...................616-526-2621
Energy Balance Therapeutic Massage 616-526-5064
    pager 616-201-9557
Touring Gear (bike rentals) 616-526-7152
Waco Air (air tours) 1-800-WACO-AIR
    or 616-922-6247

"Familiar acts are beautiful through love."
- Percy Bysshe Shelley

The Upper Peninsula -

Michigan's Upper Peninsula (affectionately nicknamed "the U.P.") is an uncrowded land of scenic splendor and sensual delights. Couples can experience a kaleidoscope of opalescent beauty, including impressive rock formations, miles of white-sand and rocky beaches, acre upon acre of magnificent forest, colorful mineral deposits, and water, water everywhere . . .

Bounded on three sides by the powerful Great Lakes - Michigan, Superior, and Huron, this spectacular peninsula offers couples The Best of The Beach! Add "rock hounding" to the usual shoreline activities of swimming, sunning, sand castles, strolling, and sunset viewing. Agates, hematite, and greenstone are unique and plentiful mementos. Offshore "sports" are abundantly available along 1100 miles of shore, too - sailing, cruising, and even shipwreck diving! - never a dull moment!

Inland areas sparkle with 4300 lakes, and 1200 miles of streams, including 16 canoeable rivers. And, over 250 waterfalls cascade endlessly down a variety of cliffs and hillsides, continuing to dazzle starry-eyed lovers. What a joy to behold!

Eighty five percent of the U.P. is forested in a beautiful array of hardwoods, pine, plants, mushrooms, and wildflowers. Mostly accessible to the public, these forests promise peaceful serenity, unequaled scenery, fabulous Fall colors, plentiful wildlife, numerous hiking and mountain bike trails, and untold photo and picnic opportunities!

Winter is normally mild, but oh, so snowy! (though roads are *very* well-maintained and accessible). Alpine skiers have several fine resorts to pick from, while sledders pick the nearest hill! Miles and miles of snowmobile and Nordic ski trails wind through stunning white landscapes, sharing the beauty with sled dog mushers, snowshoers, and couples crunching on the snow! Frozen falls, ice caves, and tranquil drifted hillsides provide the perfect background for romantic trysts!

Interesting cities, tiny villages, museums, and over 40 lighthouses, ghost towns, and general stores sparsely pepper the landscape, and invite visitors to touch on some history and take home a memory!

Highlights of the **Eastern U.P.** include, of course, the "Mighty Mac" - one of the world's largest suspension bridges, and an awesome sight lighted by the sun or by its twinkling "night lights". Overlook the bridge, and surrounding lake and countryside vistas, from the top of Castle Rock.

Head East through small lakeshore towns for a peak at the beautiful Les Cheneau Island Chain, and to peaceful Drummond Island. History buffs of man-made wonders may value a side trip Sault Ste. Marie for a Soo Locks tour.

Heading West? Take the scenic route - U.S. 2 following Lake Michigan's dune-lined shore - and stop for a break at one of the roadside parks at Cut River Gorge. Stop for lunch at quaint Cut River Inn, or for skiing, hiking, or mini-golf at Michihistrigan's Michigan-shaped course! (Gould City)

The *Manistique Lakes area* is a great home base for exploring the awesome wonders of popular Tahquamenon Falls. An inspiring sight in any season, the falls are viewed from river boat, trolley and train rides, or by huffing and puffing up the countless stairs to up-close viewing areas. Make a refreshing rest stop at Camp 33's enchanting new Brewery & Pub. Relax on the deck, or snuggle up to indoor and outdoor stone fireplaces!

For more "Lakes of the Northwoods Area" fun - take a gander at Whitefish Point Lighthouse & Great Lakes Shipwreck Museum; dive down to explore Lake Superior's Underwater Preserve; stop in at Newberry's Logging Museum; drive, hike or bike through Seney National Wildlife Refuge; or canoe Hemingway's romantic Two-Hearted River!

You won't want to miss the "superior" splendor of Lake Superior's shoreline between *Grand Marais* and Munising. Just on the inland side of Grand Sable Banks and Dunes lies one of the most picturesque, unspoiled and idyllic lakes in Michigan - Grand Sable Lake. Add just a few extra stops to your tour - Lake Superior Brewing Co. for lunch (take note of the back dining room tables, and sample some *fresh* whitefish!); Grand Sable Falls; and the fabulous Log Slide overlook. Hug the shoreline on H-58 for a leisurely

(though sometimes dusty!) 40 mile motor tour of Pictured Rocks National Lakeshore. Its colorful sandstone cliffs, a top U.P. attraction, are visible from turnouts, and overlooks - especially famous "Miner's Castle - from forest hiking trails, and from boat and plane tours departing from *Munising* . . .

Bring your camera! "Anchoring" Pictured Rocks, and promising bountiful inland and shoreline scenic "jewels", this friendly town is a storehouse of exceptional beauty. White birch forests, hardwood-blanketed hills, rocky coasts and dunes, and a multitude of waterfalls beckon.

Nearby Au Train Bay is a gorgeous spot for a beach outing, with its broad sandy shore, gentle dune-slopes, river mouth, and *solitude!*

You might even do a little year-round "Christmas" shopping in the next door town of that name.

Take a cruise to Grand Island National Recreation Area for sightseeing by tour, rented bicycle, or hiking trail. Winter ice formations on the island are said to be stunning (though getting there may be a bit tricky!) At island's edge the Alger Underwater Preserve shares its secrets of the deep with snorkelers and those aboard a glass-bottom boat tour - a different kind of fun! Or, get your shipwreck tour on land at Au Sable Lightstation, where several marked and visible ruins are buried in the sand or shallow waters.

Make Munising memorable as a quiet overnight getaway - or a day trip, heading back to "homebase" at *Curtis* or *Blaney Park . . .*

Continuing West on U.S. 2 brings you near Big Spring (Kitch-Iti-Kipi). Take your picnic to the tiny Palms Brook State Park, and take a ride on the hand-powered-rope-pulled wooden observation raft over the clear spring pool.

Beyond that, on Lake Michigan's small Garden Peninsula at Snail Shell Harbor, is the fascinating Fayette Historic Townsite.

Spend a few hours exploring the ghost town "museum", its charcoal iron kilns and restored buildings, by carriage ride or walking tour.

Moving on into the **Western U.P.** - *S*ince *truly* romantic lodging choices may be scarce, you may want to stop only briefly for a panoramic view and a picnic at Stonington Peninsula's Peninsula Point Lighthouse; a hike to the "Hemlock Cathedral" at Little Bay De Noc Recreation Area; for a stroll around historic Escanaba, with a lunch break at Tommy's Restaurant diner, or dinner at Hereford & Hops brewery/restaurant, or The Log Cabin Supper Club; hiking and biking, sightseeing and skiing, or whitewater rafting in "The City of Trails" Norway-Vulcan area, Piers Gorge, and Iron Mountain; for canoeing, hiking, horseback riding, dogsledding, snow sports, and snacking at "The Depot" dining cars in Iron River; or for a tour of Cisco Chain of Lakes, and Sylvania Recreation Area in Watersmeet. Wow!

Steer your trusty chariot North to **Ontonagon**, a great central launching point for your Westerly adventures. This is "Big Snow Country", so winter is important here, and this is your chance to live it up with Alpine skiing, snowmobiling, snowshoeing, Nordic ski touring, and cuddling around the pot-belly stove!

Fabulous in Fall, Spring, or Summer, too, this far-West section is famous for 13,380-acre Lake Gogebic - a mecca for water recreation; the lakes, streams, forest wilderness areas, river, headwaters, five impressive "see-'em-all" waterfalls of unbelievable beautiful Ottowa National Forest Blackriver National Scenic Byway (county road 513) Whew!; the 3-state/2-county view from Copper Peak Ski Flying Hill; and for the unequaled natural esthetics of the 58,000 acre Porcupine Mountains Wilderness State Park . . .

The mysterious "Porkies" are spiderwebbed by 15 hiking trails (1-16 miles long), 42K of groomed xc ski trails, and winding roads leading to ultra-scenic locales like placid Lake of the Clouds, the Union Mine Trail, Summit Peak observation tower, Union Spring, and Presque Isle Falls.

Groves of 300 year old Eastern Hemlock brilliant hardwood forests, and wild rivers and streams form a thrilling background for a heavenly breath of solitude . . . to share!

Pack up your two-person tour group and make your way back East through Old Victoria, a primitive ghost town of hand-hewn log cabins, rock runs, and a resident historian, near Rockland.

Forge a "trail" Northeast to stunning, rugged Sturgeon River Gorge country, Silver Mountain, and more of Michigan's hypnotic natural magic.

Take a sort of "break" from nature while you spend a little time wrapped in the history of the **Keweenaw Peninsula.** This area's mining heritage is evident in Keweenaw National Historic

Park, and museums, mine tours, and the opulence of once-proud mansions, theaters, and commercial buildings of peninsula cities and towns. Hop a replica trolley for a tour of **Houghton**, and a trip to the campus of hallowed Michigan "Tech". Do a little shopping (or admiring) in this historical city and its "twin" city, **Hancock** - area artisans produce an intriguing array of painting,

 copper sculpture, wood carving, and Native American birchbark and quillwork artistry. Houghton is home port to the M.V. Ranger, where you can "sign on" for a voyage to the wilderness of Isle Royale National Park, or for a Sunset Cruise in Summer. Hancock's McLain State Park calls to couples for dazzling Gitchigumee sunsets, and a beach picnic near a shelter's fireplace.

Just North of Hancock, sits one of the state's most beautiful lookout points (especially during Fall's splendor!), the Quincy Lookout - Historic Monument, and the "astounding" Quincy Mine Hoist. The entrance to the mine, one of the world's largest, is now accessible by a new "cog" railway taking visitors down the side of the mountain!

Circle the wagons in **Laurium** and **Calumet** for another hike down history's path. Take the Laurium Manor mansion tour, take in a show at the beautifully restored Calumet Theatre, take a mine tour, or lose yourselves in a museum. Want some fun? Drive to nearby Lake Linden and stop at Lindell's Chocolate Shop for some homemade ice cream or a cozy lunch in a high-back booth among the leaded glass windows, memorabilia, and the nickelodeon's tunes!

From there, continue North via the scenic Sand Dune Drive between Eagle River and Eagle Harbor, or the stunning view of Brockway Mountain Drive. Make a stop at the Jampot for a bakery or jam treat! Hold up for awhile in *Copper Harbor,* at the peninsula's tip, for a host of romantic opportunities! You could cruise to Copper Harbor Lighthouse at sunset, clamber onto a seaplane and head to Isle Royale, take a nature tour, picnic on the shore, try out a kayak, snowshoes, a dogsled, or mountain bike. Then again, you could . . . visit Ft. Wilkins living history museum, hike through impressive Estivant Pines, take a mine tour, investigate a ghost town, cross-country ski, settle into the Brockway Sauna, or watch the Milky Way and those magical Northern Lights!

Make your way East to Lac La Belle's Haven Park for a picnic near a shaded waterfall or scenic wood bridge. Afterwards, the drive South to Gay provides a wealth of sights to satisfy your scenery cravings, but one more helping - in a hot air balloon - wouldn't hurt!

Baraga County - the "Land of Legends" - has a few surprises waiting, too. Stop off in lovely L'Anse on the bay for a U.P. delicacy - the ever present pasty - or for a monstrous cinnamon roll at Hilltop Restaurant. Close-by Canyon Falls & Gorge, Hanka Homestead living museum, secluded Silver Falls near Skaney , and Baraga's Shrine of the Snowshoe Priest offer interesting diversions along your journey.

Yes, you're "on the road again", but those endless miles of pure and bountiful beauty are interrupted by these fun stops: moose "hunting" (armed with camera, please!) in Michigammee, followed by a casual repast at rustic Mt. Shasta restaurant, one of the filming locations for *"Anatomy of a Murder"*; a humorabilia stop at Da Yooper's Tourist Trap - with "free tours, free restrooms", a wonderful giftshop, and fun and fascinating displays of U.P. history; or cross-country skiing atop the granite cliffs of Negaunee with a warm up at the ski center lodge, or a refreshment stop at Jasper Ridge Brewery.

Twelve marvelous waterfalls, miles of Lake Superior Shoreline, the Huron Mountains, and numerous wilderness playgrounds welcome you to **Marquette Country.** Take a guided tour, auto-cruise the forest byways, or hit the trails for an inspirational sojourn through sensational backcountry. Do the bikepath, a lighthouse cruise, a canoe trip, a ski adventure, an antique or artwork hunt, or a mountain hike. Then wash down the trail dust in the "urban hub", **Marquette.**

Pack a picnic and venture North on Big Bay Road. Stop! Look! And listen for a band concert at beautiful Presque Isle Park. Or admire the 360° view at Sugar Loaf Recreation Trail. Why not take a moonlight sea-kayak cruise for unique fun! Oh, you're there in the Winter? One of the most beautiful snowmobile trips is through the Yellow Dog Wilderness! However, and whenever, you reach **Big Bay,** get a dose of nostalgia at Thunder Bay Inn. The hotel, and the town, were the setting for Jimmy Stewart's classic film *"Anatomy of a Murder"*. Spend some time on the shores of peaceful Lake Independence. Be sure to include an afternoon tour of Big Bay Point Lighthouse in your plans, too.

Western U.P. or Eastern U.P., your stay will be a memorable one, filled with "Yooper" hospitality. If your goal is captivation of your darlin's heart, this is the place!

Upper Peninsula Travel & Recreation Association
1-800-562-7134

Drummond Island Tourism Assn.
1-800-737-8666 / www.drummond-island.com
Sault CVB
1-800-MI-SAULT / www.saultstemarie.com
Manistique Lakes Area Tourism Bureau
1-800-860-3820
Curtis Area C of C
1-800-OK-CURTIS
Newberry Area Tourism Assn.
1-800-831-7292 / http://visit-usa.com/mi/newberry
Paradise Area Tourism Council
906-492-3927
Munising Visitors Bureau
906-387-3536
Delta County C of C
1-800-531-9591 / www.deltami.com
Tourism Assn. of Dickinson County
1-800-236-2447 / www.ironmtntourism.org
Iron County Tourism Council
1-800-255-3620
Iron County C of C
1-888-TRY-IRON
Western U.P. CVB
1-800-272-7000 / www.westernup.com
Keweenaw Tourism Council
1-800-338-7982 / www.portup.com/snow
Baraga County Tourist & Rec. Assn.
906-524-7444
Marquette Country CVB
1-800-544-4321 / http://visit-usa.com/mi/marquette

The Lodge at Woodmoor Resort -
DRUMMOND ISLAND
"natural-ly romantic"

*W*hat could more portray the picture of romantic solitude than a wilderness lodge on a quiet, wooded island? Reach Drummond Island via a 10 minute car ferry ride, and take the scenic 12 mile drive to Woodmoor. Of course, you may also arrive by plane or boat.

The 40 room log lodge blends perfectly in this woods and water setting, In-

side, the comfort of Northern Lodge-style furnishings will put you instantly at ease. Warm and inviting, the common room beckons, with soft leather sofas, a massive stone fireplace, twig furniture and card tables, accented with colorful dhurrie rugs and pillows. The second floor outdoor deck is a fine place for watching the sunset or passing boats. You'll find it furnished with cafe tables and chairs.

Guests may take a dip in the outdoor pool, or mellow out in the whirlpool or sauna. You could rent a boat or bicycle, and explore the island, or Potagannissing Bay. Winter enthusiasts may cross-country ski on Woodmoor's 2,000 acres, or snowmobile local trails.

Return to your room and you'll return to tranquillity. The lodge-style furnishings include log beds, wood floors, and Hudson Bay blankets with antique snowshoes, skis, and golf clubs as imaginative accessories. Most often requested are the Boathouse (large sunlit room with kitchenette and deck), or the Hermitage Log Cabin (1 bedroom, bath, and living room with fireplace). You'll find it easier to get a specific request if you reserve 3 months in advance. Rates vary from $69-109 for rooms, $150 for Boathouse and Hermitage.

Invite up to 150 guests for your Wilderness Wedding at the outdoor chapel in the cedars. Receptions and anniversary parties are easily accommodated here, and honeymooners are treated to a bottle of champagne.

Breakfast and lunch are available at the Pine Bar & Grill adjacent to the lodge, while dinners are a woodland experience at The Bayside. This hunting-lodge style dining spot blends casual wilderness appeal with fireplace, candlelight and linens. Midwest regional gourmet specialties are prepared fresh daily. Start with a daily flatbread feature, and add a seasonal "Chef's Vegetarian Pasta", or "Pan-seared Michigan Whitefish with roasted pepper orzo and autumn vegetable ragu". All breads and desserts are made on the premises. Dinners ($14.50-18.50 ala carte) are served nightly from May-October. Dine indoors viewing bay and beautiful gardens, then adjourn to the deck for after-dinner cocktails or coffee, with a glorious sunset chaser!

Dining Delights

For the glimmer of stars, and the gleam of romance, try . . .

The Lodge at Woodmoor Resort
906-493-1039 or 1-800-999-6343
33494 S. Maxton Road, Drummond Island 49726
www.drummondisland.com

Inn-spired Activities ————————————

Rent a boat or bicycle; swim, sail, or rent a pontoon to enjoy our secluded harbor; go bowling, hiking, snowmobiling, xc skiing; get together! - on 84,000 acres of state land and 150 miles of fabulous shoreline!

Blaney Cottages - BLANEY PARK

"cupid's hideaway"

*T*his collection of tiny cottages is so inviting you won't be able to resist! Built in 1938 as part of the famous Blaney Park Resort, each one has been recently restored to modern comfort.

You can cozy-up in your separate efficiency or one bedroom cottage. Simplicity, warmth, and pure comfort are the hallmarks here. Lazy-boy® style living rooms, TV, queen beds

with shams, ruffles, and thick comforters all combine for the "at home" feeling. Reasonable year-around rates for two range from $45-70, depending on the cottage size.

The number one attraction here? Romantic gas log fireplaces in each unit. Use is optional, at an extra charge of $7 per night, but this *is* your *romantic holiday,* isn't it?

Settle in, then take a hike! Nature trails on the property lead right to beaver dams. After enjoying this, and all the area's wonderful attractions, come "home" for a cookout if you like. The picnic area has gas grills and tables for guest use. You may even want to have a little "play time" (the playground is for children *and* adults!), with volleyball, badminton, horseshoes, or swings. Or, snuggle around the bonfire - a common nightly event.

Each morning, your host will deliver a Continental Breakfast right to your door, including coffee, juice, and their famous "Yooper Muffins".

Call to discuss any arrangements you'd like your host to make for your special occasion. But do expect to have *any* stay here be special. Your hosts are dedicated to giving all their guests "service and warm feelings", at . . .

Blaney Cottages
906-283-3163
U.S. 2 & M-77, Blaney Park
R.R. 1- Box 55, Germfask Post Office 49836
Smoking and non-smoking cottages available

Inn-spired Activities ————————————

Enjoy snowmobiling, swimming in Lake Michigan, and touring the area; pedal local bike paths; hike or ski our own trails to the beaver pond!

"Love is a butterfly, which when pursued
is just beyond your grasp, but if you will
sit down quietly it may light upon you.
- Nathaniel Hawthorne

Celibeth House - BLANEY PARK

"every stay a cherished memory"

Another refurbished landmark from the famed old Blaney resort is the beautiful Celibeth House. This nostalgic Inn makes use of a fabulous antique and art collection to help recall the genteel hospitality of a bygone era.

This is a perfect setting to forget about the cares of the outside world and slow your pace. Spend some time together in the quiet reading room, keeping company with each other, (and the animals of the U.P.) . Peruse Celibeth's collection of books

and antique magazines. On a crisp evening, sit next to your sweetie in front of the living room fireplace, and listen to the crooning of the old Edison record player. The romantic mood is enhanced by the soft glow of large electric torchiers framing the mantle. Hold it! Now smile, and have your picture taken in one of two antique cutter sleighs displayed on the comfortably furnished front porch.

Most romantic of the eight Victorian-style rooms is the aptly named Victorian Suite. With separate sitting room and dressing room, this spacious enclave is sure to make your romantic memories special. You may even find a single, mysterious rose on the fainting couch!

Each of the seven remaining rooms is tastefully furnished, with its own private bath. Available from May 1-November 1, they are reasonably priced at $50-78.

Enjoy your Continental Breakfast of fresh fruit, juice, coffee, tea, rolls, and muffins in the Breakfast Room or on the deck. Watch the hummingbirds from your own small intimate table. What a delightful, sunny way to start your day!

Celibeth House is well known for its quiet, relaxing ambiance, and for its great home-baked treats.

You, and your true love, should know it, too!

Call . . .

Celibeth House
906-283-3409
Blaney Park Road (M-77), Blaney Park
Rte. 1 - Box 58-A, Germfask Post Office 49836
Smoking outdoors only, please

Inn-spired Activities ————————

Have fun with mini-golf, xc skiing, horseback riding; tour Pictured Rocks, Fayette Historic Village; Seoul Choix lighthouse, Soo Locks, Tahquamenon Falls, Whitefish Point Shipwreck Museum, and of course Big Spring!

Chamberlin's Ole Forest Inn - CURTIS

"a gem in the forest"

*W*ake to the call of the loons at this classic 19th Century hotel-style Inn on Big Manistique Lake (or is that "On Golden Pond"?) Guests arrive by car, boat, snowmobile, or even dogsled for a meal or an overnight stay at the former railroad-passenger hotel.

Beyond enjoying the area's many wonderful sights, there are plenty of options for entertainment. The two of you could paddle one of Chamberlin's canoes to explore the islands of the lake. You could snowmobile or ski Nordic-style right from your door, or, in Summer, ask your hosts about the secluded Lake Michigan beach they recommend. You might sit on the porch with a drink and gaze at the sunset.. Or, you could even be dazzled by the Northern Lights as you soak away your tensions in the outdoor Hot Springs® hot tub. You could, that is, if you were here!

Make your reservations 2-12 months in advance for one of the four rooms with private bath (shared-bath rooms are also available). One corner room features a Jacuzzi® for those very special occasions.

Brass or iron beds are the focal point for these uniquely decorated antique-filled rooms. Each has its own sitting area, floral wallpapers, and rich, soft carpeting. Most have old-fashioned clawfoot tubs! Ole' Forest Inn takes reservations for every month but April, and promises a relaxing stay for $90-95 including breakfast for two.

Chamberlin's lobby-lounge is home to the bar, a 10 foot stone fireplace, and small gift shop area. Since a portion of the lobby also serves as one of the dining rooms, you can request an intimate fireside table.

Your Full Breakfast is selected from a menu with choices like omelets, pancakes, waffles, oatmeal, and "Cinnamon Swirl French Toast", plus beverages. Weather permitting, enjoy your breakfast, lunch, cocktails and appetizers on the wicker-filled porch.

Dinner features daily specials and a large, varied menu including "Stuffed Whitefish with smoked trout stuffing", and "Raspberry Chicken Alfredo". Soup or salad, and warm  *Dining Delights* bread, are served with your meal for $8.95-16.95. Luncheons are moderately priced selections of Salads, Sandwiches, homemade Soups, and daily specials. Wedding receptions and anniversary parties? Yes! 100 guests max., please.

Evening's romantic atmosphere extends even to the yard - with colored lights and glowing bonfires. Christmas is a perfect time to visit this "gem in the forest" and enjoy their "romantic decor". Ask, too, about New Year's Eve and Sweetheart's Getaway Packages!

Anytime you visit, it'll be "fantastic ... again", at . . .

Chamberlin's Ole Forest Inn
906-586-6000 or 1-800-292-0440
One mile N. of Curtis on H-33, P.O. Box 307, Curtis 49820
No smoking in bedrooms, please

Inn-spired Activities ———————————————
Do it all, but don't miss beautiful Grand Marais, and Curtis' Annual Winter Carnival, and July 4th Celebration!

Homestead Bed & Breakfast -

"a secluded love cocoon"

Quiet, comfortable, informal, and "laid back". Sounds like Grandma's house, but it's actually a restored 1890's home providing gracious accommodations with those unexpected extras.

Soft, simple decor sets the stage for a display of dramatic Alaskan artwork and accessories. Take an armchair video "tour"

of Alaska anytime, right here in the living room. Learn of wildlife, and sea life, admire Danali Park and the Aurora Borealis. Ask your hostess for a few personal tales of Alaskan lifestyle.

A collection of brochures will direct you to all the area's wonders and activities. In spring, participate in "Sugarbush" (maple syrup processing). After a full day, though, you'll eagerly return to the peace of your private quarters. While the Homestead offers three shared-bath rooms for $55, you'll want to book

4-6 weeks in advance to assure your privacy in one of three deluxe rooms with private bath and TV ($75).

Each guest will feel very special indeed with treats like candies in your room, shampoo and soap gifts, and chocolates on your pillow. Fresh, clear ice water is provided to refresh you. Should you decide to bring back a sample of the local specialty - pasties - it will be heated for you at the Inn.

Though the atmosphere is casual, the "Advanced Continental" Breakfast is served in semi-formal style. Fresh fruit, homemade muffins, a variety of breads, cereal and juices may be topped off with bagels, cream cheese, and Alaskan smoked salmon!

Choose this 28 acre hideaway as your base to celebrate an anniversary or honeymoon, and you'll celebrate with complimentary flowers in your room, and a bottle of champagne. Or, tell your hostess your occasion, and your desires, in advance so special arrangements can be made for you. Ask about availability of special packages, too.

Perfect anytime of year, for any occasion, the Homestead represents the hospitality and proud family heritage of America, Alaska, Canada, and Newfoundland. You're invited to travel to another state (that of pure relaxation!) Travel to . . .

Homestead Bed & Breakfast
906-387-2542
713 Prospect Street, Munising 49862
Non-smoking accommodations

*Inn-spired Activities*

Take a bike tour of Grand Island; enjoy a Pictured Rocks or Shipwreck tour; go antiquing; rent a snowmobile; take the driving tour through Seney refuge; seek out our trails and waterfalls!

$\mathcal{T}imber\ \mathcal{R}idge$ - MUNISING

"a golden place"

$\mathcal{F}$ ar off the beaten path, in the heart of the Hiawatha National Forest, this motel-style hideaway offers nine private and very comfortable suites, with all the contemporary comforts. Built on a ridge overlooking small but picturesque Hovey Lake, Timber Ridge's three-room suites feature individual decks for holding-hands relaxin'! Or, cozy up on the sofa in your living room, complete with TV and mini-kitchen. No cooking required, of course!

Easy access to all the special attractions of the Munising area will assure you're as busy as you wish to be. Timber Ridge

is ideally located at the edge of cross-country ski and snowmobile trails, and provides easy access to hiking or secluded forest picnic spots as well. The ten mile drive from Munising on Hwy. 94 takes you past two waterfalls, and through the beautiful woodland hills. The tranquil forest surrounds you.

Schedule a romantic ride around the lake with your darlin' on a paddleboat or rowboat. Then relax in the sauna or rec-room. All for a very reasonable $45.

All during Winter's soft white beauty, and Spring's sparkling renewal; through Summer's glowing days, and Autumn's brilliant colors, this place, this perfect place is here for you. Make it yours!

Call . . .

Timber Ridge Motel and Lodge
906-387-3790
HCR 1, Box 52, Munising 49862

Inn-spired Activities —————————

Get "lost" in Au Sable sand dunes, the White Birch forest, or among dozens of inland lakes and streams; look for agates on Lake Superior beaches; go canoeing, or to an indoor ice arena; explore the Rock River ice caves and surroundings - together!

Northern Light Inn - ONTONOGAN

*"where the focus is the thoughtful balance
of privacy and personal attention"*

*T*urn of the century style blends with renovated interior comfort at this small town U.P. getaway.

Five "sensuous", "seductive", "dreamy" rooms invite you - each with private bath, two with Jacuzzi® and sitting area. For a very special rendezvous, however, reserve the whole third floor! This extremely private Jacuzzi® suite is plush, yet "woodsy". For an extra surprise, you can mail your memorable items, cards to your sweetie, or flowers, to the Innkeeper in advance for placement in your room or suite.

Rates ranging from $65-125 include a Full Gourmet Breakfast served in the dining room. Sample such specialties as "Baked Apple Pancake", "Cheddar & Bacon Quiche", or "Eggs Florentine".

Evening pleasures in the attractive and spacious common area will be enhanced by a roaring fire, hot apple cider, popcorn, or chocolate cake in Winter. Iced tea or sparkling mineral water refreshes in summer.

Your host recommends Ontonogan's "Sunset Walkway". Lovers of all ages can walk on the beach (one block from your Inn), select a driftwood seat, and watch the sun drift into Lake Superior. What a spectacular uncrowded place for sunsets, bonfires, and moments of magic!

Northern Lights welcomes weddings or anniversary celebrations. Parlor ceremonies can host 30-35 guests, or they can easily accommodate 75 in the garden.

Inquire about Spring "Wildflower Photography" weekend packages. Or, simply savor this wonderful place - just the two of you!

For deluxe accommodations mixing modern convenience, traditional style, and an *adult* atmosphere, call . . .

Northern Light Inn Bed & Breakfast
1-800-238-0018 or 906-884-4290
701 Houghton Street, Ontonogan 49953
Search the world wide web on Lake to Lake or
B & Bs of the U.P. site
A smoke free Inn

Inn-spired Activities ———————————

Discover the riches of area history via mine tours, museums, and ghost towns; ski, snowmobile, and hike in the nearby Porkies; hit the beach; shop our unique stores in Silver City and Ontonogan; share a stroll on Ontonogan's "Sunset Walkway"!

Charleston House HISTORIC INN -

"the very essence of romance"

*T*his stately copper-roofed Northern mansion has all the historic appeal of a Southern plantation home. You can almost picture Scarlet and Rhett sipping a julep on the white-columned double veranda. On a warm Summer evening perhaps you could join them - settling into white wicker

rockers and cooling yourselves under the ceiling fans, or the shade of 95 year old trees.

On those cooler days, enjoy the Library's simple traditional style, piano, books, and cozy fireplace with carved mantel. Throughout the Inn, historic formality mixes with extreme comfort to create a welcoming, casual ambiance. Rich wood trim and original paneling, a grand staircase, beveled and leaded windows, and hardwood floors complete the picture of classic beauty.

Though the formal dining room provides a "class setting" for weddings, receptions, and parties (25 guests max indoors, lawn 200), a Full Breakfast is delivered to your door in a charming ample picnic basket. Such specialties as "Finnish Pancake with warm raspberry sauce" will round out your choices of "make-your-own-granola", fresh bottled orange juice, and a fruit cup.

Each of four guestrooms features thoroughly modern amenities such as phones, cable TV, new private bath (with lighted showers), coffee pots, and tea bags, and even lights on dimmers for that softer, more romantic mood!

On your bed, you'll find a copy of the "Charleston House Notebook", designed to give guests a bit of the history, and an orientation of the amenities, of the Inn and the community.

The first-floor Remington Room is cozy and so, so inviting with its beamed ceiling, paneled walls, and private fireplace. Or, you may enjoy The Owner's Room, upstairs, with sitting area and bay window overlooking the canal in Winter. Each of these has a king-size canopy bed, as does the Daughter's room - the perfect haven for anniversary or honeymoon. Its private 38' porch invites you out to swing awhile in secluded bliss!

Choose one of these, or choose the Guest Room (with its mystery closet!), but do choose early. It's possible the Inn will be full 1 year in advance during peak times (1 1/2-2 years for Winter Carnival). Standard rates are $88-110, however special package rates are in effect for University events.

For Northern-style hospitality and a smile of welcome when you arrive, . . . let your imagination carry you to . . .

Charleston House Historic Inn
906-482-7790 or for res. 1-800-482-7404
918 College Avenue, Houghton 49931
Smoking limited to garden

Inn-spired Activities ————————————

Enjoy the State Parks, lighthouses, copper mines, and spectacular scenery - especially Brockway Mountain Drive!

Laurium Manor Inn - LAURIUM

"your ideal romantic rendezvous?
Could be . . ."

*T*his magnificent copper baron's mansion is so unique and imposing they offer afternoon tours! Make *your* tour more intimate, though, with a stay in one of ten fantastic guestrooms.

Laurium Manor, a 13,000 sq. ft., 45 room testament to

opulence, was built in 1908 Art Nouveau style. One of the most unusual features? The wallcoverings. Aside from any woodpanels and moldings, all walls are adorned with either canvas or hide, and finished with hand-painted murals, stenciled designs, or gilded finishes. The dining room walls are elephant hide! Canvas covered ceilings with carved plaster moldings, gilded detailing, handcarved cabinetry, oak and maple fireplaces, stained glass, and oak floors create a rich, warm feeling of pure elegance. Architecture and decor here is magnificent, and the history fascinating, but comfort and service are also most impressive.

Large and distinctive common rooms are guaranteed to encourage conversation about the building, so for privacy you may want to look for a quiet nook - perhaps fireside in library or den, or on the covered porch.

Premier room here is the Laurium Suite, done in deep, rich colors with high antique bed, traditional details, and private fireplace, sitting area, and bath. You're the master of the Manor!

The Guest Suite, also with fireplace and sitting room, features a delightfully old-fashioned clawfoot tub. Each room is uniquely decorated to fit the feel of its available space - perhaps large and airy with deep woods or white wicker, perhaps cozy and simple with cedar walls and deep plaid fabrics. Eight rooms have private bath, all have a very special flair.

Don't be disappointed! Reserve your choice of rooms at least 2 months in advance, and plan to have a memorable "gilded" holiday for $49-119 per night.

Innkeepers at Laurium Manor are experienced counselors for wedding preparations. Your ceremony may be held in the library, or outdoors on the porch or balcony. Sit-down dinners for up to 100 guests are arranged in dining room and library, while dancing, and socializing are best suited to the third floor ballroom!

Overnight guests awaken to a Full Buffet Breakfast served in the dining room. You can just smell the sweet delights such as "Butter Pecan Pancakes" or "Nutmeg Spice French Toast" that highlight a full array of cereals, juices, sausage, and breads. For more intimate dining, you're welcome to take a tray to your room. At Laurium Manor they serve (and sell) their own home-made jams. Gift shop sales of jam, shirts, etc. help to finance further restoration efforts.

You'll have an "unforgettable glimpse of turn-of-the-century Copper Country wealth", and an unforgettable romantic odyssey at . . .

Laurium Manor Inn
906-337-2549
320 Tamarack Street, Laurium 49913
Smoking outdoors only

Onn-spired Activities ————————

Hit the trails! Nordic skiing 1 mile away, snowmobiling 4 blocks; be entertained at the Calumet Theatre! For more inviting activities, see the suggestions of our Sister Inn . . .

Victorian Hall B & B - LAURIUM

*"or could **this** be
your special place?"*

*J*ust across the street, (from Laurium Manor), and equally enchanting, this 7500 sq. ft. Victorian-style mansion offers seven guestrooms, each with private bath.

Imagine yourself a copper mining magnate, accustomed to the finest in service and surroundings. You won't be disappointed here!

Bask in the luxury of your own very romantic hideaway - the Superior Suite. A stunning king-size canopy bed graces your spacious "bedchamber", and a private fireplace sets your separate sitting room alight with its warm glow. Morning sunbeams play upon the gold colored crownwork.

Room #11, downstairs, provides a cozy hideaway, with rich, glowing colors, and its own intimate fireplace. The second floor's "Dutch Room" (room #15) is warmed by a fireplace as well. Painted birch woodwork sets off the hand-brushed blue and white mural of Dutch Delft design. Deep, glorious red walls add drama to Room #12. In cooler months, the flames of a private fireplace reflect on these walls and add a warming glow! Rates vary from $69-109.

As if your private accommodations aren't luxurious enough, return to the common rooms for a relaxing evening of fireside conversation in the library or parlor. Magnificent stained glass sets off the hand-carved fireplaces, and adorns this exquisite mansion everywhere. Here, also, the walls are covered in canvas, some with original artwork murals, and some in simple Victorian splendor. Common rooms are cozier here, though no less imposing than those of Laurium Manor. Painted hand-cast plaster moldings, and designs decorate the ceilings. Imported woods from Germany's Black Forest are used artfully for fireplaces and trim work.

Guests in Victorian Hall receive the same outstanding service, and are invited to enjoy Laurium Manor's ambiance and hospitality for their Breakfast service.

A very grand diversion, a very perfect love awaits, at . . .

Victorian Hall Bed & Breakfast
906-337-2549
305 Tamarack Street, Laurium 49913
Sorry, no smoking indoors

Inn-spired Activities ————————————

Go Alpine skiing, cycling, antiquating; check out our museums, festivals, ghost towns, and fabulous Fall colors!

Keweenaw Mountain Lodge -

COPPER HARBOR
"the lure of solitude, the lure of love."

*F*or the rustic charm of log cabin lodgings in the perfect woodland setting, reserve a private cottage at this depression-era lodge.

Encircled by the great Keweenaw forests, your wilderness getaway begins with check-in at the Club House. Its deep brown logs, beamed ceilings, and massive fieldstone fireplace also provide a fantastic backdrop for the huge dining room, open from 8 am to 9 pm. Dinners "From the Heartland . . ." include such "Tasty Temptations" as "Broiled Lake Superior Trout or Whitefish", Prime Rib, and a "Homestyle Turkey Dinner" from $9.25 to $15.95.

Dining Delights

From mid-May to mid-October, you may stay in one of twenty three cabins, or eight motel-style rooms, for rates from $60-82. One, two, or three bedroom cabins are cozy, with living rooms furnished in overstuffed comfort. Most offer tempting stove fireplaces and a rack of firewood.

Step out on your porch for a refreshing breath of clean morning air, and head to the tennis or shuffleboard court, or the resort's own nine hole golf course. A network of hiking trails is mapped out for your pleasure, including a wooded path to nearby Copper Harbor.

Surround yourself with peace and serenity. Surround yourself with an aura of romance . . . at . . .

Keweenaw Mountain Lodge
906-289-4403
Copper Harbor 49918
Smoking facilities available

Inn-spired Activities ————————————

Join us for a golfing, hiking or dining adventure; relax here, or enjoy all the delights Copper Harbor and the Peninsula have to offer!

Sand Hills Lighthouse Inn-AHMEEK

" 'capturing the romance of a bygone era.' . . .
It called to ships . . . it calls to you."

*B*y your heart, you're summoned - to the Gitchegummee shore. By your hosts, you're welcomed - to all the history and majesty this historic lighthouse Inn displays.

With 35 acres, and 3,000 feet of frontage on Lake Superior, Sand Hills exhibits a special charm year-round. Spring wildflowers paint the beautiful, romantic woodland trails where "you

are alone in the world". Collect agates and driftwood on your Summer shoreline stroll. Watch the building of a "long-abandoned" garden in the woods. Admire Autumn's blazing palette, and watch the wildlife scurry into Winter. Crashing waves and ice formations will set the stage for a dramatic cross-country ski adventure, and fabulous, quiet cold-weather escape.

Hand-tooled woodwork, ornate crown moldings, and art nouveau accessories accent the old-world comfort of the common areas. Warmed by the fireplace, charmed by the music of grand piano or victrola, and captivated by views of the lake, you'll drift into serenity on soft leather sofas.

Eight sequestered rooms with private baths set the tone for romance, and create an eclectic Victorian ambiance, punctuated with nautical lighthouse artifacts, antiques, and artworks.

While guests in the Northwest and Northeast corners enjoy whirlpool tubs and private balconies, and East Wing guests may have a private entrance or separate sitting rooms, most enchanting is the King Room. You'll feel like royalty in a velvet-draped canopy bed, and warm gold-trimmed setting. Enjoy your private remote control fireplace, and a commanding view.

Before retiring, though, don't miss viewing the spectacular sunset from the 101 foot tower! Rates vary from $132.50-200 (tax included), but call 6-8 months in advance to assure an opening for your special nights. The Inn is open all year, guaranteeing guest tranquillity with no phones and no TV.

Speak your vows in the tower - so unique, so intimate (20 guests only, please), or on the lawn or shoreline. Honeymoon or anniversary couples are gifted with wine or champagne. Whatever the reason, whatever the season, this is a truly beautiful place to be.

"Become a keeper of the light". Become a romantic, at . . .

Sand Hills Lighthouse Inn
906-337-1744
Five Mile Point Road, P.O. Box 414, Ahmeek 49901
A smoke-free bed & breakfast Inn

Inn-spired Activities ———————————————

Take a copper mine or museum tour; take Brockway Mountain Drive; cross-country ski or comb the beach; catch the sunrise, sunset, Northern lights, or "the magical majesty of a starlit Keweenaw night"!

Landmark Inn - MARQUETTE

*" exquisite restoration . . .
intimate surroundings."*

*T*his "boutique-style" first-class historic hotel is completely restored, and "overlooks nothing but Lake Superior"! Enter the lobby and step into the 1920s splendor of marble stair-case, brass railings, regal wood paneling, and crackling fireplace. Admire leaded glass, crystal chandeliers, and the comfortable elegance of traditional antique seating groups.

Sixty two private accommodations, range from standard rooms, two-room suites, and honeymoon Jacuzzi® suites, to a luxury sixth floor penthouse apartment. Each is decorated in its

own individual period furnishings complemented by locally hand-crafted birch furniture in some suites. Motif rooms include themes such as Amelia Earhart, Dandelion Cottage, and Rydhom Camp. Twenty one feature fire-places, nine have separate sitting rooms, and five have Jacuzzi® tubs. Favorites are the Tavernini, and Kawbawgam suites for you romance-seekers!

Rates, depending on amenities and lake views, will vary from $95-210, with Penthouse at $455-595 seasonally. Please reserve al least one month in advance for peak times. All rooms/suites include a nightly "turn-down" service and good-night dessert for that extra special pampering. Suites and lake-view rooms have VCRs and plush terry robes as well.

Treat your love to some time in the Hotel's spa, complete with massage therapist, Jacuzzi®, exercise equipment, sauna, and tanning booth.

Dining Delights

Dining here is an equally elegant experience in the dramatic Heritage Dining Room, or the gourmet sixth floor Sky Room. The Heritage Room serves standard breakfast fare including "Belgian Waffle", "Club Breakfast", and "Mediterranean Omelet" for $5-6.75; luncheon specialties including "Lake Superior Whitefish" and "Grilled Portabello Sandwich" for $5.95-7.95; and an International mix of dinner favorites including "Medallions of Turkey stuffed with dried cherries, scallions, baby spinach and Montrechat cheese, ground cashews, and sauce Mornay" for $13.50-19.50. On Sunday, try the spectacular Brunch Buffet.

The Skyroom - your ultimate romantic dining choice - features two walls of windows overlooking Marquette Harbor,

New England decor, fireplace, and a hand-painted ceiling mural. Serving a daily-changing variety of gourmet specialties Thursday, Friday, and Saturday only. You can expect first class service in a quaint, unpressured setting.

For more casual, lighter fare, stop in the classic English-style Northland Pub & Grill. Or, enjoy a lakeview cocktail from the sixth floor North Star Lounge. Entertainment is available in the Pub only.

As expected from a fine hotel, full catering services are available in a private banqet room for your 120 guest sit-down (plated) reception, or your 200 (standing) guests for cocktail service and hors d'oeuvres.

So, why not go first class? At the . . .

Landmark Inn
906-228-2580 or 1-888-7-LANDMARK
230 N. Front Street, Marquette 49855
www.thelandmarkinn.com
email: lpeterson@thelandmarkinn.com
Smoking: in lobby, Pub, North Star Lounge and
designated guestrooms

Inn-spired Activities —————————

Take a boat tour or waterfall tour; go horseback riding; take a carriage ride or a special Sugar Loaf hayride!

ℬig ℬay ℂoint ℒighthouse BED &

BREAKFAST - Big Bay
"a safe haven . . . for undimmed romance."

*W*hat better way to experience all the romance of the "Inland Seas", than a stay in this unique B& B? Fulfill your yearning for deep solitude and unspoiled natural beauty - you'll be inspired!

Stroll along the windswept cliff and gaze at ships, or maybe ghosts of ships, on Gitchegumee's horizon.

You may find yourself engrossed in the area's many natural wonders, perhaps enjoying a canoe trip, or a picnic alongside a spectacular waterfall - but you'll soon return.

Back at the Lighthouse, explore 40 acres of wooded trails, then relax in the sauna or library with TV/VCR, games,

books, selected CDs, or just each other. On cooler days, warm yourselves by the living room fire. sip hot or cold refreshments, and sample homemade cookies anytime.

For a real taste of the lighthouse-keeper's life, climb the 120 ft. tower, enjoy the view - the forests and fields, the Huron Mountains and constantly changing Lake Superior, the storms, the stars, the ice, and the Aurora.

Then settle into one of seven cozy, country-style rooms (each with private bath). Snuggle under your quilt or down comforter, and admire the carefully selected antiques and lighthouse-themed accessories. The tariff? $85-175 depending on room and season. Book 6-8 weeks in advance, and remember, the Inn is closed from the Monday before Thanksgiving to December 26.

Guests will greet the glorious Lake Superior morning with a Full Breakfast, served family style in the Lighthouse dining room. Enjoy fruit, cereal, muffins, jam and special Berry Butters, as well as a hot main dish such as "Stuffed French Toast".

For those of you celebrating a special occasion, ask about gift baskets which can be ordered from Attitudes of Marquette.

This may be the perfect setting for a unique and special tower wedding ceremony, though guests are limited to a maximum of four.

Here, alone, let Lake Superior's glittering waves reflect the shining beacon of your love!

Big Bay Point Lighthouse
Bed & Breakfast
906-345-9957
3 Lighthouse Road, Big Bay 49808
No smoking indoors, please

Inn-spired Activities ——————————————

Canoe Iron River; enjoy our trails and spectacular shoreline; picnic by a waterfall!

$\mathcal{T}hunder\ \mathcal{B}ay\ \mathcal{I}nn$ - BIG BAY

"the perfect picture of romance."

$\mathcal{P}$icture the balconies draped in green holiday garland punctuated with red-bowed wreaths. Picture the spectacular view of Lake Independence, shimmering in the Summer sun. Picture the historic lobby with a crackling fire in the fireplace. And picture yourself a guest, with your true love, at this "comfortable, friendly" country Inn.

Picture it as a one-time company store for local lumber concerns. Picture it in the 1940s as Henry Ford's vacation retreat. Then picture it as the setting for that classic 1959 film *"Anatomy of a Murder"* starring Jimmy Stewart and Lee Remick.

Thunder Bay Inn is certainly known for its past, and for its present purpose of pure Northern hospitality! Twelve comfortable guest rooms are furnished in ruffled curtains, antiques, quilts, and hardwood finishes. Only seven have private baths (six full baths, 6 partial baths), so you may want to reserve your "love nest" 3-6 months in advance. (The Inn is closed in April.) The "picture-perfect" favorite for romantic escapes? The Henry Ford Room, of course.

Rates vary seasonally from $55-115, and include a Continental Plus Breakfast buffet of juice, cereal, granola, bakery treats, coffee, and sometimes fruit. Most guests enjoy breakfast in the lobby, though some prefer the porches in Summer, or a private in-room repast.

Pull up a cozy chair in the Great Room during breakfast, and listen to your Innkeeper's fascinating "history lesson" of the area, the Inn, and the *"Anatomy of a Murder"* movie magic. Or, settle back with your complimentary popcorn later for a showing of the film - a fun and welcome addition to historical displays and scrapbooks on the movie.

Special occasions are celebrated with a gift of wine or champagne in your room, dessert *Dining* with dinner, and an Inn coffee mug. Small *Delights* weddings in the porch or in the Great Room (max guests 35-40) may be followed by a small dinner reception.

A large, casual pub/restaurant, built for the movie filming, serves a pleasing fare of homemade Soups, Salad, and Pizza, with Sandwiches for $3-6 per plate. Dinner menu includes such standards as "Lake Superior Whitefish", Steak, Chops, and Chicken for an average of $8-10. Full beverage service is available.

Yes, you can picture Thunder Bay in Winter white, or golden Autumn glow, and framed by Big Bay's scenic hills and lakes. Then picture yourselves, here . . . and in love!

Thunder Bay Inn
906-345-9376
Box 286, Big Bay 49808
www.bigbay.com
Smoking only on first floor; designated restaurant
areas; and outdoors

Inn-spired Activities ————————————
Hike to waterfalls in the area; this is a "Northwoods" kind of place!

Yet a third historic Blaney Resort showpiece! A little out of the way, "a little out of the ordinary" they say. Known throughout the area as *the* choice for elegant fine dining, this popular summer eatery may feature broiled "Fresh Great Lakes White-fish", "Nutty Chicken", "Homemade Blaney Sausage on pasta with marinara, sautéed peppers, and onions", and other Steak, Seafood, and specialty dishes ($8.95-14.95 - menu changes yearly). Candlelight reflects on knotty pine walls, wood-view windows, and your partner's eyes!

Open Tues.-Sun. Mothers' Day through Labor Day - call for September hours / Private parties in Special Occasion Room May 1-Oct. 31 for up to 350 - dance can be arranged / Full bar

1 Mile N. of U.S. 2 on M-77 • 906-283-3417

Dining Delights

Tahquamenon Falls Brewery & Pub - at Camp 33, the Falls

The focal point here is the blazing fire - a logging camp tradition in any season - indoors and out. Fresh contemporary flair, added to the warmth of wood and stone, create a casual, comfortable atmosphere to enjoy dining treats like "Chicken Cranberry Salad", "Brew Pub Cheese Soup", "Pub Burger", "Pork Tenderloin Medallions", "Pasta Primavera", Pasties, Steaks, Shrimp, and Lake Superior Whitefish and Trout (open for lunch and dinner - prices from $5.50-15.95). Be sure to sample the camp's own latest micro-brews!

Open all year / Seasonal micro-brewed beer and home-brewed root beer / Outdoor dining on deck

At Camp 33, Upper Tahquamenon Falls • 906-492-3300

Dining Delights

The Brownstone Inn - Au Train

Serving "exceptional food and drink" in the warmth and charm of a wood-lined, fireside-lit stone enclave. A variety of luncheon offerings like "Jamaican Steak Caesar Salad", Burgers, Whitefish Sandwiches, and "Brown Rice and Lentil Sandwich" ($3.50-7.95); a nightly list of dinner specials like "Stuffed Pork Chop with dried Michigan cherries and walnuts", "Spinach Lasagna", and "Stuffed Chicken Breast with tomato, basil, feta cheese and ham", plus Beef, Seafood and Pasta specialties ($5.95-15.95); starters like "Shrimp Jammers", "Cheese Battered Broccoli", and "Laughing Whitefish Salad"; and sweet endings like espresso, cappuccino, and "Profitirolli - cream puffs with ice cream and hot brandy fudge sauce". Truly special!

Closed for 2 weeks before hunting season / Reservations recommended / Small private parties possible / Very large beer menu & wine list, plus full bar and specialty drinks

M-28 West • 906-892-8332

298

Dining Delights

Sydney's - Munising

G'day, Mates! Kangaroos. Boomerangs. What more could you ask from a "visit" to Australia in this casual, candlelit eatery. Featuring a variety of Seafood, Steaks, and Sandwiches, and very large Omelets for breakfast. Lunch is different everyday in the "specials" department - try Mexican Day or French Dip Day. You'll really enjoy the bountiful Friday night Seafood Buffet, and Saturday's Prime Rib Buffet (both $11.95) (breakfast $4-6, lunch specials $4.45, sandwiches under $5, dinner menu $8.95-10). Finish it all with a "Chocolate Wonder from Down Under" (brownie, ice cream, fruit, chocolate sauce and whipped cream)! Blimey!

Open all year / Smoking in designated areas / Reservations accepted / Full bar / Catering hall upstairs - max guests 200
M-28 East, 400 Cedar Street • 906-387-4067

Dining Delights

Candlelight Inn - Ontonogan

Relax and watch the birds at this contemporary casual North woods restaurant. Candlelight? Of course! With firelight and fresh flowers to "enhance the romance"! House specials like BBQ Ribs, Prime Rib, and Fresh Lake Trout ($9-16 + senior prices), add to regular delights of the Friday evening Land & Sea Buffet ($9.95) and Sunday Brunch ($5.95). Finish with "Peanut Butter Ice Cream Pie", or "Fried Ice Cream"! Mmmm!

Open all year except Christmas Day / Smoking in designated areas / Reservations accepted / Full bar / Private dining room seats 30, or parties in main dining room for up to 200
2077 M-37 • 906-884-6101

Dining
Delights
                Ming Garden - Houghton

Sit beside the peaceful, flowing rock wall waterfall and meditate together! Then try an Oriental feast of "Crispy Orange Chicken", "Shrimp in Cheerful Spring", "Sweet and Sour Pork", "Hot Hunan Beef", or "Sizzling Subgum", just to mention a few choices from the extensive menu (lunch $3.25-6.25, dinner $7.50-15). For a really cozy repast, order chopsticks and feed each other "Seven Stars around the Moon" ($23 for two)!
Open seven days / Smoking in designated areas / Take out avail.
1301 Ridge Road, off M-26 • 906-482-8000

Dining
Delights
    Northern Lights Restaurant -
7th Floor, Franklin Square Inn - Houghton

For "7th Floor Dining, served with a slice of the Keweenaw sky", and a fabulous view of Lake Superior and the peninsula, be sure to try this one. Newly redecorated in vibrant sea green and plum, with faux green marble wainscot, the dining room provides a simple, upscale setting for breakfasts like "Banana Walnut Silver Dollar Pancakes", Omelets and Fritattas; lunches of perhaps "Chinatown Nachos", and daily Quiche specialties, or the fun eclectic tavern menu & premium beers in the lounge; or dinners like "Chicken Amaretto", or "Shrimp de Jonghe" (breakfast & lunch $4-7, dinner entrées under $15). Sunday Brunch includes breakfast & lunch items with fresh fruit, salad & dessert bars. 365 Days a year it's always "fine dining with a casual edge"! (You may even want to check into one of the hotel's romantic Jacuzzi® suites!)
Open all year / Full bar and wine list / Reservations accepted / Private banquet room seats 250 / Smoking in designated areas / Guitarist in lounge Friday evenings
820 Shelden Avenue • 906-482-4882

*Dining
Delights*   濼he 濼Cut-濼nn - *Kearsarge*

This long and low contemporary "house of warmth and friendliness" offers something different for the health-conscious diner". How about "Nut & Cheese Loaf", "Grilled Chicken a la Orange over rice", "Lasagna or Veggie Lasagna", "Grilled Chicken Salad with honey mustard ranch dressing, greens, egg. cucumber, tomato, and dilled havarti cheese", or "Grilled Prime Rib" ($4.25-8.95).
Open for lunch and dinner Tuesday - Sunday
U.S. 41 North • 906-337-1133

*Dining
Delights* 濼he 濼ld 濼ountry 濼Caus -*Kearsarge*

With a log cabin atmosphere that's both casual and inviting, this nicely remodeled peninsula landmark is "a favored place of the Copper Country for nearly 50 years". Feast on Trout and fresh Lake Superior Whitefish, as well as German American specialties like "Knackwurst", "Rouladen", and "German Combination Platter - Smoked Pork Chops, Sauerbraten, and Weinerschnitzel", and "Steak Au Poivre with green peppercorn brandy sauce" (lunch $4-7, dinner $9-18). Sip German beer and have a piece of signature "Black Forest Cherry Torte" by the stone fireplace. Say "Danke"!
Open year-round / Smoking section available / Reservations accepted though not for Saturday evening or Sunday Brunch 11-2 / Full bar, wine, and wide variety of German beers and imports / Parties up to 90 guests can be accommodated
U.S. 41 North • 906-337-4626

*Dining
Delights*

*Fitzgerald's Restaurant -
at Eagle River Inn - Eagle River*

Candlelight, linens, fine china, stemware, and an unbelievable Lake Superior view of gorgeous sunsets, Northern lights, and passing oreboats! Slip in for some intimate nautical drama, and "Truly terrific" food like "Spinach Salad with fresh strawberries", "Fresh Breadsticks with sundried tomato pesto and garbanzo bean spread", "Fresh Lake Trout and Whitefish", handcut Steaks, "Baby Back Ribs baked in dark beer", or "Moroccan Vegetable Stew with couscous cheese crust" ($12.50-20.50). Listen for the sound of waves crashing on the beach. Listen for the occasional call of the loons, or ghostly ships. Listen to your heart!

Call for seasonal hours / Reservations accepted for parties of 6 or more only / Full bar and wine list and micro-brew beer / Smoking in designated areas / Outdoor dining on the deck
100 Front Street • 906-337-0666

*Dining
Delights*

Harbor Haus - Copper Harbor

Fresh, from scratch specialties like Lake Superior Fish, Rabbit, Venison, "Warm Chicken and Rotini Salad" and many German delights, are served by friendly dirndl-dressed waitresses. Look for lots of weekend and daily specials. Fresh berries dress up the Summer menu in special treats like "Berry Crepes". Outstanding!

Open seven days from June to October 15 / Full bar / Reservations only required for large parties / Smoking in designated areas
Brockway Avenue • 906-289-4502

302

Dining Delights   *Northwoods Supper Club - Marquette*

For the ambiance of a log cabin structure, offset with linens, and richly colored carpets and wallcoverings. For a mood set in candlelight and a terraced garden waterfall view. For classic fine dining featuring "Escargot & Artichokes Parmesan", Prime Rib, Pasta, handcut Steaks, Poultry, fresh Fish and Seafood, and gourmet delights like "Tournedos ala Bernaise", and "Stuffed Shrimp with crabmeat, cheese, and sour cream" ($9.95-27.95). For a delightful "Luncheon Buffet with soup, salad & sandwich fixins", or dishes like "Monte Cristo Sandwich" ($2.45-8.75). For detailed service, and for "an experience rather than a meal!"
Open all year / Smoking permitted in designated separate room/ 2 Banquet rooms seating up to 200 / Full bar and very extensive wine list / Outdoor dining in garden / Weekend entertainment
260 Northwoods Road • 906-228-4343

Dining Delights   *The Office Supper Club - Marquette*

Who would have thought going to "The Office" could be so enjoyable? Settle into a velvet-draped booth, a cozy "white linen" table, or the horseshoe bar, and let the wait staff do the work! This classic steakhouse offers a "big-city menu" in a relaxing small-town atmosphere. Certified Angus Beef, along with Seafood, and such specialties as "French Cut Spring Lamb Racks from New Zealand", Prime Rib, "Veal Chops and Veal Filet Mignon", "Chicken sautéed in wine sauce", and "Australian Coldwater Rock Lobsters", complement a "12 oz. Pork Chop that re-defines the pork-chop", and special occasion dishes like "Beef Wellington", Alligator, or Ostrich ($10.95-25). Delightful!
Closed rarely / No smoking effective Jan, 1, 1999 / Full bar and quite nice wine list / Private parties possible 24-30 guests max. Reservations accepted
154 W. Washington Street • 906-228-9335

À Deux Adventures

- Eastern U.P.

Sault Ste. Marie - Curtis - Blaney Park
Soo Locks Boat Tours 906-632-2512
Fish & Hunt Shop (snowmobile, pontoon, jet boat
  rentals) 906-586-5531
Germfask - Seney
Big Cedar Canoe Livery 906-586-6684
Northland Outfitters (bike, canoe, kayak, raft rent) 906-586-9801
Seney National Wildlife Refuge....................................906-586-9851
Newberry
Mark's Rod & Reel (canoe rentals)...............................906-293-5608
Tahquamenon Boat Service, Inc. (Toonerville Trolley & Scenic
  Riverboat Trip .... 1-888-77-TRAIN or 906-876-2311
  if no answer, call 906-293-3806
Tahquamenon River Logging Museum..........................906-293-3700
Two-Hearted Canoe Trips, Inc. (at Rainbow Lodge)......906-658-3357
Wolfsong Outfitters (dog sled adventures) 906-658-3356
Paradise
Great Lakes Shipwreck Museum...................................906-635-1742
Superior Coast Divers, Inc. (rentals) 906-492-3534
Tahquamenon Falls State Park 906-492-3415
Tom Sawyer Riverboat & Paul Bunyan Timber Train.......................
  .... 1-800-732-2331 or 906-876-2331 and 906-632-3727
Whitefish Point Underwater Preserve 906-492-3445
Grand Marais - Munising - Au Train
Lake Superior Brewing Co. at the Dunes Saloon..........906-494-BEER
ALTRAN Bus (Grand Island Tours)..............................906-387-4845
Dogpatch Restaurant (casual FUN dining)....................906-387-9948
Grand Island Ferry Service...906-387-2433
Grand Island Shipwreck Tours (glassbottom boat & scuba
  trips)...906-387-4477
Pictured Rocks Cruises, Inc. (scenic boat cruises)..........906-387-2379
Pictured Rocks National Lakeshore .... 906-387-3700 or 387-2607
Riverside Resort (canoe rentals)...................................906-892-8350
Skylane Air Tours (Pic. Rocks & Grand Island).............906-222-8367
Au Train Songbird Trail 906-387-3000

304

À *Deux Adventures*

-Southern Shore & Western U.P.

Southern Shore - (Cut River, Gould city, Garden, Escanaba)
Cut River Inn 906-292-5400
Michihistrigan 1-800-924-8873
Fayette Historic Townsite 906-644-2603
Hereford & Hops 906-789-1945
Hiawatha National Forest.................................906-786-4062
The Log Cabin Supper Club...............................906-786-5621
Tommy's Restaurant.....................................906-786-1983

WESTERN U.P.
Norway-Vulcan Area
Argosy Rafting Adventures 715-251-3886
Da Do Wop Malt Shop (sandwiches, ice cream) 906-563-9786
Norway Mountain (ski area)..............1-800-272-5445 or 906-563-9700
Iron Mountain - Iron River - Lake Gogebic
Northwoods Wilderness Outfitters, Inc. (dog sled, snowshoe, xc
  ski)..906-774-9009
Pine Mountain (ski area) 1-800-505-PINE
George Young Recreational Complex and Wolf Track
  Nature Trail 906-265-3401
Iron County Historical Museum................. 906-265-3942 or 265-2671
Partridge Pines Trail Rides and Scenic Guided Tours
  at Ski Brule ....1-800-362-7853 or 906-265-4957
The Depot Restaurant & Bakery 906-265-6341
The Pasty Corner 906-265-3022
Mt. Zion (ski area)................... 906-932-9879 or 932-4231
Wakefield/Ironwood - Bessemer
Indianhead Mountain Resort (ski area) 1-800-3-INDIAN
Big Powderhorn Mountain (ski area) 1-800-222-3131
Blackjack Ski Resort 1-800-848-11125
Copper Peak Ski Flying Hill............................906-932-3500
Ottawa National Forest (Black River Area)................906-667-0261
Ontonogan - Rockland
Porcupine Mountain (ski area) "The Porkies" 906-885-5275
Porcupine Mountain State Park...........................906-885-5885

À Deux Adventures

- Western U.P. - Keweenaw Peninsula & Baraga County

Houghton

Isle Royale National Park 906-482-0984
Isle Royale Seaplane Service 906-482-8850
Lake Superior Boat Cruises (to Isle Royale) 906-482-0984
Marie's Deli & Restaurant (light meals) 906-482-8650
Michigan Tech's Walker Theatre (university) 906-487-1885

Hancock

Arcadian Copper Mine (tours) 906-482-3101
F. J. McClain State Park .... 1-800-44-PARKS or 906-482-0278
Quincy Steam Hoist & Mine Tours 906-482-3101

Calumet - Laurium - Lake Linden - Ahmeek

Calumet Theatre .... 906-337-2610 or 487-2073
Coppertown USA Mining Museum .... 906-337-4354 or 337-4579
Laurium Manor (tours) 906-337-2549
Lindell's Chocolate Shop 906-296-0793
Delaware Copper Mine Tours .... 906-289-4688 or 337-3333

Eagle Harbor - Copper Harbor

Jampot Bakery - The Society of St. John Monks .... no phone
Eagle Harbor Lightstation Museum (late June-late Sept)
Estivant Pines
Astor House Museum 906-289-4449
Copper Harbor Lighthouse Tours 906-289-4410
Fort Wilkins State Park 906-289-4215
Isle Royale Queen III (cruises to Isle Royale) 906-289-4437
Keweenaw Adventure Co. (sea kayak tours, mountain bike
    rental, dog sledding, xc ski) 906-289-4303
Keweenaw Bear Track Eco Tours 906-289-4813
"Spirit of America" (lighthouse & sunset cruises) 906-289-4996
The Boat Co. (kayak tours) 906-289-4515

Baraga County

Hanka Homestead 906-353-7116
Hilltop Restaurant (L'Anse) 906-524-7858
Mt. Shasta Restaurant (Michigamme) 906-323-6312
Superior Balloons (hot air balloon rides - Chassell) 906-334-2906

À Deux Adventures

- Marquette Country - Marquette - Big Bay

Marquette Country
Da Yooper's Tourist Trap 906-485-5595
Jasper Ridge Brewery (Ishpeming) 906-485-6017
U.S. National Ski Hall of Fame......................906-485-6323
Granite Pointe Nordic Ski Center (Negaunee).......... 1-800-55-XCSKI
or 906-475-8200
Michigan Iron Industry Museum (Negaunee) 906-475-7857
Marquette Country Tours (various types of tours and
  equipment rental).....................................906-226-6167

Marquette
Attitudes Gift Baskets 906-228-2068
Marquette Mountain (ski area)...............1-800-944-SNOW
Marquette Side Treks (sea kayak tours).........906-228-8735
Uncle Ducky Cruises (lighthouse tours)..........906-228-5447

Big Bay
Big Bay Point Lighthouse Tours 906-345-9957
Huron Mountain Outfitters (wilderness and waterfall
  tours)......................................906-345-9265 and 345-9552
North Country Outfitters (kayak, canoe, and mountain
  bike rentals and tours.............................906-345-9504

For complete information on lighthouses, waterfalls, parks,
and snowmobile and cross-country ski trails, please contact:

The Upper Peninsula Travel & Recreation Association
1-800-562-7134

Mackinac Island

T̄his is it! Michigan's ultimate romantic getaway. So much beauty, history, and magic is packed into this small space! The sparkling blue water - reflected like diamonds in the eyes of your love. The peaceful emerald forests - enfolding you like a tender embrace. The stunning limestone rock formations - a testament to forever. The Fort, the stately Victorian mansions, and of course the lack of automobiles - all reminiscent of a simpler, slower time . . . a time for romance!

Most Island visitors arrive by boat, and dock in the center of a bustling shopping district filled with antique, clothing, gift, art, curio and candy stores. Select a keepsake, while away some lazy time, and watch the making of some famous Mackinac Island fudge!

Stroll through the colorful past, examining Missionary Bark Chapel, the museum homes and government buildings of Market Street, the working Benjamin Blacksmith Shop, the Indian Dormitory, the Governor's residence, the churches, and that hilltop treasure - Fort Mackinac (admission fee applies - ticket includes

Original watercolor by Carolyn Scott Risk - Copyright © 1997

entry to other attractions). In the fort, tour administrative buildings, soldiers' quarters, the post hospital, schoolhouse, and parade grounds. Exhibits, demonstrations, and reenactments give you all the flavor of a 19th century soldier's life. Lunch at the Fort Tea Room, and marvel at the spectacular view from this natural fortress.

A large part of the unbelievable charm of this island is the old-fashioned "horse and buggy" transportation. Take a narrated Carriage tour for a pleasant ride and overview of island life, or hire a carriage and drive it yourself for a truly unique experience. Carriages act as "taxi" service here, as well, providing historic transportation to island attractions.

The island was once inhabited by Native Americans. They named it Michilimackinac, meaning "Big Turtle", a tribute to the part of nature it most brought to mind. Later renamed Mackinac, the island became Michigan's first state park. Eighty percent of this most unusual "park" remains a wilderness, offering glimpses of unequaled forest and lakeside beauty, including wildflowers, expansive Lake Michigan and Lake Huron vistas, caves, and magnificent limestone rock formations.

These unusual natural attractions inspired many Indian legends. The 75' high limestone "tower, Sugar Loaf, is said to have been "filled with honey, and the home of Manibozo, the Great Spirit". Famous Arch Rock has its own romantic story ...

" . . . a beautiful young Indian maiden called Ne-Daw-Mist (She-Who-Walks-In-The-Mist) was gathering wild rice, and came upon a handsome young brave - son of a sky spirit. They fell deeply in love. The maiden's Father forbade her marriage to the non-mortal brave. He beat her cruelly and tied her to a high, rocky bluff on the Island of the Turtle. As she wept for her lost love, her tears washed away the stone, forming the arch. Her dashing brave found and rescued her, taking her in his arms. They returned together to the home of his sky people, leaving behind a dazzling monument to true love".*

All the history and magic of Mackinac Island is easily accessible by carriage, saddle horse, bicycle, or footpath. Miles of trails direct you to natural highlights and viewpoints such as Point Lookout, the 320 foot "top of the island" overlooking Bois

Blanc island, Round Island with its memorable lighthouse, Mackinaw City, and the "Mighty Mac" bridge. Visit the Scout Barracks, Skull Cave, cemeteries, Fort Holmes, British Landing Nature Center, and the battlefield - all "Down the Middle" of the island.

The "Round the Shore" road (8.2 miles) creates a fantastic bicycle trip, with stops at lovely Dwightwood Springs, Arch Rock, Sugar Loaf, the 300 yard pond-side Wildflower Nature Trail, Point Aux Pins (point of pines), the State Park Nature Center (with restrooms), the 1/2 mile British Landing Nature Trail, Brown's Brook (a non-potable, year around spring-fed stream), Devil's Kitchen rock formation, Lovers' Leap, and several perfect picnic spots!

The ultimate man-made island attraction is the Grand Hotel - "crown jewel of Mackinac". Stop in for a tour ($7), a stroll through magnificent gardens, a spectacular dining experience, High Tea, or evening cocktails. An elegant departure!

If you're staying on the island (Don Davis, Grand Hotel, says "you haven't been to Mackinac Island unless you've stayed on Mackinac Island!") many hotels, restaurants, and bars offer various evening entertainment options. Dining, dancing, and music to suit all tastes are pleasant options, as are outdoor passions like star-gazing, moonlight strolls, sunset cruises, and lantern-lit carriage rides!

June's Lilac Festival is a favorite and exciting time to visit.

Helen Martineau, an English writer, said it best in 1836, "The Island is the wildest and tenderest little piece of beauty that I have seen on God's earth." You, and your true love, deserve a wild, tender, and beautiful escape - the ultimate romantic experience. You deserve Mackinac Island!

Mackinac Island C of C
1-888-MAC-ISLE
www.mackinac.com/visitorsbureau

Bayview at Mackinac -

"come sail with me . . .
to our castle by the 'sea'"

$\mathcal{P}$erched at water's edge on Michigan's most romantic island, the Bayview calls all lovers home.

Of the twenty deluxe rooms in this charming Victorian Inn, four have whirlpool tubs. Each room offers a private bath, the most modern amenities, and spectacular "seascape" views. Most romantic? Any of three Executive/Bridal suites, or the Master suite. Rates vary from $95 to 295. Open from May to October, the Inn is usually quite busy, so plan to book your reservations as early as possible.

Complimenting the fine accomodations will be your Full Buffet Breakfast, served on deck, veranda, or in the dining room. Bay View Blend coffee highlights a daily specialty like "Cheesy Potato Casserole", "Bayview Peach French Toast", or "Bayview Quiche". Homemade pastries, cinnamon rolls, muffins, biscuits, tea and juice complete your morning feast.

While all the guests here are considered VIPs, special occasion or VIP service *is* available. Perhaps a bottle of wine or champage, sweet, lovely flowers, or a gift basket will enhance your visit. Wedding (or 50th anniversary)? Twenty guests may attend your vows, and toast your love on the most special day of your lives together. Choose a setting of porch, veranda, sundeck or parlor.

Settle on one of the beautiful porch verandas, or even the sundeck. Gaze at the sailboats, the lighthouse, the sunset. Gaze at each other! Sip a lemonade or iced tea and sample a cookie or brownie. While away the afternoon together!

Hire a private carriage for an unforgettable evening. Dining, dancing, romancing. Star gazing, embracing, making a wish.

Experience the Mackinac magic at . . .

Bay View at Mackinac
906-847-3295
Huron Street, Box 448, Mackinac Island 49757
Smoking outside only (in common areas)

Inn-spired Activities —————————

Ask the Innkeeper for suggestions of things to do; "Mackinac Island is as romantic as it gets"!

"Love is like the magic touch of stars."
- Walter Benton

Haan's 1830 Inn -

"an island fantasy"

*P*romising to blend "the charm of the old and the convenience of the new", this Inn welcomes guests to "come home" to a bit of history mid-May to mid-October.

Though restored and newly re-decorated, Haan's is a tasteful representation of Island hospitality in the 1800s. With the Inn's cozy parlor offering antique game, books, and stereo-

optican viewers; the dining room offering a warmly glowing fire in Spring and Fall; and the porches offering wicker rockers, settees and swings, history and relaxation-abound! Guests settle back on private screened-in porches, content to watch the comings and goings of ferries, boats, and passers-by.

Featuring antiques and authentic period decor, seven light and airy rooms with hand-tied quilts or crocheted coverlets offer guests a simple pampered comfort. Five of the rooms have private baths, and rates varying from $120-130. For a quiet couple's rendezvous, reserve the Colonel William Preston suite - an English-style room with sitting area, sleigh bed, and fully furnished kitchen. Honeymooners *may* be able to enjoy the spacious Vernon Haan room with its whirlpool tub, though it's mostly reserved for the owner's use.

Each morning, wonderful tempting aromas waft through the Inn and mix with an ever-present light, sweet potpourri scent, to tempt you to Breakfast! Your formal buffet-style repast may be enjoyed on the porch, or on the lantern-lit dining room's long harvest table. China and crystal gracefully display the fresh "from scratch" muffins, "Poppy Seed Cake", bagels, cereals, fruits, and beverages. Enjoy!

Haan's is conveniently located close to everything, and right next door to St. Anne's Church for weddings! Ask your hosts to assist with arrangements, dining reservations, or simply calling a horse-drawn "cab". Honeymooning? Let them know, and enjoy a beautiful surprise in your room!

Be sure to call early in the year for a weekend with all the flavor and romance of the past - "behind the white picket fence" at . . .

Haan's 1830 Inn
906-847-6244
Huron Street, P.O. Box 123, Mackinac Island 49757
Winter address: 3418 Oakwood Ave., Island Lake, IL 60042
847-526-2662
Smoking on porches or in yard only, please

Inn-spired Activities ———————————

Go to nearby Mission Point for sunrise and watching the freighters pass, or for casual romantic dining; enjoy sunset at Sunset Rock, cocktails at the Grand Hotel, or a 1/2 hour champagne carriage ride to the Woods restaurant; find your way to "Lover's Leap", look around, and get a hug from your honey!

Metivier Inn -

*"for those quiet evenings . . .
wrapped in history"*

*T*his charming Inn is "peaceful and quiet even in busy summer". Set back in the delightful historic district, its casual, laid-back appeal is accented by a large "people watching porch" (protected in inclement weather).

Breakfast on the porch is most popular, though another favorite place is the lobby common room with its cozy wing-backed chairs, intimate tables, and quaint wood stove. Choose from a large selection of games to amuse you, or get comfortable in the TV room. Or, stroll through the gardens - glorious in Summer.

Original watercolor by Carolyn Scott Risk - Copyright © 1992

Twenty one rooms promise romance in the style reminiscent of those old days on the island. Antiques and period reproductioins complement the thoroughly modern convenience of private baths, ice makers, and different decor on each floor - enjoy white wicker, canopy beds, or four-poster beds. Treat yourselves to the luxury of a Turret Room with canopy bed and chaise lounge, or, reserve the Metivier's Grandview Room, with floral decor, TV, Jacuzzi®, private yard and porch. Rates May - October range from $115-245, but do ask about off-season specials. Reserve by March for Turret Rooms, and at least one month in advance for standard rooms.

The friendliness and personal touch here extend to the buffet-style Deluxe Continental Breakfast. A minimum of three fresh fruits, bagels, English muffins, coffee cake, and other bakery treats, cereal, and perhaps a surprise addition, will start your day's adventure well. They're flexible here, serving 7:30-10, and leaving out the gourmet coffee and tea throughout the afternoon.

Whatever you may desire can be arranged for you, gladly. Fresh flowers and a champagne package will please the couple who wish a celebration, or plan fruit, crackers and cheese if you prefer. Plan a picnic, plan a special dining experience (Innkeepers have menus for "previewing"), or simply plan to relax and listen to the "clippity-clop of an occasional horse and carriage". Whatever you plan, "you'll hate to go back home" after you try . . .

Metivier Inn
906-847-6234
Market Street, Box 285, Mackinac Island 49757
www.mackinac.com/
Smoking on porches only, please

Inn-spired Activities —————————————

Rent a carriage to drive yourself; take an easy bike trip around the outside of the island (8 mi) - take a picnic lunch; go to the Oyster Bar & Pub - a small, noisy, fun place with tin ceiling, mirrors, big old bar, and great food; charter a boat for a sunset cruise to the bridge (or even a moonlight cruise)!

Grand Hotel -

"the ultimate romantic destination,
on the ultimate romantic isle"

"I am a grand lady, a legend, a landmark, a refuge. After one hundred eleven years I still stand sentinel. I still welcome many travelers - the young, the old, those in between - but my favorite guests are lovers. They smile, they laugh, they gaze at one another and imagine only they exist. They stroll hand-in-hand through my glorious gardens, then toast each other in my elegant dining room. They embrace on my magnificent porch, and drift, enraptured to a private tryst in one of my enchanting suites.

Yes, those who love are special here. I shall promise to forever inspire them, to make their memories sweet and joyous, and offer them a place for loving, that place they'll return to. . . 'Somewhere In Time' . . ."

"a legendary setting . . ."

There is nothing like it - the Grand Hotel - "America's Summer Place", and Michigan's *ultimate romantic getaway!* This picturesque and imposing classic Greek-Revival-style hotel stands as bluff-top guard over Michigan's most romantic isle.

Horse-drawn Victorian carriages, with candle lanterns and top-hat coachmen, deliver guests into that "elegant ambiance"... that is the Grand Hotel.

Up to 1400 bright geraniums decorate the 660' porch, their signature beauty repeated in the carpet design of the Grand parlor. Stunning works of art complement world-famous designer Carlton Varney's exciting yet stately decor, and spill into a twenty-four hour gallery display which varies yearly.

There's a new "place" to discover around each corner: A shop with gifts or clothing, flowers or food, news, art or necessities; The "Audubon Wine Bar" with it's cozy library (take books or puzzles to your room and return on check-out!) - open twenty-four hours with beverage service only in the evening; or even the small, cozy "Card Room" - open at all times for play or conversation.

"colorful diversions . . ."

Grand Hotel guests may be found languishing amid cool lake breezes on the magnificent porch, or strolling the fifty acre manicured grounds to admire over 100,000 fabulous floral plantings or fascinating topiary displays.

They sample old fashioned outdoor pastimes like bocce ball, croquet, or clay court tennis. They delight in sunning and swimming at the 220' serpentine "Esther Williams Pool", or relaxing in the adjacent sauna and whirlpool.

They rent a bicycle at the Hotel Tennis Shop, and request a box lunch for the perfect picnic. They golf. They exercise on the "Vita Course", or a selection of equipment. They try out duck-pin bowling. They take advantage of pampered salon and spa services - a manicure, a massage, or a whole new look.They tour the hotel stables and antique carriage collection. They take in a movie at 9 p.m. in Heritage Hall.

They relax! They dream! They escape to a simpler time!

"gracious service . . ."

Overnight guests at Grand Hotel are served a hearty Full Breakfast, and an incomparable five-course Dinner (included in the room rate). Start your day with a choice of fresh fruit, breads and pastries, omelettes and eggs, cereals, quiche, crepes and more.

Dining Delights

Over fifty Jamaican waiters cater to your every desire in the white-linen elegance of the Salle à Manger dining room, where dressing for dinner is required, and a highlight of the day! Dinner, featuring the highest quality cuisine, offers a wide selection of seasonal and regional specialties from three rotating menus. While the dining room is known for it's Prime Rib, Grand Hotel's chef creates many other culinary delights including perhaps: "Smoked Salmon Custard", "Duck Terrine", or "Pineapple Kirsch" as appetizers; "Chilled Cucumber and Sweet Onion Soup", "Vichyssoise", or "Chilled Apple Cinnamon Soup"; Caesar and daily Salads;, "Pistachio Crusted Breast of Chicken with port wine glaze", "Grilled Swordfish Filet with roasted pepper coulis", or "Peppered Venison Loin with huckle-berry compote" (ask about non-guest dining rates - reservations are recommended). Complement your meal with a selection from the Hotel's extensive and "guest-friendly" wine program.

Detailed descriptions, specific suggestions to enhance each entrée, and a twenty-eight wine "by the glass" (or even a taste!) menu, make it an easy task to decide.

After dinner demitasse, as well as 3:30 p.m. High Tea, are served in the parlor, complete with entertainment.

Though you needn't stay the night to visit Grand Hotel, there is a nominal charge ($7) to access public areas and enjoy the unique atmosphere and experiences to be found here. Luncheon, golf, shopping, High Tea, or dinner in the main dining room are offered to "day guests", as well as the opportunity to enjoy the "Grand Luncheon Buffet" - truly a dining event. $30 includes gratuity, and entitles guests to sample overflowing tables of salads, cheeses, meats, seafood, oven-fresh breads, and tempting pastries - and to be treated like royalty!

Lighter, more casual lunches and dinners are available at Carleton's Tea Store, Geranium Bar, The Jockey Club at the Grandstand, Pool Grill and the nearby Hotel-owned Woods restaurant.

The Old-world tradition of High Tea is observed daily, serving fine wine and champagne, finger sandwiches, scones, pastries, and of course tea - as you like it!

Beverage, luncheon, or tea service may be charged to your room for payment on departure.

Late afternoons and evenings are a great time to visit the Cupola Bar - sip a beverage, enjoy the sunset or the lights of Mackinac Bridge, and chat awhile - all to the accompaniment of mood-setting piano music. Or, take an after-dinner spin around the Terrace Room dance floor, in the arms of your love. Keep time to the lilting strains of Bob Snyder and the "Big-Band"-style Grand Hotel orchestra.

Receptions and private parties can be accommodated, provided Hotel terms and time constraints can be met. Discussions and quotes will be entertained after December 1.

"Nothing is overlooked!" From fresh flowers daily, to red-carpet treatment every moment, Grand Hotel offers the ultimate in luxurious style and genteel service.

Each of the Hotel's three hundred thirty rooms reflect its traditional elegance in a unique way - "no two are alike"!

Perhaps you'd like the "China Suite" - its oh-so-unusual king size canopy bed, hand-carved Oriental furnishings, and private patio are intoxicating. Or maybe The Lodge of Teddy Roosevelt - a wildly masculine retreat. Does the oppulent Napolean Suite appeal, or the delicate intricacy of Josephine's Suite? Or would your romantic spirit be best set free amongst the simple extravagance and panoramic views of the Milliken or Woodfill Suites. Even the smaller, simple rooms are beautifully done. High ceilings, private baths, and *"abundant amenities"* ensure your comfort and pleasure in each.

Remember, rates of $320-590 double include meals, and vary depending on dates requested. Many off-season special event and package rates are available, including annual art and music celebrations, holiday, murder mystery, and "Somewhere in Time" weekends, and "Touch

of Romance" packages with wine, flowers, and fudge! (Since tipping is neither expected nor permitted, a service charge will be added.) Balcony rooms may be requested, but not guaranteed, and all reservations for weekends should be planned at least six months in advance. Last minute cancellations happen, but it's risky. Weekday stays present a real value possibility with chance of upgrade, easier booking, and better deals possibly available. Grand Hotel is open from early May till late October, but begins booking November 1 for the following season.

Each guest is very special here, and Grand Hotel staff promises they'll "do whatever it takes to make sure your expectations are met or exceeded."

Yes, this is a Grand Hotel - "turn of the century elegance and charm . . . (with) the best of contemporary living" . The perfect place to celebrate the days of yesteryear . . . love of today . . . together . . . "Somewhere in Time".

Create a legendary love, at . . .

Grand Hotel
906-847-3331
Reservations 1-800-33-GRAND (1-800-334-7263)
Mackinac Island 49757
Winter address: 2177 Commons Parkway, Okemos 48864
517-349-4600
www.grandhotel.com

Inn-spired Activities ——————————

Hire a carriage or drive your own rented "hack" for an island tour; explore 40 miles of bridle path upon a rented "steed"; visit the fort, hike the woodland trails, "shop for antiques, curios & world-famous fudge"; see Arch Rock, "island gardens, and splendid 19th century cottages"; "There is a quaint magic on Mackinac Island"!

The Carriage House Dining
Room - at Hotel Iroquois

On the water's edge, and serving food as great as the view - in a setting graced with floral decor, and a mellow piano bar. In the morning, how about the "Mackinac Breakfast - pancakes with Bois Blanc maple syrup", or another A.M. treat? ($8-12) For lunch, try "Onion Soup", "Gazpacho", or Soup of the Day, "Grilled Crab, Lobster, and Shrimp Salad", "Fresh grilled Lake Superior Whitefish Sandwich", or choose another specialty ($8-15). All entrées, accompaniments, breads and desserts are made fresh right here (even roast turkey!). Dinners are special, with elegantly served entrées like "Barbecued Tuna with green onion

butter and fried oysters", "Roasted Chicken with fuselli pasta, mushrooms, spinach, and gorgonzola cream sauce", "Grilled Lake Superior Whitefish", "New York Strip with match stick onions", Prime Rib, and "Filet with herb garlic butter" ($30-45). They're famous for their desserts, and feature their homemade hot fudge sauce. Incredible!

Open 7 days - from just before Memorial weekend through mid-October / Reservations recommended / Smoking in designated areas / Limited special parties / Patio dining - weather permitting / Full bar and wine list

Huron Street - on the Waterfront • 906-847-3321

Dining Delights ***Point Dining Room*** *-Mission Pt. Resort*

"Casual elegance, rustic beauty, and turn-of-the-century charm" combined with fine dining selections such as "Mission Point Corn and Potato Chowder in Sourdough Bowl", "Parmesan Chicken", "Penne Pasta with roasted red peppers", "Grilled Marinated Twin Veal Chops with pollenta and apple curry sauce", or "Broiled Bahamian Lobster Tail with herb garlic sauce and lemon risotto" (average dinner $18).

Open seasonally / Full bar & wine list / Parties possible - inquire for details / Smoking in designated areas / Outdoor dining / Live entertainment / Casual deli and bar & grill also available / Waterfront lodging available

Lakeshore Drive • 906-847-3312 • www.mackinac.com/

Dining Delights ***Woods*** *- a Grand Hotel Property*

A taste of Bavaria! With charming Chalet-style ambiance - imposing stone fireplace, antlers and animals, beamed ceilings - and legendary Grand Hotel service. Tempting starters like "Duck Terrine", or "Sweet Corn & Roasted Red Pepper Soup" whet your appetite for entrée specialties like "German Bratwurst", "Red Deer Medallions with sweet potato fritters", "Parchment Baked Mackinac Whitefish", "BBQ Filet of Salmon", "Grilled Venison Chops with red currant glace and wild mushroom stew", and "Weiner Schnitzel with red cabbage and potatoes" (dinners $11.95-24.50). Top it off with a "delectable dessert". Decidedly unique!

Open Memorial Weekend to mid-October / Also serving a limited casual luncheon menu / Smoking in designated areas / Full bar and Grand Hotel wine list / Reservations suggested - especially weekends / Chalet Banquet Room seats 50 / Piano entertainment nightly / Cocktails & appetizers in Bobby's Bar

At the Woods nine golf course • 906-847-3699 or 906-847-3331

À Deux Adventures

Ferries

Arnold Mackinac Island Ferry...................................... 1-800-542-8528
    Mackinac Island Office 906-847-3351
    Mackinaw City Office 616-436-5542
    St. Ignace Office..906-643-8275
Shepler's Mackinac Island Ferry.............................. 1-800-828-6157
    Mackinaw City 616-436-5023
    St. Ignace 906-643-9440
Star Line Mackinac Island Ferry 1-800-638-9892
    Mackinaw City 616-436-5045
    St. Ignace 906-643-7635

Bicycle Rentals

Hotel Iroquois...906-847-3321
Island Bicycle Rental..906-847-6288
Lakeside Bikes..906-847-3891
Orr Kids 906-847-3211
Ryba's..906-847-6261

Carriages and Horses

Arrowhead Carriage 906-847-6112
Carriage Tours Livery 906-847-6152
Chambers Riding Stable 906-847-6231
Cindy's Riding Stable..906-847-3572
Gough Livery...906-847-3435
Jack's Livery Stable 906-847-3391
Mackinac Island Carriage Tours Taxi 906-847-3323
Mackinac Island Carriage Tours Tickets.......................906-847-3325
    winter..906-847-3573

Additional Adventure Resources

Fort Mackinac Tea Room..906-847-3328
French Outpost (pub & restaurant)................................906-847-3772
Horn's Gaslight Bar (sandwiches & dinners).................906-847-6154
Pub & Oyster Bar 906-847-3454

DNR Rec. Division (marina information).......................906-847-3561
Mackinac Island Airport..906-847-3231
Professional Marine Services (cruises, charters, after hours ferry)
    .... (May-Oct) 906-847-6580 or (Oct-May) 517-733-8569